WELFARE AND RELIGION IN
21ST CENTURY EUROPE

-k S†

The editors would like to thank the Bank of Sweden
Tercentenary Foundation and the Foundation Samariterhemmet,
without whose generosity this book would not have been possible.

This book has been written within the framework of Impact of Religion:
Challenges for Society, Law and Democracy, a multidisciplinary research
programme at Uppsala University, funded by the Swedish Research
Council 2008-2018.
See www.impactofreligion.uu.se

THE IMPACT OF RELIGION

Challenges for Society, Law and Democracy

Welfare and Religion in 21st Century Europe

Volume 2

Gendered, Religious and Social Change

Edited by

ANDERS BÄCKSTRÖM
Uppsala University, Sweden

GRACE DAVIE
University of Exeter, UK

NINNA EDGARDH
Uppsala University, Sweden

PER PETTERSSON
Uppsala University, Sweden

ASHGATE

Published by
Ashgate Publishing Limited
Wey Court East
Union Road
Farnham
Surrey, GU9 7PT
England

Ashgate Publishing Company
Suite 420
101 Cherry Street
Burlington
VT 05401-4405
USA

www.ashgate.com

British Library Cataloguing in Publication Data
Welfare and religion in 21st century Europe.
   Volume 2, Gendered, religious and social change.
   1. Public welfare--Europe--Cross-cultural studies.
   2. Public welfare--Religious aspects. 3. Church and social
   problems--Europe--Cross-cultural studies. 4. Religion and
   sociology--Europe. 5. Women in church work--Europe.
   6. Theology, Practical--Europe.
   I. Backstrom, Anders, 1944-
   261.8'32'094-dc22

Library of Congress Cataloging-in-Publication Data
Welfare and religion in 21st century Europe / [edited by] Anders Bäckström and Grace Davie ; with Ninna Edgardh and Per Pettersson.
          p. cm.
      Includes bibliographical references and index.
      ISBN 978-0-7546-6107-8 (v. 2 : hardcover) — ISBN 978-0 7546-6108-5 (v. 2 : pbk)
      1. Public welfare—Europe—Religious aspects. 2. Welfare state—Europe.
I. Bäckström, Anders, 1944– II. Davie, Grace, 1946– III. Edgardh, Ninna, 1955–
IV. Pettersson, Per, 1952–
   HV238.W426 2009
   361.7'5094--dc22

                                                                      2009020283

ISBN 978 0 7546 6107 8 (hbk)
ISBN 978 0 7546 6108 5 (pbk)
ISBN 978 0 7546 9257 7 (ebk)

MIX
Paper from
responsible sources
FSC® C013056

Printed and bound in Great Britain by
TJ International Ltd, Padstow, Cornwall.

Contents

List of Figures and Table   *vii*
Preface   *ix*

1   The WREP Project: Building Bridges   1
     Anders Bäckström, Grace Davie, Ninna Edgardh and Per Pettersson

2   Majority Churches as Agents of European Welfare: A Sociological
     Approach   15
     Per Pettersson

3   A Gendered Perspective on Welfare and Religion in Europe   61
     Ninna Edgardh

4   Thinking Theologically about Welfare and Religion   107
     Thomas Ekstrand

5   Welfare and Religion in Europe: Themes, Theories and Tensions   151
     Anders Bäckström and Grace Davie

Appendix: The WREP Team   *173*
Bibliography   *175*
Index   *193*

List of Figures and Table

Figures

1.1	Map of case study locations	3
2.1	Four sectors in the provision of welfare services	29
2.2	Four possible positions regarding the churches' roles as social agents	39
3.1	The existing and the ideal regarding gender roles in church-related social work	84
4.1	The vision and mission of the churches as welfare agents	141

Table

2.1	Majority church membership/affiliation in the WREP case studies	22

Preface

This book is the second of two volumes, both of which can be read in different ways.[1] At their simplest, they constitute an account of a comparative study on welfare and religion across eight western European nations. This study – Welfare and Religion in a European Perspective: A Comparative Study of the Role of Churches as Agents of Welfare within the Social Economy (WREP) – is itself the second of three related projects, all of which have emerged from the Uppsala Religion and Society Research Centre. The genesis of each of these projects is briefly set out in the following chapter, as are the details of WREP itself.[2]

These books quite deliberately bring together very different fields of social-scientific enquiry – welfare, religion, gender and the social economy – which have, all too often, been kept apart. The reasons for these enforced separations are not hard to find. In terms of the first two (welfare and religion), they lie in an understanding of the modernization process in which one of these replaces the other as the dominant player in the field. This is especially true in those parts of Europe where the welfare state has substantially taken the place of the church as the effective means of care for European people – a process unlikely to be reversed in the foreseeable future. Why, then, should there be a study which focuses specifically on the interconnections between welfare and religion in the early years of the twenty-first century? Has something significant happened to demand this? And if so, how can this shift be explained?

The question of gender adds a further dimension. Even a cursory glance at the institutions of welfare and religion in Europe reveals a strikingly similar pattern: in both systems, women are disproportionately present at the point of delivery, but under-represented in management. Once again, it is important to ask why this is the case and how it is best understood. Is this a persistent pattern, or is it likely to change; and, if so, when? How, moreover, is this pervasive imbalance legitimized? Is the legitimization process the same in each area of enquiry, or is something rather different at stake? Such questions will resonate repeatedly in the following pages.

All of these interests come together in a specific 'field' – the sector that is variously termed civil society, the third or voluntary sector, or the social economy. Welfare is 'relocating', but in different ways in different places; the churches have increasingly ceased to be a 'sacred canopy' for the whole of society, but remain

---

[1]   For the first volume, see Bäckström and Davie, with Edgardh and Pettersson (2010).

[2]   A much fuller account is given in Volume 1.

both active and effective at local level; and women – both paid and unpaid – are more likely than men to be engaged at the level of delivery which is necessarily local. It is this that accounts for the stress in our writing on both the individuals and organizations that make up the social economy and the variety of forms that this takes in different parts of Europe.

There is, however, a further dimension to our work: that is, its *theoretical* significance. The logic of WREP demands that we address not only the changing nature of the institutions in question, but also the conceptual frameworks that must be brought into play if we are to understand fully what is happening in late modern European societies. It is clear that conventional theorizing about the welfare state, just like the welfare state itself, has come under strain in recent decades. Pressures from within the system (notably the marked changes in European demography) and outside it (a shifting global economy) require that we rethink the assumptions on which the welfare state is built – a fact that becomes ever more urgent, almost by the day. Coincidentally, or perhaps not, standard theorizing about religion has been subject to similar pressures. No longer is it possible to talk simply in terms of secularization. The patterns of religion across Europe are changing rapidly as the religious factor once more asserts itself in public as well as private life – the outcomes of this situation are increasingly uncertain.

Hence one of the central questions of the WREP enquiry: what is the place of religion in Europe at the start of the third millennium, and what role does it play in the wider society? In engaging these issues, the final chapter of this volume places the findings of our research and our subsequent analyses into a broader theoretical perspective. In so doing, it draws on a wide range of ideas, some of them innovative, and becomes in itself a creative exercise. At the same time, it reveals the incompleteness of the work and the need for further developments in the field. One of these can be found in a further study from the Uppsala stable – Welfare and Values in Europe (WaVE) – which is introduced briefly in Chapter 1; a second lies in the work currently being carried out in a recently established Centre of Excellence at Uppsala University. This is a major interdisciplinary programme concerned with the continuing impact of religion on modern European societies.[3]

It is important to grasp that the two volumes emerging from the WREP project embody different approaches. Volume 1 set out the parameters of the project in some detail. The introductory chapters described the background to the study, including its genesis, structure and scope. They also explained the details of the methodology – not least the advantages and disadvantages of the comparative method as it was used in this project. The core of the book resides, however, in the eight case studies, each of which described the connections between welfare, religion and gender in a 'representative' town in eight European societies. The final chapter contained some initial reflections on these data. Volume 2 tackles the

---

[3]   This Centre of Excellence – The Impact of Religion: Challenges for Society, Law and Democracy – is funded by the Swedish Research Council. Its work began in 2008 (see http://www.impactofreligion.uu.se for more details).

same material from a thematic point of view. Three approaches are taken in turn to identify and to explain the various strands within the data. A sociological analysis comes first, followed by an approach which concentrates on gender. The third way of working is somewhat different: it looks at the material from a theological perspective, asking in particular what motivates and sustains the actions of the churches in the field of welfare, and how the formal or 'official' statements of the churches are worked out in practice.

The last point requires a little expansion. The theological dimension is not an optional extra tagged on as an afterthought; it has been integral to the study right from the start, and is carefully referenced in almost all of the case studies. As the churches engage in welfare, for example, theological ideas are present in the motivations of both individuals and organizations – though not always in similar or predictable ways. Quite apart from this, it is clear that different theologies account for both commonality and difference across Europe. Greeks and Finns, for instance, quote similar verses from the Bible in seeking justification for their work, or more precisely their care for those in need; conversely, Luther's doctrine of the 'two kingdoms' leads to a considerably more amicable division of labour between church and state in the Nordic countries than that found in, say, France.

None of these activities would have been possible without a number of key people – most of all the international and interdisciplinary team brought together in Uppsala in order to carry out the project. The details of the team and their respective responsibilities can be found in the Appendix. Here, however, it is important to acknowledge the core group – those who conceived of the idea in the first place, set about finding the necessary resources and dealt with both the intellectual organization and the day to day management of the project. They are Anders Bäckström, Grace Davie, Ninna Edgardh, Thomas Ekstrand and Per Pettersson. Between us we represent a range of different disciplines and have – consequently – made different contributions to the project, which has been housed in the Uppsala Religion and Society Research Centre. The support staff of the Centre, notably Barbro Borg and Maria Essunger, deserve our warmest thanks; in sustaining the ongoing administration of the Centre, not to mention the numerous research meetings held there, they have played a vital role in the success of the whole undertaking. It is important, thirdly, to acknowledge the financial support given to the project from the Bank of Sweden Tercentenary Foundation and the Foundation Samariterhemmet – without whose exceptionally generous assistance very little of the work would have been possible. Additional grants came from the Academy of Finland (for the Finnish research) and the Diakonische Werk Württemberg (for the German case study). When it came, at last, to publication, Sarah Lloyd at Ashgate has proved an imaginative and very helpful editor. Rebecca Catto and Susannah Cornwall have put in long hours perfecting our English and Anders Sjöborg worked tirelessly on a complex multilingual bibliography.

This preface must include a final point, which reflects our way of working: that is the training element built into the WREP project and its successor, WaVE. Each national team had a senior and junior member: the senior member is an established scholar in the field (trained for the most part in sociology or theology); the junior researchers were doctoral or post-doctoral students. One of the most pleasing aspects of the whole venture has been the emergence of a new generation of scholars, as, one by one, these 'junior' researchers acquire their doctorates and launch their careers. Their enthusiasm, and a growing rapport between them, has been a crucial factor in sustaining not only themselves, but their senior partners – indeed, in permitting the project as a whole to come to a successful conclusion. In total, 24 researchers from Sweden, Norway, Finland, Germany, England, France, Italy and Greece have been involved – a team with growing competence in the field. Their names, the institutions in which they are based, and their disciplinary backgrounds are listed in the Appendix.

As the Director and Assistant Director, we would like to thank all those who have contributed to WREP in whatever way and have helped us to bring the project to a successful conclusion.

Anders Bäckström

Grace Davie

2011

Chapter 1
The WREP Project: Building Bridges

Anders Bäckström, Grace Davie, Ninna Edgardh and Per Pettersson

This book, together with its partner volume (Bäckström and Davie 2010), is concerned with the project known as Welfare and Religion in a European Perspective – or WREP for short. The goal of the project is easily summarized: it is to discover exactly what happens on an everyday basis in the fields of welfare and religion in Europe in the first decade of the twenty-first century, and to ask what our findings can tell us about the changing nature of European societies.

WREP was designed to build bridges – between different research fields (notably welfare and religion) and between different disciplines (the social sciences, gender studies and theology), bearing in mind that research fields and disciplines are overlapping categories at least to some extent. Very fruitful syntheses have emerged from these collaborations. This introduction is designed however to build a bridge in a different sense: its primary aim is to 'connect' the first and second volumes of *Welfare and Religion in a European Perspective*. In so doing it works on a 'need to know' basis. In other words it introduces sufficient contextual material for this book to make sense as a free-standing volume. The reader who wishes to know more should refer to Volume 1, where the genesis and development of WREP are set out in detail and where both the rationale and the methodology of the project are described in full.[1]

The chapter starts by reviewing the case studies that lie at the heart of the WREP project. This is followed by a short section that underlines the increasingly apparent links between Europe's major theological traditions and the different welfare regimes that have been identified in different parts of the continent. In this, two distinct bodies of literature (those relating to welfare and to religion) are brought together in innovative ways. A third section introduces the thematic analyses that form the core of Volume 2. What insights emerge if the extensive data produced by WREP are examined from the perspectives of sociology, gender and theology? The final section is in two parts. It looks first at the common themes that emerge from the preceding chapters; it then introduces the developed theoretical analysis that will form the conclusion to the project as a whole.

---

[1] See also the final section of this chapter where the organizational elements of WREP are summarized.

Eight Case Studies in Eight Medium-sized Towns

The core of WREP lies in a detailed examination of the social economy of a single locality in eight European countries: Sweden, Norway, Finland, Germany, England, France, Italy and Greece. Our intention has been to map the place of both welfare and religion in the town in question; to note the similarities and differences across Europe regarding the responses of the state (in its local forms), the churches, and a range of voluntary organizations to the current situation; and to ask what this information can tell us about the changing nature of European societies, which are clearly facing similar issues. Our questions included the following. How do these various actors respond to the pressures that they face, and what resources do they have at their disposal? To what extent do these resources depend on the fact that the modern welfare state has developed differently in different parts of Europe – developments which leave distinctive 'spaces' not only for the churches to contribute, but for their role to adjust as circumstances require? And how, finally, might this situation evolve?

The case studies themselves are described in detail in the partner volume; so also are the reasons for choosing these particular examples and the various methodologies employed to understand them better. Here they are simply summarized, as a backdrop to the thematic analyses that follow.[2] The precise location of each town can be seen in Figure 1.1. In terms of timing, it is important to note that the detailed fieldwork took place between 2004 and 2005 – in what follows the contextual information has been updated where appropriate, but not the data themselves.

The Swedish case was located in Gävle, a town situated near the east coast of Sweden, and approximately 180 km north of Stockholm. Since the 1950s this former industrial town has gradually metamorphosed to become part of the new service economy. As in Sweden generally, Gävle is a place where the labour movement and the Social Democrats have dominated politically. Also typical is the numerical dominance of the Church of Sweden, to which about 75 per cent of the population belong and pay an annual fee (about one per cent of their income).[3] Currently 92,000 people live in the municipality of Gävle, including 10 per cent from outside Sweden (mostly refugees from the Middle East and Africa); three quarters of the population reside in the urban area. The WREP enquiry concentrated on the latter and drew on a variety of sources, including a close analysis of documents concerning the welfare situation and the role of the church within this and a series of interviews with both employed and elected representatives from the public authorities and the Church of Sweden. Group

---

[2]   Reference should also be made to the very detailed working papers of the WREP project (Edgardh Beckman 2004; Yeung et al. 2006a; 2006b). Much of the data cited in the following chapters comes from these papers.

[3]   At the time of the fieldwork, this figure was noticeably higher (80 per cent) – a reduction in membership that is repeating itself all over Sweden.

Figure 1.1   Map of case study locations

interviews were also carried out with representatives from the population as a whole. Broadly speaking, these methods were repeated in every case, bearing in mind that the available documentation varied very considerably from place to place – the reasons for these differences are worth pondering.[4]

The Norwegian enquiry was carried out in Drammen, a town of about 57,000 inhabitants some 40 km south of Oslo. Drammen is an old port, closely connected to a range of industrial and commercial activities in the southeastern part of Norway. The town, however, has undergone significant structural change in the last 20 to 30 years to become primarily a regional service centre. Traditionally, the Social Democrats have had a majority in the town but this is also changing. Drammen is noteworthy in that it hosts a wide variety of religious (both Christian and non-Christian) and philosophical communities. The Church of Norway, however, is by far the largest of these, comprising 77 per cent of the population.

---

[4]   Unsurprisingly, the further south that you go in Europe, the sparser the documentation becomes. There is also a close relationship with finance: wealthier churches have more resources available for this kind of work.

Also present are Muslims, Buddhists, Hindus, Sikhs and Jehovah's Witnesses. Unsurprisingly, Muslims comprise the largest religious group outside the Church of Norway, which reflects the significant immigration of ethnic minorities into Drammen. Among the Christian denominations outside the Church of Norway, the Norwegian Pentecostal movement is the largest. The presence of Muslims and Pentecostals in Drammen corresponds more or less to the relative strength of the two groups at national level. It is important to note that the local parishes and the voluntary organizations of the Church of Norway have a long tradition of engaging in social work.

The Finnish case study took place in Lahti, a town with circa 98,000 inhabitants and located 100 km north of Helsinki, with a history dating back to the fifteenth century. In recent years, Lahti has undergone rapid and troublesome economic change. Currently the main source of employment lies in service provision, and the majority of the municipality's employees are social and health care workers (53.9 per cent). At the time of the fieldwork, the local council was dominated by Social Democrats together with the National Coalition Party, a typical collaboration in towns of this size. Lahti is also representative of Finland with respect to socio-demographic variables and in the fact that 84 per cent of the population belongs to the Evangelical Lutheran Church. The parishes have a long tradition of engaging in social work, in cooperation with the municipality and other organizations. And as in the rest of Finland, the church has assumed an increasingly active role as the town has faced economic challenges. Lahti contains examples of all the major issues represented in this project: structural change, difficult economic adjustments, pressures from outside as well as within and a desire to find new (and affordable) ways of organizing the welfare sector.

The German case is one of the most striking in WREP given the distinctive and highly significant role of church-related organizations (both Catholic and Protestant) in the welfare systems of Germany. About 60 per cent of welfare is provided in this way, financed by a variety of insurance schemes. This situation was very apparent in Reutlingen, a town with 110,000 inhabitants. From the early sixteenth century, Reutlingen was a bastion of the Reformation and a strongly Protestant identity still persists. After the Second World War, however, the town became more and more mixed from a denominational point of view. Currently, the Protestants remain the largest religious group with 42.8 per cent of Reutlingen's citizens belonging to the Evangelical-Lutheran church compared with 23.9 per cent who are Catholic. Over and above these two groups, public statistics also reveal the so-called 'others' (33.3 per cent). This highly varied category comprises other Christians (such as the Orthodox or members of the free churches), Muslims, Jews, Buddhists and Hindus, but also people who do not belong to any religion at all. Interestingly the last named are the most numerous among 'the others' in Reutlingen (Stadt Reutlingen 2005). Immigrants make up approximately 10 per cent of the population and are mainly of Turkish or Greek origin. It is also important to note the presence of ethnic Germans who have returned from the former Soviet Union.

The town is situated in the industrial region known as the 'Mittlerer Neckar' (in Baden-Württemberg) which is currently dominated by the car industry. Following crisis and decline in the textile industry the biggest employer in Reutlingen today is Robert Bosch GmbH (a hi-tech firm). In the field of higher education Reutlingen offers a recently founded college for economic studies; conversely a college for teachers was closed in the mid 1980s. Independent welfare organizations in Reutlingen are represented by (among others) a large diaconal institution which employs about 2,500 people, who work as carers for the elderly and disabled and in education. The current re-organization of the local welfare model into smaller units is also significant. Increasingly public welfare authorities, independent organizations and commercial firms compete to provide services within these units. On the one hand this change encourages greater co-operation, but on the other it increases the economic regulation of social work and health care. It has also undermined the monopoly of the diaconal institutions in certain areas.

The English case is very different – here the presence of volunteers rather than paid employees is at its most developed. It was carried out in Darlington in the northeast of England. Once a manufacturing town, Darlington has undergone significant change during the late twentieth century. In 2004 the town had a population of about 98,000 and 80 per cent of jobs were in the service sector. The relatively deprived northeast is traditionally a Labour stronghold and this is also true of Darlington, though the presence of Labour, Conservative and Liberal Democrat representatives on the local council witnessed to the mixed social make-up of the town. As in most of our cases, Darlington mirrored the nationally relevant issues that derive from the shift from an industrially-based to a service-oriented society – these include an ageing population, unemployment and inequalities in health and wealth. There are examples of real social need in the area. Quaker families played a major role in the social history of Darlington, but a Church of England presence has also been significant. Our enquiries revealed that the local parishes are involved in both independent and cooperative initiatives in the areas of social welfare and community development; the role of the church in education is particularly important in the English case.

The French enquiry took place in the town of Evreux, which lies 100 km northwest of Paris, and has approximately 100,000 inhabitants. This formerly provincial city is gradually being incorporated into the suburbs of Paris; the city has, however, considerable significance in France both politically and religiously. In 2002, after more than 20 years of Communist government, the city elected as *député* Jean-Louis Debré – a prominent, and at times controversial, member of the political right, and from 2002 to 2007 the President of the French National Assembly. In 1995, Monsignor Gaillot (the Catholic Bishop of Evreux) was sharply criticized by the Vatican, and eventually removed from his post, for (amongst other things) his views on contraception and the ordination of women. His condemnation raised unexpectedly strong reactions throughout France. The Evreux case study reflects on the influence of this episode on Catholic activities at local level. That said, Catholic organizations have been present for a long time in this city. Very largely, they concentrate their efforts on those who are deemed marginal in French society: on prisoners, on long-stay patients in hospital (notably in psychiatry and geriatric medicine) and on the new immigrant populations (especially the *sans-papiers*). The presence of Islam is of particular significance in France, as it is in Evreux itself – most Muslims in the town live in the district known as La Madeleine.

The Italian case study was conducted in Vicenza, a city in the Veneto famous for its outstanding Palladian buildings. Today it is a medium size town of 110,000 inhabitants, typical of the urban northeast of Italy, a region which is experiencing rapid socio-economic change. Traditionally it was a bastion for the Christian Democratic Party. At the time of the WREP enquiry, however, it was governed by a centre-right majority, composed of Forza Italia, Alleanza Nazionale and Lega Nord. The church's presence in welfare includes a wide variety of agents: first of all the many parishes, with their various charitable practices, which are difficult to know and to classify even for the Diocese of Vicenza; then the religious institutions of many different kinds (including the religious orders), operating mainly in the field of education; and finally the heterogeneous world of Catholic associations – among them Caritas-Diaconia, which is currently the principal church-related actor in Vicenza's welfare system. Central to the Italian case is a continuing debate about who or what constitutes 'the church' – a question that reflects ongoing confusions between the religious and the secular.

The Greek case study – our only example of the Orthodox tradition – took place in Thiva and Livadeia, towns which are located 85 and 135 km, respectively, northwest of Athens. They are the two largest towns in the prefecture of Viotia.[5] Thiva has approximately 23,000 inhabitants and Livadeia is a little smaller. A moderate Socialist party has prevailed in the area for a considerable period. The main sources of income in both places are agriculture and industry. Major social problems include unemployment following factory closures in the 1990s; financial concerns specific to the agricultural industry; the integration, employment and social inclusion of immigrants; family-related problems, especially care for children and the elderly; and drug abuse. As such, Thiva and Livadeia are broadly representative of the social difficulties present in Greece more generally – difficulties which came to a head in 2010. The local church and monasteries are, however, unusually active in the domain of social work, as are some local and national governmental agencies. Attitudes towards the local church are correspondingly positive, whereas the national church incurs considerable criticism – a point explained in detail in the Greek case study.

---

[5]   Prefectures are regional divisions introduced by the Greek state; there are 51 prefectures in Greece.

Theological Traditions and Welfare Regimes

It is clear even from this short résumé that the WREP case studies were selected in order to cover the major theological traditions of European Christianity: Lutheran, Anglican, Catholic and Orthodox, though there was no direct representation of the Reformed or Calvinist tradition, which is regrettable (see Manow 2004 for a discussion of this point). A second omission must also be noted: the WREP enquiry did not deal in detail with Europe's religious minorities, whether indigenous or recently arrived. It is not that such minorities are insignificant – they most certainly are in a complete analysis of religion and welfare in Europe. Quite apart from anything else such minorities have increased the visibility of religion right across Europe. Indeed for precisely this reason, they became the topic of a *separate* enquiry by the Uppsala team, known as WaVE (Welfare and Values in Europe). The material from WaVE is referenced in passing in the present volume, but it is not developed in detail (see below).[6]

At the same time, care was taken to ensure that the WREP cases covered the different welfare regimes of post-war Europe, as these are identified by Esping-Andersen (1990). These include the social democratic model of northern Europe, represented by Sweden, Norway and Finland; the conservative model found in the Catholic countries of Europe, including the more rudimentary forms of this located in southern and southeastern Europe (the former are represented by Germany and France, and the latter by Italy and Greece); and finally the liberal model typical of Anglo-Saxon countries, represented by the English case. From this point of view the spread of case studies is good, though a little over-weighted towards the Nordic countries – an imbalance explained by the location and funding of the project as a whole. It is widely recognized that Esping-Andersen's work is pivotal for the understanding of Europe's welfare systems, a fact dealt with in some detail in the early chapters of Volume 1, which includes an overview not only of Esping-Andersen's own contributions, but also of the major criticisms of his work and his responses to these (Jeppsson Grassman 2010). There is no need to go over that ground for a second time. It *is* important, however, to appreciate the connections between the two factors so far outlined in this section: theological traditions on the one hand and welfare-regimes on the other.

The conclusion to Volume 1 began to reflect on this relationship, building on the relatively recent work of Philip Manow (2004; Van Kersbergen and Manow 2009a) and Sigrun Kahl (2005), both of whom recognize the significance of religious ideas in the formative period of the welfare state from the nineteenth century onwards. Attention should also be paid to the contributions of Birgit and Elisabeth Fix who emphasize very similar connections, but employ a very

---

[6]   For more details, see 'Welfare and Values in Europe' (WaVE), a project funded by the European Commission (EU) through the 6th Framework programme – see http://www.crs.uu.se/Research/Concluded+projects/Welfare_and_Values/.

different methodology in their empirical investigations (Fix and Fix 2002; 2005).[7] Most important of all for the WREP enquiry, however, are the links between Gøsta Esping-Andersen's analyses of welfare-regimes on the one hand, and David Martin's work on secularization on the other, noting especially Martin's magisterial *A General Theory of Secularization* (1978). Social policy experts are very familiar with the former; scholars of religion continue to engage with the latter. Very seldom, however, are the two bodies of literature brought together.

Martin's central thesis is easily summarized: the process of secularization – strongly associated in the European case with the onset of industrialization and urbanization – is common to the continent as a whole, but unfolds differently within particular cultural contexts (Martin 1978: 4–5). These contexts are determined by identifiable factors, for example the precise timing and the nature of what Martin terms 'crucial events' – namely the English Civil War and the American, French and Russian Revolutions, and the place of religion in these. Did these cataclysmic struggles occur over religion, against religion or through religion? The *absence* of such an event in the Lutheran countries of Northern Europe is just as significant. The details are complex, but the underlying idea is simple enough. Emerging, in the fullness of time, from these various upheavals, are specific – and up to a point predictable – variations in the secularization process.

The crucial point is the following: these variations mirror very closely the regime-types initially identified by Esping-Andersen and exemplified in the WREP case studies. The pathways of secularization on the one hand 'match' the distinctive patterns of welfare that emerge on the other. Had there been a Calvinist example in WREP, yet another variation would have become apparent. It is simply that the story is told from different points of view: one scholar documents the influence and the adjustments of a territorially-based church to the upheavals and dislocations of the industrialization process; the other observes the emergence of the secular institutions required by a modern industrial society. The reasons for this parallel thinking are clear enough: they lie in the fact that both 'theories' (the contrasting processes of secularization and the very different welfare regimes that have emerged in different parts of Europe) draw on the same underlying alignments and cleavages in European society, initially identified by political sociologists in their work on the nineteenth century. Especially significant in this respect is the pioneering work of Lipset and Rokkan (1964). Such cleavages are, in turn, determined by the 'crucial events' already outlined.

One element in this transformation is the process of institutional separation or differentiation, in which tasks or areas of activity traditionally undertaken by the churches move bit by bit into the secular sphere.[8] Such areas of activity include education, healthcare and – of course – welfare. In each situation, a particular

---

[7]   Fix's and Fix's conclusions are based on survey data collected in 2001–2002; the questionnaire was administered at national level in six European societies (Austria, Belgium, Germany, the Netherlands, Norway and Switzerland).

[8]   See Casanova (1994) for a full discussion of this point.

variant of the welfare state emerges, as a similar goal (the separating out of welfare from the influence of the churches and the creation of an autonomous sphere with its own institutional norms) is achieved, or semi-achieved, in somewhat different ways. As we have seen, the role of both theology and ecclesiology in determining these pathways – albeit as one factor among many – is not only increasingly recognized in the literature but is more than apparent in the material emerging from the WREP case studies.

This leads us to a crucially important question. What happens, or will happen, when the work of the churches in the sphere of welfare begins to expand rather than contract? Or to put the same point even more directly: what will happen as the role of religion as a whole becomes more rather than less visible in modern Europe both as a social provider and as a significant voice in public debate? This possibility was alluded to briefly in the final paragraphs of Volume 1. It will be developed in detail in the conclusion to this book. In the meantime, it is important to engage the cross-cutting themes that constitute the central chapters of Volume 2. There are three of these, written from the points of view of sociology, gender and theology.

Cross-cutting Analyses

In Chapter 2, Per Pettersson sets the empirical results from the eight European localities into a sociological context, paying particular attention to the pressures of globalization, the processes of religious change, and the role of religion in late modern society. The chapter works at three levels. It starts with societal factors, noting in particular the position of the majority churches as unique institutions in European societies, in the sense that (despite everything) they still attract the passive allegiance of a large majority of Europeans – far more than any other institution apart from the state. The chapter then turns to organizational questions, examining in some detail the role of the churches themselves, together with the many different associations linked to them, in the social economy of each of the WREP case studies. From this point of view, the churches are seen as simply one organization amongst others. Interestingly, very different opinions emerge regarding the role (or more accurately roles) of the churches – this is even more the case if their contributions to the practical provision of welfare are distinguished from their involvement in public debate. Thirdly, the chapter engages the parts played by individuals as both the providers and recipients of welfare. In this respect one point is very clear: individuals matter and a particular person can make a considerable difference to the profile of the churches in welfare activities at the local level. For precisely the same reason, however, some (though by no means all) church-related welfare has an ad hoc and rather personal character.

In the final section, these analyses are drawn together and reset into the broader debate regarding religious change and the role of religion in late modern societies. What emerges, both from WREP itself and from the growing body of material in this field, is the increasingly ambiguous place of religion in modern Europe. Religion is not so much disappearing as changing in its form, function and content. For this reason the notion of 'religious change' emerges as a more appropriate label than 'secularization' when describing the role of religion and religious organizations in the WREP enquiry – a point strongly echoed in the theoretical discussion which concludes this book.

Chapter 3 finds its point of departure in the ongoing debate concerning the significance of gender in European policy-making, particularly in relation to welfare and social care. The challenges created by permanently rising expectations regarding welfare, at a time when resources are shrinking, form a crucial part of this discussion. The situation, moreover, includes a very 'human' (and necessarily gendered) element – namely the provision of care by one human being for another. This in turn relates to the sometimes heated debate concerning the role of the churches in welfare and its possible futures. Given the taken-for-granted association between women and caring, the churches are faced with some difficult decisions: who, precisely, will be responsible for their growing contributions in this field? These challenges, however, take on different meanings in different parts of Europe – a point well-illustrated by our case studies.

With these questions in mind, Ninna Edgardh examines our results in innovative ways, revealing both the surprising similarities that can be found across Europe alongside some very striking differences, noting in particular how apparently similar findings may have very different implications depending on the context in question. Amongst other things, these contrasts reflect the extent to which the churches make use of voluntary contributions and/or paid employment in the work that they undertake. The chapter ends rather differently, however, with a primarily theological discussion about a possible 'third way': one which might enable the churches to avoid a division that is becoming increasingly apparent in modern Europe. This division reflects two ideal types of church life. On the one hand can be found a church 'with a female face', which is committed to social activities; on the other is a church 'with a male face', which is more likely to be expressed in traditional forms of liturgy and institutional structures.

In parenthesis it is worth noting at this point both the pervasiveness of gender in our material but, at the same time, its apparent elusiveness. Gender differences are found everywhere in the data, as the imbalances between women and men make themselves felt in divisions of labour (in work and family life), in religious activities, in forms of social commitment, in the care for vulnerable people and indeed in neglect. Such imbalances, however, are frequently so taken for granted that for many of our interviewees they are almost invisible – for the great majority of our respondents what they see is simply the natural way of doing things rather than a constructed social order that requires reflection. Almost all of the challenges currently facing those responsible for welfare have, however, to do with radical changes in work and family life which have far-reaching effects for both women and men. It is for this reason that debates about gender relations are so central to European policy-making, indeed to European life as a whole – hence their importance for our work.

In WREP, gender has been approached as a social practice, continually constituted and reconstituted by the activities of individual women and men, as well as by social institutions. The decision to include gender as a key variable in the project was taken right at the start. The reasons were several. Based on previous research we could expect both religion and social care to be highly gendered areas, but the specific intersection between gender, welfare and religion in Europe seemed to be something of a blank spot. Given our proposed methodology, we were hopeful that we might achieve a more nuanced picture of how the churches are part of the more general gendering of care, through their practices as well as through their theological motivations. This has indeed been the case. The researchers have been able to map and to analyse these very intricate relationships in innovative ways. As a result, every aspect of our work (theoretical, methodological and substantive) has reflected the initial decision.

The approach in Chapter 4 is equally distinctive: it offers a theological interpretation of the motives for, involvement in and views about welfare provision among Europe's majority churches. It starts with an overview of the various church traditions covered in the study, describing and explaining their official doctrines in so far as these can be found in documents issued by churches, confessional publications and similar texts. This is a substantial body of material. In the second section of the chapter, Thomas Ekstrand draws on the empirical evidence from the case studies, using this to reflect on both the explicit and implicit theologies of the churches in question, and how each of these are worked out in practice. This section includes some very rich data, which reveals (amongst other things) the possibility – indeed the likelihood – of tensions between local applications and official or traditional teaching. Finally, the chapter identifies a number of specific theological problems facing the majority churches when they choose to become involved in welfare provision and opinion-forming activities – these problems are brought together under the concept of identity and are best expressed in the form of questions. Are churches putting their religious identity at risk by becoming large welfare providers? Or do they express their 'true' identities by embracing this role? Not everyone agrees about these matters.

Theorizing Welfare and Religion

The conclusion to this volume is divided into two unequal parts. The first section draws the threads of the previous chapters together, identifying the points at which the various approaches adopted in this book overlap or intersect. The crucial role of volunteers and volunteering in the welfare systems of Europe offers a good example. Who are these people and what are their motives for doing what they do, and why are so many of them women? A related issue lies in what can and cannot be taken for granted in the present situation. The taken-for-granted, moreover, is often 'invisible', a fact with important implications for methodology. A third theme relates to the shifting identities of religious organizations in modern Europe and how these might change as new functions are assumed. Lastly, it is important to capture the sustained tension between the prophetic or critical role of the churches and their hands-on experience as welfare agents. These are not easily reconciled.

The core of the chapter lies, however, in the exploration of a series of interrelated issues that emerge from the WREP data, all of which expand into larger questions concerning the nature of religion in late modern Europe. The relationship to welfare forms one part of this thinking (a major part), but the chapter goes further than this, in the sense that it opens up new fields of research for scholars of all disciplines who are struggling to keep up with the growing significance of religion in late modern societies.

The first question is simple enough: is there more or less religion in Europe than there used to be? The answer, however, is complex, not least with respect to the WREP material itself. In almost every one of our case studies, the role of the churches in the delivery of welfare is expanding rather than contracting, but in a situation where the churches themselves are struggling to meet the increase in demand, given that their resource base (in terms of both money and manpower) is reducing. In other words, there is a demonstrable increase in welfare provision on the part of the churches and in the demand for this, but against an overall decline in the number of people actively involved in the churches.

The second theme relates to the shift from a culture of religious obligation to one in which the populations of Europe are able to make their own decisions with respect to their religious lives. Almost nobody (or to be more precise, almost no adult) is *obliged* in late modern Europe to go to church for whatever reason – to get a house or a job, or even to acquire or maintain a degree of respectability. Almost all commentators agree, moreover, that this is a good thing: there is no place for religious coercion in a modern democracy. At the same time, welfare systems are far less monolithic than they used to be, and in theory at least, are designed to 'serve' customers or clients who are free to make choices about how to access the things that they require from the welfare sector. In other words, instead of one comprehensive system replacing another, both institutions (religious and secular) are subject to similar pressures as the public decide for themselves the particular packages that they require. The 'markets' that emerge, moreover, increasingly overlap as the churches join other service providers in the social economies of Europe's towns and cities. With this in mind, a primary task of WREP has been to describe and to explain the local situation regarding welfare and religion in eight European localities. One conclusion is very clear: in each of these places the secular and the religious are mutually constituted: each builds on to the other, and each reflects the characteristics displayed by the other – a point that needs developing in some detail.

If this kind of *inter*relationship is true of the secular and the religious, it is also true of the public and private. Initial (i.e. mid-twentieth-century) interpretations of this situation went as follows: scholars of religion very largely agreed that religion was disappearing from the public sphere in Europe, but that it continued to endure in the private lives of many Europeans. Our own view is that this is true to a certain extent, but it is not the whole truth. One reason to hesitate can, for instance, be found in Chapter 2. Given that very many Europeans maintain at least a nominal or passive link to their respective churches – which are themselves public institutions – it is clear that the notion of privatization needs immediate qualification. Much more radical, however, are the very visible changes that began to appear in the final decades of the twentieth century and which are, if anything, intensifying at the present time: religion for a wide variety of reasons is now central to *public* debate in almost all European societies. This rebalancing requires an explanation; it also takes many forms. Particularly interesting for WREP is the fact that religion is also growing in visibility in the social economy quite apart from its place in public debate (both local and national) – once again this challenges the notion of privatization.

The *visibility* of religion, however, needs careful interpretation. Is religion more visible because it is present in a way that had not previously been the case? Or is it more visible because we (European populations) now choose – for various reasons – to take notice of something that has always been there but that we have chosen to ignore? Or is it a combination of both these factors? The notion of the *post*-secular will be used as a pivot for this discussion and will lead in turn to the final pairing introduced in the conclusion: namely the intersection of recent changes and long-term trajectories.

The re-appearance (real or imagined) of religion in public debate is an example of relatively recent change. The long-term trajectories are, however, rather different and relate to the particular circumstances of each nation state in which this process takes place. Clearly these contextual issues return us once again to the 'crucial events' of Martin's analysis and the pathways of both secularization and welfare that develop as a result. The question can, however, be opened up in new ways: to consider the future as well as the past of religion in Europe. How, in other words, is the situation likely to develop as the twenty-first century progresses and what are the most effective ways of preparing for this? But once we step down this road, it is hard to avoid a second set of issues: those that interrogate the adequacy of social science to comprehend what is happening. Do we have the tools and concepts that are necessary for a proper understanding of religion in twenty-first-century Europe? A good start, surely, is the approach adopted in WREP: that is to appreciate that both religion and religious organizations have the potential to contribute to democratic society in Europe, understanding religion not only as a challenge, but as an available and effective resource in the lives of both individuals and the communities of which they are part.

An Institutional Note

As indicated in the Preface to this book, WREP is the second of three projects to emerge from the Uppsala Religion and Society Research Centre. The first formed part of a broader initiative funded by the national Swedish Research Council under the title 'The State and the Individual: Swedish Society in the Process of Change'. Within this, the Centre was responsible for the research that related to the constitutional changes that took place in Sweden in 2000 – the moment when the Church of Sweden ceased to be a state church (Bäckström 1999). The publications from this project are listed in Volume 1.

The WREP initiative was a natural extension of this work, in terms of both organization and content, in the sense that particular themes within the State Church project effectively acted as pilot studies for WREP. Specifically, they paid attention to the place of the majority church in the changing nature of Swedish society following the recession of the 1990s – an adjustment that included initial steps towards the privatization of welfare. Both projects, moreover, built on to established traditions of research, and on to studies that dealt both with the place of religion in late modern societies and with the role of the churches as active voluntary organizations.

WREP in turned begat WaVE (Welfare and Values in Europe), a project funded through the Framework 6 programme of the European Commission at a time when interest in and concerns about religion in Europe were developing rapidly. Some elements of WaVE are very similar to WREP but not all. Most important are the two 'extensions' to the earlier project: that is the decision to include both the religious minorities which now exist all over Europe, and four examples from the post-communist parts of the continent (namely Latvia, Poland, Croatia and Romania). The group of researchers has been enlarged accordingly. In WaVE, moreover, welfare has become more the 'prism' through which core values are perceived – those, for example, of inclusion and exclusion – than the focus of the research as such.

The Uppsala team is currently responsible for 'The Impact of Religion: Challenges for Society, Law and Religion'. This is an ambitious ten-year research programme funded jointly by the Swedish Research Council and Uppsala University and includes within it a variety of themes relating to welfare and well-being in religiously plural societies. The work on religion and welfare, therefore, is not only ongoing, but increasingly recognized as a central field in the inter-disciplinary study of religion and society. Further details of all these endeavours and the publications they have engendered can be found on the website of the Uppsala Religion and Society Research Centre.[9]

---

[9]   See http://www.crs.uu.se/Impact_of_religion.

Chapter 2

Majority Churches as Agents of European Welfare: A Sociological Approach

Per Pettersson

Introduction

In this chapter, the empirical results from the eight case studies in WREP will be analysed in light of the sociological literature on religious change, globalization, and the position of religion in late modern society. The analysis reflects the increasing number of studies which indicate the multi-faceted and ambiguous development of religion in present-day Europe (see for example Martin 2005; Berger 1999; 2001; Herbert 2003; Habermas 2005; Casanova 2006; Pettersson 2006; Davie 2007b; Berger et al. 2008). Our results confirm the view that modernity does not necessarily entail the disappearance of religion, but is more likely to mean a change in its form, function and content. 'Religious change' is therefore a more helpful label than 'secularization' when describing the position and role of religion and religious organizations in late modern European societies.

For example, our data tell us that there is both an increasing and a decreasing role for the majority churches in contemporary Europe. On the one hand, churches have a steady, and possibly increasing, role to play both in social cohesion and as welfare agents. At the same time, however, their membership is diminishing. But even with their reduced capacity (financial as well as human), they are expected to handle increasing social needs. In all these respects, our results reveal both similarities and differences across a wide variety of traditions and in different parts of the continent (compare Davie 2000; Eisenstadt 2003).

The following analysis is structured at three levels: the societal, the organizational and the individual. At the societal level, the challenges to Europe's welfare systems and questions about the position and role of each majority church in its respective society and culture are discussed. The subsequent section (the organizational level) focuses on the churches as one organization among others in society. At the individual level, the roles and perspectives of individuals in the context of church and welfare are introduced. The final part of the chapter summarizes the discussion from the previous sections, and relates this to a broader theoretical framework regarding religious change and the role of religion in late modern society.

Welfare and Religion at the Societal Level

As indicated, this section examines the current challenges to European welfare systems, and the relationships between the welfare systems and majority churches in the eight countries that are the focus of our study. The similarities and differences between these churches, their relationships to the state, and their roles in the respective welfare systems are carefully scrutinized.

Challenges to European Welfare Systems

In all of the eight countries, welfare conditions and the future of welfare systems are high on the public agenda. The specific nature of the debate varies, however, and is related to the historical background of the country in question, current welfare arrangements and the national political situation. That said, some challenges are common to all cases. Perhaps the most urgent of these is posed by the demographic changes taking place right across Europe, which have led to a rapidly ageing population, which causes pressure on all welfare systems. Medical and pharmaceutical improvements, combined with rising living standards, have hugely increased life expectancy in every European society, leading to radical changes in age structures. This tendency is exacerbated in countries with very low birth rates, such as Italy or Greece. Global migration, which increases the need for social and financial assistance among newly-arrived groups in all European countries, must also be taken into account. Equally important, finally, are the growing economic and social 'gaps' emerging in society, which are caused by new types of social exclusion and new forms of poverty – those, for example, which result from long-term unemployment.

A rather different type of challenge comes from transnational financial and political structures – organizations such as stock markets and the European Economic and Monetary Union (EMU). Standardized policies put pressure on all countries to adapt their economies to supranational principles, which more often than not means reducing their public expenditure – a tendency made considerably more urgent by the recent (2008) economic crisis and the excess of debt which has followed. At the same time, the implementation of market- and competition-based models in the organization and management of welfare causes further tensions. Traditional values underpinning public and voluntary non-profit management can easily come into conflict with the ethos of the 'for profit' commercial sector.

This combination of increasing pressures on welfare and the need to reduce public expenditure has provoked a number of critical issues, which churches as well as states have to deal with. A major question for the majority churches, for example, is how to react to cutbacks in welfare provision. Should the churches adopt a critical role in relation to the reduced ambitions of the state, or should the churches enter the stakes themselves as welfare entrepreneurs, taking over areas of service abandoned by the state? Should the churches speak out as a voice in public debate, or act as agents in social provision, or both (Lundström and

Wijkström 1997; Fokas 2009)? It is well-known that the German churches (both Protestant and Catholic) have acted as agents of the state in the delivery of welfare for several decades. Might this become a more general model? And what might be the conditions (formal and informal) of such agreements? And how might the contractual procedures work in practice? So far there are more questions than answers.

Other, deeper, issues follow from this. What would happen to the identity of the church if it began to provide basic welfare activities on behalf of the state? And why are states interested in churches as welfare providers in the first place? Are there particular characteristics of church-run welfare services that differ from the characteristics or qualities of public services? If so, what are these, and how can they be put to good use? The material from WREP should be looked at in this light. What overall tendencies, similarities, differences and tensions can be detected in the empirical material, and how do these results contribute to a general understanding of both welfare and religion in late modern society?

The Distinctive Character of European Welfare

One point is very clear: our data reveal a common, if at times uneven, European understanding of the relationship between the individual and society, which implies that no-one in need should be left without help by society as a whole – a fact already established in a number of more quantitative enquiries (De Moor 1995; Halman 2001; Davie 2002). The 450 Europeans interviewed in our case studies display, in their different ways, a common value base which attaches great importance to care for the weak and a sense of solidarity between people. Following this logic, it is not only up to the individual to take care of him or herself. Society at large, that is the state and other collective agents, are expected to assume at least some responsibility for those in need. This point is nicely illustrated by an Italian representative of the public authorities who says, '[I]t is a matter of civilization. People have the right to be assisted by the stronger parts of society, through all possible means, public and private' (Frisina 2006: 188). Similarly, a Finnish respondent declares quite simply that '[W]elfare means that the municipality can take care of all basic needs' (Yeung 2006: 180).

Such an understanding of solidarity between people is deeply-rooted in Europe – the more so if seen from outside. Exactly the same idea can be found, for example, in several national constitutions as well as that of the European Union itself.[1] Indeed the whole idea of the European Union, at least in theory, reflects the notion of commonality and sharing beyond national borders. Such values are implemented in various ways and to various degrees in European welfare systems

---

[1]   Article II-94:2 of the EU Constitution states, 'Everyone residing and moving legally within the European Union is entitled to social security benefits and social advantages in accordance with Union law and national laws and practices' (European Union Constitution 2004).

– in marked contrast to cultures where individuals *are* obliged to take care of themselves, and where society is not expected to act to support and care for people who cannot manage alone. Strikingly, both the debates surrounding President Obama's attempts to introduce health care reform in the United States in 2010, and the European commentaries on these, epitomize such contrasts.

It is clear that this common basis of solidarity, with its largely Christian roots, is upheld by the public authorities in Europe as well as by the majority churches. There are, however, significant differences in the manner in which these values are expressed, deriving at least in part from the ways that the historic churches interact with their respective states. In the north, for example, the comprehensive welfare systems of the Nordic countries endorse the role of the state in handling collective responsibility. Conversely, needy individuals in Italy and Greece are normally absorbed into the extended family. In this part of Europe, welfare organizations exist mainly to care for those without such a network. The role of the churches also differs: in Germany, the churches themselves are major practitioners of collective solidarity, while the Church of Sweden is an active supporter of a strong welfare state. In Italy and Greece respectively, the Catholic Church and the Greek Orthodox Church underline and guard the role of the family as a primary welfare agent, whilst providing emergency help for those in need.

This emphasis on solidarity is regarded as distinctively European. How, then, will this feature be managed by the European Union in terms of the gradual move towards convergence with respect to social policies?[2] What, conversely, will happen to common European values in an increasingly multicultural and religiously diverse society? Will this mean the introduction, even the imposition, of religiously-linked values on social policies? If so, how will negotiations about different religious values take place in the arena of welfare? Alternatively, will a growing respect for religious differences mean an increasing separation of religious values from the public sphere, including the provision of welfare? How, finally, will the influence of transnational organizations – such as large companies, financial bodies and the agents of standardization (for instance the International Organization for Standardization) – affect these inherited values?

The Particular Qualities of the Majority Churches: Unique as Institutions

A further distinctive feature of Europe is its relatively homogeneous religious history – i.e. of dominant Christian churches with close relationships to the nation state. There can be no doubt that a Christian heritage is a formative factor in the construction of Europe, in terms of cultural norms as well as institutional structures (Davie 2000). It is equally true that the quasi-monopoly status of Europe's Christian churches diminished considerably in the nineteenth and twentieth

---

[2] Even if there is no explicit programme for policy convergence, such a process is implicitly taking place – for example, in the need for shared norms regarding labour mobility. This will have consequences for social policy all over Europe.

centuries, through the gradual separation of church and state, a loss of overall authority and a corresponding growth of religious minorities. None the less, a majority of Europeans are still in some sense attached to these churches, which continue to play a significant role (both formally and informally) in almost all European localities, regions and nation states. Historically, moreover, the majority churches have been the providers of education, medical care and charity. Through these actions, and by the thinking that underpins their work, these institutions have contributed significantly to the European understanding of solidarity and social responsibility.

This is clearly demonstrated in our case studies. Over and over again in our interviews, respondents mention the role of the majority churches in the transmission of cultural values. For example, a Swedish director of a public authority in Gävle says, 'The Christian message is the foundation of our culture to a large extent … the church has had such a great influence on our views and our way of being' (Edgardh Beckman et al. 2006: 48). Indeed, many interviewees stress the churches' role as the bearers of what they consider to be fundamental *human* values, not only European ones. What is more, the provision of such values, and a framework to maintain them, is seen as an essential contribution to the welfare and well-being of society. Precisely this is noted by a Finnish public authority representative, who says, 'The church is a central part of our society. It still is – we see the church as provider of our guidelines for life. People do still listen to the church and its pronouncements' (Yeung 2006: 171).

Increasingly, however, Europe is becoming religiously diverse. The change takes two rather different forms. It comes, first, from the growing number of immigrants arriving in Europe from many different parts of the world. Most striking in this respect are the highly visible Muslim minorities all over Europe – noticeable, among other things, in terms of buildings and in terms of dress, both of which are at times contentious. In France, 6–7 per cent of the population are of Muslim origin; in Sweden, England, Germany and Greece, 3–4 per cent; in Norway and Italy about 2 per cent; and in Finland about 1 per cent.[3] Despite the fact that these percentages are small and that a significant number of these people are not practising Muslims, this minority constitutes an important sign of Europe's increasing religious diversity.[4]

A second and equally important change – one in fact that penetrates even more deeply – is the growing cultural and religious pluralism among Europeans themselves. The loss of traditional, and often hierarchical, forms of social control

---

[3]   It is important to note that there are no official comparable statistical data on the numbers of Muslims in Europe. These percentages are estimated from the different sources provided by the European Monitoring Centre on Racism and Xenophobia (EUMC 2006) and Nielsen (2009).

[4]   As was made clear in the previous chapter, the focus of WREP lies on the majority churches of Europe. The follow up study – Welfare and Values in Europe (WaVE) – paid particular attention to the religious minorities of Europe.

over cultural resources enables individuals to pick and choose on their own terms from an ever growing supply of cultural goods (Giddens 1991). The globalization of cultural communication – accelerated by media, travel and the availability of the internet – simply encourages this trend. As a result, Europe's common historical traditions are increasingly mixed with new forms of religious pluralism, caused on the one hand by immigration, and on the other by internal fragmentation and the growth of more individualized forms of spirituality (Heelas and Woodhead 2005).

Taking all these things into account, and recognizing the extent of the changes that are taking place, we maintain none the less that the majority churches remain unique as institutions – largely because of their critical role in the development and formation of European society. It is important to remember that these churches still span the whole of Europe. Their distinctive buildings can be found in every locality (parish), region (diocese) and country (national church), as can their personnel. In most settlements (large or small), the oldest building still being used for its original purpose is the church (Bäckström and Bromander 1995; Davies 1994). This fact alone underlines the role of the churches in providing links to the past and aspirations for the future. At the same time, the churches' personnel offer liturgies to mark the beginning of life (baptisms) and the end of life (funerals) – the latter in particular remain a significant point of reference for most Europeans. Such liturgies are linked to the deepest realities of human living, and for this reason alone, they function (if only implicitly) to integrate the majority churches into society at large (Davie 2000; Hervieu-Legér 2000).

More concretely, the churches offer an impressive variety of religious and social activities, forming a major part of Europe's social and cultural capital – the case studies in Volume 1 offer a huge range of illustrations in each of the eight countries. Interestingly, however, it quickly became clear to us that many aspects of the church's social role are so much taken for granted that they are not referred to directly in the interviews; instead they are communicated indirectly, often in the form of an understatement. In other words, just as beliefs are implicit rather than explicit, certain kinds of knowledge are passive rather than active.

Churches as Significant Agents in the Social Economy

In everyday discourse, the churches are generally described as institutions in decline, increasingly marginalized from mainstream society. This image is correct in some respects, but it is a view which finds its point of departure in the historically dominant role of the churches. It does not take sufficient account of the churches' current position as one voluntary organization among others in modern society. In fact, in comparison with other such organizations, it is clear that the majority churches are not only holding their own, but are maintaining a relatively dominant position – not least with reference to the issues under review in the WREP project. The following paragraphs reflect on this shifting and somewhat ambiguous situation.

In most of our eight cases, the churches are formally constituted as voluntary organizations placed between the individual and the state, and are regarded as part of the voluntary sector; in a few countries they still hold the position of state churches. Even the state churches, however, perform much of their activity through associated voluntary organizations. Very often, moreover, such organizations have a rather more neutral image in terms of religion than the churches themselves. This is especially the case in the field of welfare, a fact frequently noticed by our respondents (see below).

In both academic and public discourse, a wide variety of labels are used to describe the organizational structures which fall between the individual or family and the state. Among them are the following: social economy, non-profit, voluntary, non-governmental, third-sector and so on. Irrespective of their formal position in relation to the state, all of our churches should be seen as part of this social economy in the sense that they both organize and produce a particular kind of 'value-creating' activities (compare Harris 1998; Wijkström and Lundström 2002). For this reason, churches can be viewed as 'service-producing' organizations, a point which is especially clear when it comes to their role as agents of welfare. Concepts from service research are therefore very useful tools in the analysis of their role (Pettersson 2000).

The social economy at large, as we define it here, consists of a number of organizations at different levels: self-help groups, networks, interest organizations, political, religious and sports organizations, co-operatives, philanthropic organizations, political parties, labour unions and many others. Nonetheless, in all the national and local contexts studied in this project, the largest institution in society apart from the state is clearly the majority church. This is particularly apparent in terms of the number of people who still claim to be members of, or affiliated to the historic churches (whether this attachment be implicit or explicit), as can be seen in Table 2.1 below.[5]

---

[5]   Statistics of affiliation to majority churches are compiled in different ways. The figures used here are taken from different sources, and are approximate estimates of the percentage of people whose primary religious affiliation is to the major religious institution in the country. Comparison between countries is difficult for a whole variety of reasons, sociological as well as theological. Further details for each case can be found in: Stathopoulou (2007) for Greece; Rapporto Eurispes (2006) for Italy; Church of Norway (2009) for Norway; Evangelical Lutheran Church of Finland (2009) for Finland; Church of Sweden (2009) for Sweden; Statistisches Bundesamt Deutschland (2010) for Germany; ISSP (2007) for France; and ORB (2007) for England. Germany must be considered a special case among the eight countries, in the sense that there are two majority (folk) churches, Catholic and Protestant. Each has regional dominance in different parts of the country, and the two combined attract 61 per cent of the total population as members. Due to the specificities of the East German case, only 25 per cent of people in that part of the country belong to one of the two major churches; conversely, in the western part of Germany, the membership rate remains at 69 per cent.

Table 2.1   Majority church membership/affiliation in the WREP case studies

Country	% Estimated membership of (affiliation to) the majority church	
Greece	Greek Orthodox (2007)	93
Italy	Roman Catholic (2006)	87
Norway	Church of Norway, Lutheran (2009)	81
Finland	Church of Finland, Evangelical Lutheran (2009)	80
Sweden	Church of Sweden, Lutheran (2009)	71
Germany	Protestant and Roman Catholic (2007) Protestant 30%, Catholic 31% Total membership: 25% in the former East and 69% in the former West	61
France	Roman Catholic (2007)	58
England	Church of England, Anglican (2007)	45

These statistics require careful interpretation. Since we are talking about majority churches, it is clear that church membership often overlaps with an individual's cultural and/or national identity. In Italy, for example, belonging to the Catholic Church is one way of conveying that you are an Italian (Pace 1998). Other churches play a similar role in their respective contexts. Interestingly, in several of the eight case studies people express such sentiments by saying that an important function of the church lies in the fact that it provides a sense of social belonging and thus of security (compare Bäckström 2001). It is clear that rites of passage play a significant role in this respect. At the same time, the churches provide – indeed in a sense they embody – a significant network of social relationships in society. Such networks (religious or other) are crucially important for social cohesion, stability, security and economic growth – as highlighted in a wide variety of empirical enquiries (Putnam et al. 1992; Putnam 2000; Castells 1996).

The aggregated social mechanisms, which link people together in any given society, are sometimes referred to as a society's 'social capital' – a term popularized through the work of Robert Putnam. Through their sheer size, the majority churches constitute an essential part of the social capital in all of our case studies. They link people together in many different ways – a facility which is directly referred to in a number of our interviews. Respondents underline the role of the parishes for more general networking at the local level. A striking illustration appears in the German case, where representatives of the *public* authorities in Reutlingen regarded the parish as an irreplaceable social network, recognizing in particular the duty of church members to care for their neighbours (Leis-Peters 2010).

A Major Institution, Second only to the State: Six Tentative Statements

It is interesting to reflect on the implications of this situation both for WREP and beyond. In order to do this, we have formulated the following somewhat tentative, but at the same time radical, statements. All of them highlight the church's presence as the largest institution apart from the state (in terms of size and nominal membership) in most European societies:

1. It is clear that an institution of this size will have at least a tenuous link to a very large number of individuals in the country in question, in many cases the majority of the population. This can be formal membership or simply a vague sense of belonging. Clearly, membership (or whatever term is used) of the various churches implies very different degrees of involvement or activity, even between adherents of the same church. That said, being a member or feeling that one belongs implies that there is some kind of attachment to be taken into account. For most people, the rites of passage are the most popular services provided by the church. It follows that those who are members, or who claim to belong, have direct contact with the churches' personnel at specified and often critical moments in their lives.

2. Through their links with so many, and such a wide variety of individuals, the historic churches are implicitly connected to almost all sections of society. This network of relationships can be seen as an invisible infrastructure, which penetrates deeply into the population. In this sense it is possible to argue that the relationships between the church and the individuals who are linked to it integrate the church into the society of which it is part.

3. As a result, the church is likely to be seen as a less controversial institution than those which represent a minority of the population. Thus the majority church is regarded as more mainline and more 'neutral' than minority religious groups. It is expected to act as the representative of society at large, and to speak on behalf of different religious groups. For this reason it is likely to become a natural partner for the public authorities, and is welcomed as a distinctive collaborator alongside other organizations. Such relationships are expressed in different ways in our case studies. In many English parishes, for example, Church of England clergy are actively involved in local primary schools and often chair boards of governors. In Sweden, church buildings are popular (though at times controversial) places in which to celebrate the end of the school year. And even in France, where church–state relationships are notoriously conflictual, the historic buildings of the Catholic Church are financially supported by the state in a way that those of the religious minorities are not.

4. A majority church tends to adopt ideological and theological positions which are consonant with the dominant opinions in the country or society

concerned. And if, occasionally, the church in question does express a more unusual or extreme point of view, it usually accepts that not all of those who belong to it will follow the same line. Indeed, the fact that an institution involves the majority of the population implies in itself that it represents a wide variety of opinions on all sorts of issues: social, political, economic, philosophical, theological and so on. We can assume, moreover, that a church will be more likely to adapt to what might be termed 'public' opinion if its structures are more democratic and less hierarchical. The more democratic the structures, the more room there is for such opinions to exist *within* the church. Thus we should expect rather more 'moderate' positions in the mainstream Protestant churches of Europe compared with the more ideological, and at times uncompromising, positions of their Catholic equivalents (Martin 1978).

5. As already mentioned, an institution which has a large number of citizens as members will generate a significant amount of a society's social capital. When using the concept 'social capital' in this context, we employ a wide definition including all kinds of social networks, not only organized forms of co-operation (Putnam 2000). The relationships that emerge from such activities connect individuals with their own history, with their relatives, with each other and with local, national and even global populations – many churches have links overseas. The implications are considerable – notably for the maintenance of shared values which become in turn the preconditions for solidarity, and some would argue for democracy itself.

6. Finally, the majority churches and the organizations and religious orders that are linked to them constitute a major part of the social economy in all our case studies. Churches are without doubt influential social and economic agents. They possess property, buildings, financial and human resources (such as local officials and volunteers), and run a huge number of economic and social activities. In this book we focus on the role of the churches as welfare agents, but they are also major cultural entrepreneurs in other fields, not least in music. In short, local churches all over Europe organize activities which are vitally important for social integration, sustainability and development.

Church–State Relationships

From a common history as institutions in union with the state, the majority churches of Europe have developed, and continue to develop, in different ways. Present church–state relationships are, however, complex: it is not easy to make a simple comparison between countries. As a first move, it is important to distinguish between the formal church–state relationship and the many informal connections that operate in daily life. Results from our case studies show very clearly the inconsistencies between these. A good example can be found in the Swedish case, which reveals that – despite the formal separation between church and state in 2000 – some kinds of co-operation between the Church of Sweden and local public authorities have in fact increased. As a Swedish church representative says, '[A] typical example is to look at the public schools coming to church, which was not possible at all for a time. Today it is a matter of course to come to Christmas services, Easter gatherings and such things' (Edgardh Beckman et al. 2006: 56). It is obvious that the position of the church in relation to the state can be stronger in practice than the legal position suggests. Conversely, a strong church–state relationship does not automatically mean a strong position in local life. The Church of England, for example, has a well-established legal position in relation to the state, but a representative of the public authority in Darlington, England is not so sure: 'I have to say that the church in general is almost never mentioned … it is not mentioned at all in strategic thinking, operational, anything' (Middlemiss Lé Mon 2010: 22).

That said, the moderately strong links between church and state give the Church of England an official, and distinctive, position in many public contexts. This is the only church in Europe, for example, with formal representation in Parliament. Every working day, parliamentary proceedings are introduced with Christian prayer and 26 Bishops sit, as of right, in the House of Lords.[6] In other respects, however, the English case is ambiguous. For a start, the state takes no financial responsibility for the church. And in many contexts (including the field of welfare), the Church of England is treated in just the same way as all other churches and religious organizations; it is simply one among many faith-based organizations that engage in welfare activities.

Of all our case studies, the Greek Orthodox Church has the strongest formal relationship with the state. Interviews from the Greek case study show that the relationship between church and state is perceived as so close that it is difficult sometimes for people to distinguish between them. Church and state are seen as a single institution, with similar expectations placed on them. Although the cases are very different, this situation is in some senses replicated in Norway, which also has a formally constituted state church, bearing in mind that the constitutional position of the Norwegian church is undergoing change – its position in Norwegian society is a much debated issue (Schmidt 2006; Norway, Department of Culture and Church 2008).

In Italy, Germany and Finland the majority churches are formally separate from the state, but the presence of the majority church in public settings is officially recognized – for example, through religious education in public schools. The separate but still relatively close relationship between church and state in Italy is regulated by an agreement established in 1929.[7] In Germany, both the Catholic

---

[6] This situation may come to an end relatively soon. The composition of the House of Lords is currently under review.

[7] The *Lateran Pact* of 1929, also called The Lateran Treaty, are three agreements made in 1929 between the Kingdom of Italy and the Holy See, ratified 7 June 1929. They consist of three documents: a) a political treaty recognizing the full sovereignty of the Holy

and the Protestant churches have been officially separate from the state since 1919. However, the preamble of the German constitution still refers explicitly to God, and the majority churches are highly involved in religious education in schools; they are also the dominant welfare providers in Germany (see below). The Evangelical Lutheran Church of Finland was separated from the state in 1870, but maintains close connections with it. Since the separation between the Church of Sweden and the state in 2000, Sweden has a weaker church–state connection than most of our case studies. All that is left of the historically strong relationship is a law stating that the Church of Sweden must remain an Evangelical Lutheran church, that it must be a democratic organization which is open to all, and that it should 'cover' the whole of Sweden geographically (SFS 1998). France, in terms of WREP and indeed in Europe as a whole, has the strictest form of separation between state and church, a division established in 1905 and underpinned by the specifically French principle of *laïcité*.[8]

It is difficult, however, to 'order' countries on a church–state relationship scale, partly because of the point already mentioned: official principles and policies very often differ from what happens on the ground. Indeed the apparently clear-cut French case offers an instructive example. Quite clearly, there is a discrepancy between the very strict principle of *laïcité*, and its application in practice. As we have seen already, the state takes responsibility for church buildings erected before 1906, and offers them to the Catholic Church without charge – at considerable benefit to the church. At the same time, the Catholic clergy benefit from the public social security system: surprising though it may seem, the clergy's national insurance and old-age pensions are substantially supported by the contributions of all citizens (Valasik 2010).

Our fieldwork revealed further noteworthy ambiguities regarding church–state connections in France and the role of the churches in welfare. On the ground, religiously-linked associations are, among others, significant providers of services in Evreux. There can be no doubt about this. Interestingly, however, in the course of the French case study, elected politicians from the locality were not only ignorant of what was happening on the ground, but declined on principle (the principle of *laïcité*) even to discuss the matter. The individual responsible for these matters in Evreux puts this as follows, '[I]'ve never asked myself what the Catholic Church did on the level of welfare. Perhaps I should have done, but no, I've never thought about it' (Valasik 2010: 138). Such sentiments were, in fact, very similar to those of the English local official quoted above.

See in the State of Vatican City, which was thereby established; b) a concordat regulating the position of the Catholic Church and the Catholic religion in the Italian state; and c) a financial convention agreed on as a definitive settlement of the claims of the Holy See following the losses of its territories and property.

[8]   The notion of *laïcité* implies the absence of religion from the public sphere. The concept was explained in detail in Chapter 8 of Volume 1.

Different Understandings of the Role of the State

When analysing the role of the churches in different national contexts, it is necessary to clarify some marked national differences regarding the state itself: its role, the expectations of its citizens regarding this role, and degree of trust that surrounds its activities. In all three respects, the divergences are considerable despite the commonalities of the European past, and concern the relationship between the state and the individual on the one hand, and the state and the churches on the other. In the Nordic countries and in France, for example, the state is not only regarded as strong but as the ally of the people. In Greece, in contrast, the state is seen as not only as weak but as profoundly unreliable (Angell 2010; Pessi 2010; Fokas and Molokotos-Liederman 2010). Germany's twentieth-century history has encouraged a view of the state as an organization which cannot fully be trusted if it becomes too dominant. For this reason it must be hedged around with checks and balances (Leis 2004). As a result, the principle of subsidiarity sits well in Germany – but for very different reasons than in Italy, where the same concept is rooted in a social policy built on the central role of the family, strongly supported by Catholic social teaching (Frisina 2004). The British view of the state[9] falls somewhere in between the Nordic countries and Germany: in Britain, the state is deemed reliable and is accepted as a *regulatory* power. Its primary role is to provide a solid framework for society, but the state as such should not enter or control people's private lives. One result of this situation is that assistance from the state is considered a favour rather than an entitlement.

In the Nordic countries, the state is commonly expected to take care of citizens throughout their lives. Unsurprisingly, therefore, the majority of Swedish, Finnish and Norwegian interviewees from the general population, as well as from the local authorities and churches, strongly defended the state as a provider of comprehensive welfare services. A Swedish representative of the population in Gävle expresses it like this: 'Swedish welfare means security from the cradle to the grave. From the moment you are born until you are laid to rest you are taken care of by the public authorities if you can't manage on your own' (Edgardh and Pettersson 2010: 39). Another example of the Nordic view is the Swedish way of labelling society a 'home for the people', an expression used especially with regard to the twentieth-century development of the Swedish welfare model. In other words, the state is thought of as a mother and father, taking care of its citizens as if they were members of a family. This way of describing an individual's relationships to the state is totally different from the view of Greek people, who do not trust a state that delivers inefficient services. A monk in Thiva puts this very directly: 'wherever there is civil servant mentality, nothing can work well' (Fokas and Molokotos-Liederman 2010: 174).

---

[9]   The references here are to the British state, though the case study in itself concerns England and the role of the Church of England in welfare activities.

Churches and the Division of Labour in Welfare Systems

In each national context, the division of roles between different agents in the provision of welfare has changed over time (Bäckström et al. 2004; Jeppsson Grassman 2004). Historically, in every one of our case studies, family members have been the main providers of assistance for individuals in need – a form of welfare provision that depends on the proximity of the people in question, and works best in stable, agricultural societies. As part of the break-up of agricultural society and the growth of industrial production, however, many people migrated from rural areas to the cities that housed the new industries. The need for new forms of social services increased in parallel with this migration; the support of increasingly isolated families was no longer sufficient.

Large numbers of voluntary organizations based on altruistic social support were formed in the context of industrialization and urbanization. These organizations, however, developed differently in different parts of Europe, depending on the particular needs of the situation in question. They were often linked to the churches. At the same time, and in parallel with the growth of voluntary organizations, nation states also expanded their social responsibilities, in order to provide security and support to people in need. In Northern Europe, the idea of a strong social state dominated. Here the expanding public sector relieved the family of several of its traditional responsibilities, as well as taking over a number of activities organized by voluntary agents. Elsewhere, as we have seen, the balance was rather different.

In addition to the family, voluntary organizations and the state, it is important to note a fourth type of welfare provider: the private sector. Private companies appear as welfare agents in two rather different respects. First, they have been responsible for services, which form part of an employee's working conditions – good examples can be found in the provision of housing or medical care, when these are linked to contracts of employment, bearing in mind that the particular nature of these services varies considerably between companies and countries. Secondly, and increasingly, private companies are offering welfare provision as their core business, competing in a growing welfare market, for example in care for elderly people, in specialized medical treatment, and in parts of the education system. In other words, welfare itself is becoming increasingly commercialized, a point covered in some detail in the following section.

Family, voluntary organizations, the public sector and private businesses, then, constitute four social sectors, all of which are involved in the provision of welfare services (see Figure 2.1 below). The division of labour between these agents within a specific welfare system is sometimes referred to as the 'welfare mix'. As is to be expected, both the historical development and the continuing changes in the precise division of labour between these agents varies considerably from one country to another. There is, however, a common trend: all of the countries in the WREP project have shifted first from an agriculturally-based to an industrially-based economy, and are subsequently transforming into

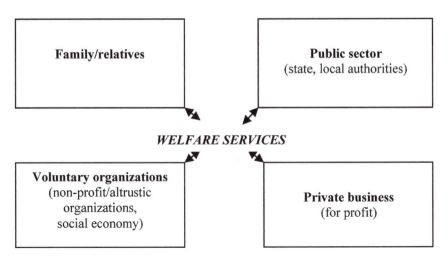

Figure 2.1   Four sectors in the provision of welfare services

societies dominated by a service economy (Bell 1973; Toffler 1980; Ingelstam 1995; Castells 1996). Their welfare arrangements have adapted accordingly.

The position and role of the churches in the welfare mix merits careful attention. It depends on a variety of factors, including the relationship of the churches to the other welfare providers, and the precise division of labour between the providers themselves at different points in their respective national and local contexts. It is equally important to grasp that the churches have affected and have been affected by all four of the contributors outlined above. Clearly they have strong links to individuals and their family networks – this has always been the case. Regarding *public* services, the churches are interlinked much more closely in some countries than others. Thirdly, the churches themselves play many different roles in the voluntary sector, and at times they co-operate with private business. Each of these points can be illustrated by the WREP data.

In the social democratic model of the Nordic countries, for example, the churches do least in the basic provision of welfare. In most other cases, the churches have a formally accepted and at times integrated role as welfare providers, based on agreements or contracts with the states in question. Germany is the most developed case in this respect; indeed it is almost an exception in the sense that the churches are responsible for a *major* part of basic welfare provision. The German churches, both Catholic and Protestant, constitute the two largest providers in the German welfare system, operating through their respective welfare organizations – for example diaconal institutions, social organizations or self-help groups, all of which are subsumed into the following umbrella organizations: Diakonisches Werk (Protestant) and Caritasverband (Catholic). These organizations belong to the voluntary sector, but most of the services that they offer are financed by the state and by state-regulated social insurance schemes. In short, the German state, together with the appropriate regional and local authorities, retains the responsibility for welfare provision, but delegates as much of the work as possible to voluntary organizations, including the churches. In this sense the German churches are effectively doing a large part of what the state does in northern Europe. In England and France, the state is clearly the main welfare agent, though in close collaboration with voluntary organizations, some of them with religious affiliations. In Britain the voluntary sector is relatively developed. In France, it is less so. In the French case, moreover, the contributions of the religious sector are at times surprising given the pervasiveness of *laïcité* in the French system (see above).

In southern Europe, individuals in need remain reliant on their families, who are supported by the churches in this role. In both Italy and Greece, the churches deem it important both to legitimate and to encourage the role of the family as the primary provider of welfare. Somewhat paradoxically, therefore, their role corresponds to that of the Nordic churches in legitimating and supporting the *existing* welfare model. It is important to remember, however, that the Catholic Church in Italy and the Greek Orthodox Church do not only focus on the part played by the family, they themselves take on a substantial role in the provision of care, both directly and through their associated organizations.

Quite apart from the welfare mix as such, the data from our case studies reveal how attitudes to and expectations of the church as a welfare provider reflect the system itself. In northern Europe, for example, where the state and the public authorities have the overall responsibility for welfare, expectations of the churches are minimal. A Norwegian politician in Drammen expresses it like this: 'I don't think that people have expectations that the church should contribute. I think that when you actually see how the church contributes, you are positively surprised. In principle the state is supposed to take care of you from the cradle to the grave' (Angell 2010: 67). In Germany, in contrast, the 'Sozialstaat' (the official welfare system) presupposes a strong involvement from major voluntary organizations. Accordingly, expectations are high regarding the capacity of the churches to undertake a significant portion of welfare services. In southern Europe, things are changing. The traditional role of the family as the major welfare provider has been eroded for a variety of reasons, themselves related to the wider processes of social change. The latter include decreasing birth rates, increasing levels of divorce, the increasing integration of women in the labour market and increasing levels of migration (both within and between countries). As a result gaps are exposed in the traditional system, which have led to rising expectations regarding other actors in the welfare mix, not least the churches. In the Greek case study in particular, people expressed high expectations of the church as an institution capable of filling the gaps in the welfare system. Indeed – as will be shown in the next section – there is a general tendency across all eight countries for the churches to *increase* their involvement in the provision of welfare, irrespective of their existing position in the welfare mix.

Welfare and Religion at the Organizational Level

It is now time to look at the data in terms of what they tell us about the majority churches as welfare providers in modern European societies. The section starts with an outline of the organizational characteristics of church-related welfare and its role in relation to other providers. In this connection, it is important to consider the majority churches both as service providers and as voices in the public debate. We will then look at how these activities are regarded, drawing on quotations from our various respondents (i.e. representatives of the general population, of the local authorities and of the churches themselves). Running through this section is an underlying question; should the churches develop their roles as service providers, or should they put pressure on the state to increase its own activities (and therefore resources) in the field of welfare? This question will not be answered directly (that would not be possible), but will be considered from a variety of angles.

Churches as 'Public' Voluntary Organizations

The observations of our case studies demonstrate that the historic churches are in many respects becoming increasingly like any other organization within the voluntary sector. At the same time, however, they are distinctive. The data reveal that the expectations placed on the majority churches are of a different kind from those placed on voluntary organizations in general. This has to do with the special character of a majority church, which for the reasons given above is culturally as well as institutionally rooted in the country in question. In this sense, these churches are seen as belonging to everyone, irrespective of religious involvement. Inevitably, therefore, the majority churches have a 'public' character, which is reinforced in organizational terms – a comprehensive network of parishes. Because of this, the majority churches interact in the welfare arena in two rather different ways: as part of the voluntary sector on the one hand, and as a part of the 'public' sector on the other. 'Public', in this respect, means something more than the state itself.

Expectations of the majority churches as public or semi-public organizations are expressed in different ways by the interviewees. Public authority representatives in Darlington, for instance, expect the Church of England to provide social services regardless of people's religious affiliation – and without 'preaching' to them. In other words, the Church of England's position as an established church implies a responsibility for all people, an obligation which is not imposed on other religious groups. At the same time, the established church has a duty to represent – and to act as the voice of – all faith communities. This is nicely demonstrated by the fact that Anglican prison chaplains have responsibility for ensuring that prisoners of all faiths have access to their respective religious representatives (Middlemiss 2004; Beckford and Gilliat 1998). This need for impartiality is confirmed by church representatives in Darlington, for example by a parish priest who says that the great advantage of the Church of England is 'that at its best it is seen as the best possibility of neutral holy ground. It belongs in that sense to everybody' (Middlemiss Lé Mon 2010: 123). Further interviews from the English and indeed from the French and German case studies reinforce this point: they repeatedly show that the buildings owned by the churches are regarded as *public* resources, essential to the community as a meeting place for all people and for many different groups.

Parishes and Church-related Organizations

The European majority churches have a common organizational form: their territorially-based parish structure which has existed for centuries. This structure, which covers the entire territory, is one expression of the public and shared character of these churches. As a result, the church is present in every single locality in Europe, a fact that was noticed in all our case studies. More often than not, this was seen as something positive: it provided a sense of belonging, a collective identity, as well as cultural and historical links.

In terms of their participation in the organizational sphere of society, the majority churches act through two different channels: the parish itself which forms a natural base and a common frame of reference for all church-related work, and a whole series of separate church-linked organizations such as religious orders, youth organizations or social action groups. The specific division of labour and responsibilities between these two organizational forms differs between the case studies and indeed between different localities within the same country. Our results reveal, however, that it is the separate church-related organizations which play the more important role in welfare provision. This is especially the case in Germany and Italy. In the Greek case, it is the regional diocesan structure of the official church which assumes the major responsibility for organizing welfare, complemented by the local parish and other organizations. Unsurprisingly, in the Catholic Church and the Greek Orthodox Church religious orders also have a central role to play. In the Nordic countries, conversely, the dominant role of the state means that the role of the churches in basic welfare provision is very limited – which might explain why separate church-related organizations have not developed to the same extent as they have in other parts of Europe.

France, as ever, is a special case, due to its strict separation of church and state. The French study clearly reveals two rather different organizational 'faces' of the local Catholic church in Evreux. These are the parish and the associations, which interact in subtle ways bearing in mind the principle of *laïcité*. In line with this principle, there must be no official collaboration between church and state. Nonetheless, co-operation does in fact take place between Catholic associations and the various levels of the state. It is almost as if the church participates in welfare invisibly, through its associations (Valasik 2006). Notably, it supports the pioneering work of new organizations or projects which arise to deal with particular problems – such as the challenges posed by illegal immigrants – by loaning premises, setting up networks, and sometimes by giving financial support. A lay worker in Evreux perceptively expresses both the importance of church-related social work and its subtle links to the official Catholic Church: '[I]f all of a sudden there were no Catholic associations working in welfare, the state wouldn't be able to cope. But people find it hard to make the link between the church as an institution and the Catholic aid organizations which help thousands of people' (Valasik 2010: 210). This division of labour between the official church and the church-related organizations in France is best understood as a practical adaptation of the principle of *laïcité*.

Churches as Agents in Social Work: What Do the Churches Really Do?

Like voluntary organizations in general, the churches have different functions in relation to the welfare system. These can be divided into four main types: vanguard roles, improver roles, value-guardian roles and service-provider roles (Kramer 1981; Angell and Wyller 2006). In the vanguard role, the church acts in the frontline, highlighting new areas of need and prioritizing forgotten groups of people. As an improver, the focus is on the enhancement of existing welfare provision in order to increase different aspects of its quality. In its role as value guardian, the church acts as a defender of, and advocate for, various human values. In parenthesis, it is important to note that if the value-guardian role comes into conflict with the existing political regime and is actively expressed, it will become a directly political role, often deemed a prophetic role (especially in a theological context). Due to the close church–state relationship in most of our cases, this type of role has been relatively undeveloped in the majority churches studied in WREP. However, as differentiation between church and state increases, the political dimension may grow accordingly.

The service-provider role, finally, can itself be of three different kinds – depending whether we are talking about a primary, complementary or supplementary provider of services. As a *primary* provider, the church is either the sole provider, or among the main providers, of a certain kind of welfare. If, on the other hand, the church is offering services which are qualitatively different from what is provided by the public welfare system, these can be labelled *complementary* services. When, finally, the church-provided service is simply an alternative choice, a substitute for the same service offered by the state, it offers a *supplementary* welfare service. It is clear that the same church may appear as a primary provider in one welfare area and as a complementary provider in another.

The mapping aspect of the WREP case studies reveals that all the local churches participated in welfare activities of one kind or another, both as part of their ordinary parish work, and through separate organizations linked to the church at local, regional or diocesan level. When comparing the degree of church involvement in practical social work between the eight localities, it is – as expected – the German case that shows the most extensive involvement and the British case the least. Before going further, however, it is important to remember that the WREP project was largely exploratory and was based on qualitative rather than quantitative methods. The comparability between the cases is therefore limited, meaning that a strict 'ranking' of the cases according to the degree of participation is not possible. Instead, the following paragraphs describe the specific character of each case, in an attempt to capture at least something of the richness of the data. A more detailed description can be found in the case studies contained in Volume 1.[10] It is important to note, finally, that each case study represents a snapshot of the locality in question. It should not be considered representative of either the country as a whole or even of the national church. That said, the following cases do give some insight into how the system operates in the eight countries represented in WREP.

Germany   In Germany both majority churches play a major part in the organization and delivery of welfare, in a way that is qualitatively different from the other countries. This is the most obvious example of a church acting as a primary provider of welfare. The churches form an integral part of the public welfare system, a situation which is underpinned by a specific contract between church and state. This way of working reflects the desire of the relatively strong German state to decentralize its responsibilities, by delegating significant sections of its work to other institutions.

The WREP case study focuses on the Protestant church in Reutlingen. This in turn forms part of the regional Evangelische Landeskirche in Württemberg, which is responsible for a broad range of welfare activities under the umbrella organization Diakonisches Werk, Württemberg. These include nursing services, care homes (for elderly people, those with disabilities and those with mental health problems), counselling services, a kindergarten for children with special needs, and a hospital for psychiatry and psychotherapy. Thus an extremely wide range of social responsibilities are delegated to the church by the state, but are, to a very large extent, financed by public resources. Many such services are provided by a church-related organization named the Bruderhaus Diakonie, which offers an excellent example of the strength of the church-related social work. In all, it has about 1,500 employees in the district of Reutlingen, yet is just one of several church-related welfare providers. A good illustration of a welfare activity run by the church district of Reutlingen can be found in a home-nursing service responsible for a population of 25,000 inhabitants (Leis-Peters 2006; 2010).

Greece   In the Greek towns of Thiva and Livadeia, too, the church carries a large part of the collective responsibility for people in need. This situation differs, however, from that in Germany, in that the Greek Orthodox Church has somehow to fill the very visible gap between acute social needs on the one hand and the inabilities of the state to provide on the other. In the Greek case study, for example, the only two homes for elderly people in Thiva and Livadeia are run by the church. None at all are run by the state (a situation that reflects a culture that assumes that

---

[10]   Longer, considerably more detailed versions can be found in the working papers of the WREP project. See Edgardh Beckman (2004) and Yeung et al. (2006a and b).

care is provided by the family). A second point is also important. As opposed to the relatively centralized Greek state, the Greek church is decentralized – as a result, a great deal of social work is organized at regional and diocesan level. Indeed each parish has its own programme of social activities, with the diocese acting largely as an organizing and co-ordinating body. The church in Thiva and Livadeia, for example, provides a wide range of welfare activities, which are less extensive overall than those in Reutlingen, but which are absolutely crucial in the local context. These include soup kitchens, financial support for poorer people, and the organization of a blood bank. In addition, and due very largely to the competence of a number of the local priests in psychology and psychotherapy, the church in this part of Greece also provides significant services for the mentally ill (Fokas 2006; Fokas and Molokotos-Liederman 2010).

In short the German Protestant church and its Greek Orthodox equivalent have similar roles in practice in their respective localities, but for totally opposite reasons. Both are *primary* providers. In Germany, this is the result of deliberate policy-making; the Orthodox Church in Thiva and Livadeia, conversely, is strong precisely because the state is weak, and can offer only minimal provision for welfare. Thus the importance of the church in this field is a direct consequence of the state's shortcomings (Weisbrod 1988; Salamon 1987). In such a situation, it is more or less taken for granted that the church should fill in the gaps in welfare which the state cannot handle, but there is no formal contract between church and state concerning this role. This could be called an implicit, rather than explicit contract of welfare provision.

Italy   Similarly, the Catholic Church in Vicenza – along with the religious orders and associations which are linked to it – provides very basic welfare in areas where the public authorities offer very little. Each parish in Vicenza, for example, has its own welfare centre, providing services such as emergency food, clothing and shelter, programmes for education and recreation, and so on. The three main religious orders are mostly involved in education, especially nursery schools. One such order also runs retirement homes for elderly people. The Catholic organization Caritas-Diakonia is currently the major church-related agent in Vicenza's welfare system, and runs the main night shelter in the town. It also organizes self-help groups among people with psychological needs, and provides counselling for adolescents and guidance for women. Thus Caritas-Diakonia has a *vanguard* role, and regards itself as an emergency organization. It often operates in areas where state intervention does not reach, and makes a point of discovering new needs and reporting them to the state sector, which is then expected to take over (Frisina 2006; 2010).

France   The Catholic Church in Evreux has made the question of welfare a core issue in its pastoral ministry. Despite the restrictions of the French system, the parishes collaborate with and support the different Catholic associations and religious orders, by providing meeting-places for their social activities (for example, activities for people with special needs). Here the church-linked associations take on a mainly *vanguard* role, running targeted short-term social actions such as assistance for asylum seekers, as well as longer-term educational and relationship-building activities. There is support for a wide range of underprivileged people, including work with alcoholics, single mothers and the disabled, assistance for children at school, literacy education and help with financial problems (Valasik 2006; 2010).

Finland In the Finnish town of Lahti, welfare work is a central part of the overall strategy of 'serving' in the Evangelical Lutheran parishes, and includes counselling, mental health care, meals, financial support, and activities for elderly and disabled people, immigrants and the unemployed. The church also runs a centre for social work volunteers (Yeung 2006; Pessi 2010). Such activities were of particular importance at the time of the Finnish recession in the early 1990s (see below).

Sweden The Church of Sweden in Gävle operates mainly through the local parishes, but there is also an important church-related foundation, the Gävle Diaconal Council, which aims to support financially individuals who are in need. The parishes run a great variety of welfare and welfare-related activities, such as social gatherings which offer an opportunity for people to meet, to socialize and to get a sense of community. These include group activities for children and young people, meetings for elderly people and family guidance. There is a chaplaincy service at the hospital, the university and the health care centre, which is run in collaboration with the public authorities. As in many other Swedish localities, parish personnel have a central role in the municipality's emergency counselling teams as well as in the municipal family centre (Edgardh Beckman et al. 2006; Edgardh and Pettersson 2010).

Norway Results from Drammen reveal two types of church-related agents: the local parishes and a small number of church-linked associations. Two of the latter operate very notable projects directed to people with substance abuse problems. Another association organizes activities for young people. Most of the parish activities are directed towards children, teenagers and elderly people. The primary aim of the latter is to bring people together and to arrange opportunities for meeting, talking and sharing. There is also a visiting service and counselling groups for the bereaved (Angell and Wyller 2006; Angell 2010).

England Among the eight cases, the Church of England in Darlington has the least involvement in practical welfare provision. But even here, the parishes organize informal activities for children and elderly people, and collaborate with the public authorities in the provision of complementary services – for example chaplaincies for the hospital, the arts centre, the local college and the police. There are, however, no major welfare organizations directly linked to the Church of England which are currently operating in Darlington. By far the most active voluntary agent in the social field in Darlington is, in fact, the local Baptist church, which runs extensive programmes for homeless people and those with drug addictions (Middlemiss 2006; Middlemiss Lé Mon 2010).

In short, in the Swedish, Finnish, Norwegian and English localities, the role of the church is mainly *complementary* to the publicly-provided welfare services. However, these churches (and church-related organizations) also take on a *vanguard* and *value-guardian* role in certain fields – a point which is particularly clear in the Norwegian case (Angell 2010). Indeed, most of the church-run social activities in these countries are focused on gathering people in the community and supporting them psychologically and socially. They do not, therefore, have the same engagement with basic provision that is found in Germany, Greece, Italy and (up to a point) France.

Bearing all these examples in mind, the churches' contributions to welfare can be categorized into two major types: material and non-material provision. The former includes food delivery to poor people, financial support to individuals in need and housing for homeless people. The latter refers to a number of organized activities, for example counselling, educational work, and activities for children, teenagers and elderly people. Symbolic and representative functions relating to psychological or social needs also belong in this category. For a significant number of people, the latter offer a sense of meaning and belonging that is hard to find elsewhere. Such a view is particularly clear in the following statement by a Greek priest:

> Furthermore, the church plays other roles in welfare provision beyond those which are normally discussed – i.e. caring for the poor, elderly and ill: for instance, aesthetics is a large part of welfare, and tradition – the church pays attention to people's such needs of places to 'soothe their souls', and it significantly provides them with their tradition (*paradosi* – the passing on of heritage, from one generation to the next; not meaning a function of looking back), linking them to this significant source of identification. (Fokas 2006: 244)

In this quotation, the provision of church buildings is clearly important, in that in themselves such buildings represent positive values and a relationship to the transcendent. It is also clear that the link to a collective identity (and associated values) can offer a feeling of security, not least in times of crisis and disaster (Berger 1969; Gustafsson 1995; Post et al. 2004).

The practical role of a church in welfare provision – as opposed to its more non-material aspects – is dependent on a number of factors. Some have been mentioned already: these include the nature of the national welfare system; the position of the church in society, both in general and in relation to welfare; and the strength and efficiency of local provision. What precisely is left for the church to do in any given situation? Further factors are, however, important, notably the availability of both financial and human resources, including volunteers. The two are closely related and will be taken in turn. It is abundantly clear that the financial situation of the majority churches of Europe varies considerably. Some are considerably richer than others, for a whole variety of reasons, and are able to do things that are out of the question elsewhere. The precise situation varies, however. In some cases, there is considerable wealth at national level, but very much less at the local – the Greek case study offers a good example of this mismatch. Conversely, the Church of Sweden and Church of Finland are relatively well endowed at local level, a situation that is highly dependent on membership rates and may change in the future (Edgardh Beckman 2004). This in turn has an effect on the number and role of volunteers engaged in the activities of the churches. In all our cases, the churches were dependent to some extent on the contributions of voluntary workers, but in Sweden – unsurprisingly – their role was relatively marginal, given the very large number of employed personnel. England lies at the other extreme: here volunteers are central to the system which would collapse without them. The wider and at time very complex implications of working with volunteers will be considered below.

One final point is, however, important. The majority churches must situate their work in relation to other local agents. In Darlington, for example, the limited role of the Church of England in welfare activities can be at least partially explained by the very active role of the local Baptist church in this field (Middlemiss Lé Mon 2010). The reverse is the case in Drammen where the significant social role of the Church City Mission is directly related to the lack of any other spokesperson for such issues in the area (Angell 2010).

Opinions on the Role of the Churches

In each case study, selected representatives from local public authorities, the church and the general population were questioned about the role of the church in welfare. Specifically, our interviewees were asked whether the church should itself provide services – for example, in running a shelter for homeless people – or whether the church's primary role is to be active in public debate as a value guardian. Or should the church do both of these things: offering services in its own right but at the same time raising its voice in public discussion? Additional questions follow from these. Should the state – supported by the church – take on full responsibility for social welfare provision? Or, should the church have an independent role in publicly defending the values on which the welfare system is based and in stipulating the kind of services that are appropriate to a late modern society? In all eight countries, and in all groups of interviewees, people were noticeably divided in their opinions.

Theoretically there are four possible positions in relation to the two main questions (see Figure 2.2 below). Position A states that the church should take on neither practical social work, nor contribute to public debate; position B states that the church should take on social work but should remain quiet in public debate;

		Churches should take on practical social work	
		No	*Yes*
Churches should speak out in public debate	*No*	A	B
	Yes	C	D

Figure 2.2　　Four possible positions regarding the churches' roles as social agents

position C argues the reverse – that the church should speak up in public debate, but not be an agent of welfare itself; and position D recommends that the church should be active in both public debate and practical social work (Yeung 2008; Pessi 2010).

Although WREP is not primarily a quantitative study, our results reveal some interesting tendencies in this respect, pointing to similarities, contrasts and (at times) tensions in the sample as a whole. Interestingly, almost no respondents among the 450 interviewees adopt position A. It follows that nearly everyone in the total sample endorses the role of the church in at least one respect. Positions B, C and D can be found in all our case studies, but in varying degrees in the different categories of interviewees and in different countries. Most respondents hold either position B or D. Many of them say moreover that some kind of social service activity is an essential part of the church's identity. An excellent illustration can be found in the unequivocal response of a Greek interviewee who declares: '[S]hould is the wrong word: there is no should about it. Church and social service are one and the same, indistinguishable' (Fokas and Molokotos-Liederman 2010: 177). Likewise, a German interviewee says: '[T]he church needs to have social activities. Otherwise it is no longer a church' (Leis-Peters 2010: 105).

Interestingly, in all the cases under review, there is a general perception among Europeans at local level both that the state is doing less than it should in the field of welfare, and that it has reduced its social activities in recent years. Although the precise point of reference varies between the countries, there is a feeling that the gap between social needs and the state's provision is getting bigger. The church representatives in particular criticize the public authorities by claiming that the latter are reducing their budgets for welfare provision and count instead on the church, expecting it to increase its own contributions. A lay person in Vicenza nicely captures this dilemma:

> They count too much on voluntary work ... I witnessed the opening of a centre for the disabled, entirely created thanks to the efforts of families and volunteers ... And there was also the inevitable politician who had the nerve to declare: 'I am proud of our people who have the strength to manage on their own!' What a cheek ... Of course, well done Veneto people, well done citizens of Vicenza! And so they [local authorities] don't spend a single Euro. (Frisina 2010: 159)

More specifically, in response to the challenge of reduced public financing and increasing social needs, a division of opinion is beginning to emerge. On the one side are people who wish the church to be more critical of the state for not taking its responsibilities in the field of welfare seriously, and on the other are those who want the church to stick to practical social work and to keep out of public debate. The details of this division vary from case to case and – as expected – are linked to both national and local factors. The reactions are bound to be different in places where there is a moderately comprehensive welfare system, compared with those where provision is not, and never has been, adequate. Predictably, Norway and Greece exemplify the two extremes.

Rather more positively, data from all our case studies reveal an *increasing* openness among local people (both from the public authorities and from the population in general) regarding the churches' contributions to welfare. Attitudes vary, however, from a flexible and relatively balanced approach on the one hand, to very high (one could even say demanding) expectations on the other. The latter can be seen especially in Germany, where – given its role as a primary welfare provider – the Protestant Church is sometimes accused of being itself responsible for cutbacks in welfare services. The public are not aware that the 'real' decisions are made by local and state authorities. The Greeks also have a great deal invested in the church: once again both those working in the local authority and the representatives of the population expect the church to compensate for poor welfare provision. And even where the church in fact provides many more social services than the state, this is still regarded as inadequate. This attitude is further exacerbated by a general assumption that the church is extremely rich, which is not the case at local level.

Results from the Italian case study show that expectations of the church in the field of welfare are not primarily directed toward the parishes but to the church-related associations and the religious orders, which are very largely taken for granted as providers of social care. The Italian case study reveals, moreover, that the relatively strong position of the Catholic Church, and its consequent involvement in official affairs, is supported by some people but strongly rejected by others. On the whole representatives of the public authorities and of the local churches promote the involvement of the church in social action. Specifically, they support the dominance of Caritas-Diakonia as a welfare agent, as well as the public voice of the Catholic Church. Conversely, representatives of private social organizations and of citizen groups argue for an increased process of secularization in Italian society, meaning by this a reduction in the institutional and political role of the Catholic Church. That said, they very often regard *themselves* (as individuals) as representative of the church in both word and deed, given their status as church members (Frisina 2010).

In France, England and the Nordic countries, expectations in the area of welfare are primarily directed toward the state. Voluntary organizations are seen as secondary, but nonetheless welcome, welfare agents. And with the obvious exception of France, the data also reveal a general openness on the part of public authorities regarding co-operation with the local majority churches – something that has increased in the last decade. Interestingly, in England and Sweden, views about co-operation are even more positive among representatives of the public authorities than in the churches themselves. This is not to say that the attitudes of church people are negative, but simply that they are more hesitant, doubting that they would be welcome in such a collaboration.

The Finnish case, finally, quite clearly illustrates an increasing social role for the Church of Finland – as we have seen, this began at the time of the Finnish economic recession in the 1990s and has continued ever since. The church played a major role in welfare during the economic crisis, which enhanced its profile in new ways. At the same time, it encouraged Finnish people to trust their church – nationally as well as locally. Since this time, the common view among Finns is that the church's welfare activities are essential if the gaps left by the state and the municipalities are to be properly filled (Heino et al. 1997; Yeung 2003; Pessi 2010).

One further – and unequivocal – point concludes this discussion. Significant numbers of those representing the public authorities in all eight of the WREP case studies maintain that the churches' contributions to social services are indispensable – for the following reasons: their inherent social capital, not least a multitude of volunteers; their economic capital, including buildings which fulfil many different functions, both symbolic and practical; and, lastly, their cultural capital, especially the values that motivate social commitment and engagement.

A Prophetic Voice or Keeping Silent?

When it comes to the more specific question of the role of the church as a voice in public debate, all our interviewees were very firm about one thing: the church should *not* involve itself in the work of political parties – indeed it should not become politicized at all. On more general interventions, however, a rather different picture emerges. Here responses vary from place to place.

In Greece, for example, there is a markedly negative attitude among all three groups of interviewees regarding the role of the Greek Orthodox Church in public debate. Such a view is related to a persistent critique of the national church and – even more specifically – to the then Archbishop, who in the opinion of many had become far too involved in political affairs.[11] And when asked about the public role of the church, Greek respondents seem automatically to think of the *national* scene. Conversely, when referring to the church's more practical contribution they connect more easily to what goes on locally. Bearing this in mind, Greek interviewees are clear that the church should not be involved in day-to-day politics; there is, however, a certain amount of support for the church's responsibility to comment on social issues. That said, a minority want the church to keep out of public debate altogether, and to stick to social work only. One Greek respondent articulates this view very clearly: '[I] would prefer if it [the church] would mainly be involved with actions, rather than with words' (Fokas and Molokotos-Liederman 2010: 178). Representatives of the local population in Reutlingen express rather similar opinions, once again expecting the church to stand up for the poor by means of practical activities rather than statements or sermons. For these people, actions most certainly speak louder than words.

In France, unsurprisingly, the principle of *laïcité* is clearly reflected in the opinions expressed by public authority representatives. Equally important in the French case is the memory of former conflicts between church and state. When asked about the role of the church in public debate, for instance, an individual responsible for welfare issues in the French town of Evreux responds as follows: '[I]f the French bishops started intervening in political debate, in my opinion that would restart wars and tensions which we really don't need – we've got other things to do' (Valasik 2010: 138).

In countries where the welfare involvement of the churches and the church-related organizations is extensive and institutionalized, their position *vis-à-vis* public debate is complex. On the one hand, the churches are fully accepted as professional actors in the field of welfare. On the other, the fact that they are so closely related to the state means that it is difficult for them to criticize the system of which they are part. To start with the more positive aspects of this situation, it is clear that representatives of the public authorities in Reutlingen regard the church as one of the few social institutions which are still able to contribute significantly to public debate on the national as well as on the local level. As one of them says:

> When I say that there are poor children in a kindergarten and they need support no-one listens. If the priest talks about the same subject everyone listens. I am not insulted by this fact. I think, we should cooperate in this matter. (Leis-Peters 2010: 109)

---

[11] At the time of the Greek case study, the Archbishop Christodoulos was the Archbishop of Athens. After his death in 2008 he was replaced by Archbishop Ieronymous, formerly bishop of Thiva and Livadeia. In 1998, Ieronymous was Christodoulos's principal rival for the archbishopric. Interviewees in Thiva and Livadeia were well aware of the tensions between the two men, a fact which undoubtedly coloured their responses regarding the national/local situation.

Similarly, the public authority representatives in Finland regard the church as having not only a right but an obligation to make a clear and visible contribution to public debate. Here is one example: 'The church should support the voice of the weak as well as the spirit of "not leaving your pal who is in need behind"'[12] (Pessi 2010: 85). A Swedish public employee reinforces the point – the knowledge and competence of the church are absolutely essential in public debate: 'I would be very disappointed if the church keeps silent and stands aside when it comes to social issues of different kinds' (Edgardh and Pettersson 2010: 49).

It is the German example, however, which reveals the more problematic side of the linkage to the state. It is true that institutionalized contracts offer the church an obvious role in public debate. Exactly the same relationship – and most importantly the financial dependency that it entails – means, however, that a critical or prophetic role can at times be tricky. It is the state which delegates certain tasks to church-related providers – a fact that undoubtedly influences the way in which the churches are able to criticize public policy. This is true even when co-operation between the churches and local authorities is seen as positive by both parties. In short, there is a risk that the churches' critical function might get lost. One of the church representatives in Reutlingen underlines this point:

> It is not easy to deviate from the social policy of the public authorities if you are closely connected to them by the finances. If I am dependent on public funding I am a partner and can criticize on a professional level. But to put my foot down by saying: 'Not with me!' That's difficult. (Leis-Peters 2010: 109)

A rather different issue is highlighted by some of the Swedish church representatives. It concerns the consequences of being a majority church where almost the whole population are members. In this situation, an opinion-forming role is problematic given that citizens of all political colours belong to the church. If the church 'contains' so many opinions, it can be difficult to pinpoint a representative figure or spokesperson to articulate a single view. A church representative puts it thus:

> We have this problem with the type of church we have, that it makes it difficult to find someone who can represent the church. We have the privilege or the problem that almost all people can say they represent church. (Edgardh and Pettersson 2010: 51)

New Forms of Contract-based Church–State Relationships

When voluntary organizations establish agreements and contracts with public authorities, they are regarded primarily as providers of certain services. In order to guarantee the quality of these services, control mechanisms are built into the

---

[12] This phrase is well-known in Finland – it was widely used during the Second World War.

contracts. It follows that the service-providing organization has to work to the standards laid down by the public authorities. Such standards can, however, restrict the organization, or oblige it to change its structure or policy in one way or another. So much so that voluntary sector researchers have noted a risk for ideologically-driven organizations, which may be forced through the contracting procedure into ways of working not suited to their primary identities (Lundström and Wijkström 1997; Olk 2001; Wijkström et al. 2004; Schulz et al. 2007). To put it bluntly, what might at first seem a good idea – i.e. enrolling voluntary organizations and churches as providers of welfare services – may end up killing the ideological heart which gives these organizations both identity and legitimacy. Indeed, some commentators have argued that contracting could even be a threat to democracy, in the sense that, by their very nature, voluntary organizations generate core and positive values, including those of solidarity (compare Putnam 2000). This may or may not be the case, but one rather more modest point is very clear from our case studies: contractual arrangements with local authorities almost always imply, either explicitly or implicitly, a reduced religious profile on the part of the church or church-related organization. It follows that such contracts oblige the church to restrict its scope to social issues only, and, in that sense at least, require a change in identity.

In the German system in particular there is an overt and 'official' competition among welfare providers, who bid for contracts to run services. A representative of the public authority in Reutlingen puts it in these terms:

> Every welfare organization, which wants public contributions for its projects, has to lobby for it. There are no exceptions from this rule any longer. Even the churches and the church-related organizations, which used to have a privileged position, have to do this today. (Leis-Peters 2010: 106)

A church representative describes the same development:

> We more and more must beg for everything. Before the budget meetings in the town council, or in the district assembly we go to the parliamentary groups to beg for funding ... Some years ago we wrote an application letter and that was enough ... Today you have to beg personally ... Once we did not do that and as a consequence we got less money than all the others. (Leis-Peters 2010: 106)

Indeed the growing influence of competition on church welfare comes through as a dominant theme in all the German interviews. Most respondents agree that welfare provision is becoming more and more of a market, a way of working that also applies to voluntary initiatives. These adaptations to economic principles have practical consequences – that is clear. More importantly, however, they also influence the welfare agents' ways of thinking, which in the long term must, it seems, affect the underlying philosophy of all such organizations including the churches.

The French case offers a revealing example of the desire of the public authorities to take control of voluntary associations by means of contracts, which lead in turn to a change of status for the organizations in question – indeed for their core mission. For instance, when a new town council in Evreux took over in 2001, it realized that the management of welfare was largely in the hands of the associative sector, and wanted to re-assert the central role of the public authority. A majority of these associations were, moreover, Catholic. An elected politician in Evreux explains:

> Some associations sometimes want to act as a filter between clients and politicians, and that's really a tendency we must resist … I think we must renew the link with democracy, and let the elected representatives take back power with citizens instead of working through this filter of the associations; that's the key issue at the local level. (Valasik 2010: 143)

A new policy of contracting was put in place, whereby financial support was offered only to those associations which could show tangible results in the short and medium term. Projects which did not correspond to the model set down by the authorities received little support, especially those whose goals were less immediate. Local politicians refused to take the risk of supporting an activity where the results could not be measured in advance. This change in political direction provoked numerous conflicts – indeed some associations rejected *any* form of scrutiny by the state. More generally a number of people raised important questions about the criteria for financial support, and argued that the town council had created a new form of clientism, whereby *only* associations which conformed to the model received assistance. A sharply critical interviewee in Evreux, questioning these new conditions, says:

> When there were people really doing a good job in the districts where there were problems, their subsidy was cut. So you have to wonder whether it was really because they considered they weren't doing a useful job, or whether it was just to make a point at the expense of the previous administration. (Valasik 2010: 143)

More generally, personnel from the associations indicated more than once that they found themselves involuntarily under the control of public bodies, and felt in consequence that they faced a process of homogenization in welfare management.

The French case illustrates a trend which raises important questions for the future at the European level. Will the implementation of new public management systems, presently taking place all over Europe through the contracting process, reduce the diversity that currently exists in the area of welfare? In other words, will the ensuing standardization force very different agents to adapt to common frameworks which require that they leave their individual ideologies and characteristics behind? Alternatively, will the distinctiveness of different agents and the variety of profiles that these represent be regarded positively – i.e. as contributions which enhance the quality of welfare by meeting individual and diverse needs more effectively? Both outcomes are possible from what we can see in our data.

The Development of Churches as Professional Organizations

In their work as social agents, churches – just like their secular equivalents – are bound to be influenced by wider trends in organizational management. New knowledge, research findings and emerging trends in this field affect all organizations, not least their leaders. At the same time, the functional differentiation and increasing specialization of late modern societies oblige such organizations to compete, and therefore to strive for continually increasing quality in their mission. Churches are not immune from these changes. It is true that religious organizations tend to implement these ideas rather later than other sections of society, but there is a steady trend within the churches, as elsewhere, related to the incorporation of recent management thinking (Torry 2005).

In short, a number of interrelated factors drive churches to develop as professional organizations within the area of welfare, including all those already mentioned: the demand for quality, the implementation of new public management, contracting arrangements with public authorities and the increasing complexity of the regulations governing welfare provision. The results from WREP touch upon many aspects of these changes. As expected, the most professionalized organizations are found in Germany, due largely to their dependence on the state for financial support. Because of this, the motivation to improve performance is very high – partly to respond more effectively to social needs, but also to qualify for continued financial assistance without which these providers cannot sustain their position (Leis-Peters 2010).

There is, however, an obvious tension between the increasing professionalization of churches and their identity as voluntary organizations. Among others things, this concerns the balance between professionalism and volunteering in welfare activities. All of the churches under review make use of volunteers who are distinct from professional employees, but in different proportions depending on their financial situation (see above). It is quite clear, moreover, that both groups of people are indispensable, but the combination is not always easy to manage. On the one hand churches are driven towards greater professionalization (and therefore to paid employment) when acting as welfare agents alongside public authorities. But on the other, the churches and church associations are particularly beneficial partners for the local authorities, precisely because of their ability to recruit volunteers (which reduces the costs for welfare provision). This dilemma is highlighted by one of the Italian interviewees, a representative of a private organization. He criticizes the authorities very directly for making use of volunteers in order to reduce public expenditure: 'Professionalism is needed, love is not enough. But love is for free, and so it is convenient for public authorities to exploit this situation using volunteers even if they end up doing damage' (Frisina 2010: 157).

In the longer term, it will be important for the churches to reflect on, and find a balance between, these two kinds of people. They must think hard about which areas in particular require professionalism, and which areas are best served by the contributions of volunteers. They must also ask what will happen if the professionals take over and adopt the standards set down by state contracts. More profoundly, in what ways is the core identity of the church affected by its increasing role as a service provider? Precisely this issue will be discussed further in the next section, in relation to the role of individuals as carriers of particular values.

Welfare and Religion at the Individual Level

The previous sections of this chapter have dealt with the role of the churches at the societal and organizational levels. In the following paragraphs we will focus on individuals: their significance, perceptions and interactions. Four themes from the cross-analysis will be highlighted: first, opinions regarding the quality of church-provided welfare services; second, the ways in which estimations of 'quality' are related to the particular people who work for the church; third, the importance of certain individuals as entrepreneurs in the welfare field; and finally, the role of the majority churches in linking the individual to the wider society.

Church Welfare Services Offer Better Quality

Very many of those interviewed judge the quality of church-provided welfare to be higher than that of a service provided by public authorities, at least in certain respects. Specifically, the church is seen as performing better than public authorities in its encounters with individuals, in the sense that each human being is regarded as a 'person'. A more holistic approach and a capacity for empathy are repeatedly mentioned in relation to the welfare provision of churches, in contrast to the more formal services offered by the state. Interviewees from every category and every case study regard the church as being 'closer' to people and their needs.

Expanding on these contrasts, many interviewees declare that church-related social services provide some kind of added value. Once again this reflects the way in which the church engages with the individual. For example, a church representative from Italy feels that practising Catholics in the sector offer 'more humane' services than those provided by the state:

> We have a vast demand for our services because here it is not like a public office; it is not cold ... They ask us for something more humane, they come in need of a saviour and we help them. Compared to public service, here we have a different fund of human experiences and a different motivation. (Frisina 2010: 156)

This view is confirmed by Catholic workers in Evreux where the holistic qualities of care are particularly valued. Above all, this means being available to listen and to support people in their daily lives – individuals should not simply be regarded as workers, as unemployed or (worst of all) as excluded (Valasik 2010).

Conversely, welfare provided by the public authorities is thought by many to imply a rather distant, impersonal (even anonymous) relationship with the client. One reason for this, according to some respondents, is that public provision is based on a professional ethic rather than a purely human one. A Greek interviewee, for example, declares that the local public welfare services function 'terribly':

> It is based on benefits which are not enough to help in any case. And the contact between the state institution and the person in need is limited to this exchange of money. It is bureaucratic. For me, it's not welfare at all. No one [in public services] looks at the state of his [the welfare seeker's] life. (Fokas and Molokotos-Liederman 2010: 173)

Such views are almost to be expected in Greece, but even in Sweden representatives of the public authority agree that state provision is at times tied rather too much to bureaucratic rules. They note that the church has an advantage in this respect, since it is less regulated by law than its public equivalent. It is freer, and thus more flexible.

Anonymity is mentioned in several case studies, but here the responses are complex. On the one hand are voices from Greece, who stress once again that the church is attractive to people precisely because it does not deal with them anonymously, which happens repeatedly in state welfare provision. The point is plainly, if rather hesitantly, expressed by a woman working in a church programme who says: 'I don't know enough. But if the employee is a civil servant, and if we judge by how the public system runs in general, it is more impersonal, more cold, more distant and foreign … or that's how I imagine it' (Fokas and Molokotos-Liederman 2010: 174). Anonymity can, however, have its benefits. Interestingly, both Swedish and English respondents argue that the church *does* in fact offer anonymity – and is preferred for just this reason. Paradoxically, they point out that state welfare providers are not obliged to guarantee anonymity for a person seeking help given that they are public bodies. The church, in contrast, given its mission to protect people, guarantees to safeguard the identity of those who seek its help. Anonymity, therefore, is regarded as both a positive and a negative factor. Either way, it is clear that the church *is* able to handle anonymity positively – to respect the integrity of its clients, but at the same time to maintain a more personal service.

On a rather different tack, our case studies reveal a variety of ways in which the specific qualities perceived in church-provided welfare connect to – and are motivated by – the wider values of the church, including those that relate to the transcendent. The reverse is also true: transcendent values are expressed in, and legitimated by the church's social activities. Symbolically, such values are discovered among other places in both rituals and buildings designed to represent the numinous (Davies 1994; Pettersson 2000). Rather more practically, many of our interviewees clearly appreciate the role of the churches in sustaining the values of care and solidarity, especially in relation to underprivileged people (often referred to as 'the weak'). In this sense the role of the churches as the upholders of symbolic or vicarious memory interacts with their welfare-provider role; each supports the other. Both, moreover, contribute significantly to the public as well a private identity of the churches (Hervieu-Legér 2000; Davie 2000).

All that said, it is important not to exclude the critical voices. One such concerns what many people regard positively, namely the informal and personal attitude of the church in the provision of welfare. A number of the Greek respondents, for example, claim not only that the church has a more personal relationship to the client than the state does, but that this is a negative thing. These respondents regard the state as being better than the church as a welfare provider, in the sense that the state is neutral and does not expect anything in return, whereas the church 'wants you on its side'. As already mentioned, this is something which the public authorities try to control: contracting processes oblige the churches to adopt a more professional and religiously-neutral approach in their welfare activities, limiting thereby their religious character.

Individuals as Carriers of Quality-forming Values

Welfare services involve human encounters, many of which are face-to-face. Positive interactions between the people concerned are therefore of paramount importance. Individuals who provide welfare services on behalf of the church are, moreover, representatives of the church itself, and thus of its identity and values – a point recognized in several of our case studies. Indeed the reason why the church is perceived as providing 'better' welfare services is often related to the specific individuals who are working for the church in a given locality. They are considered to be doing their jobs well because of their strong personal interest in the needs of their clients, whereas public service employees are said to be motivated more by their salaries than by empathy. From this point of view, the quality of church-provided services is thought by many interviewees to stem from a higher degree of altruism. Others see it as linked to the 'spirituality' of church representatives, which adds a certain quality to the encounter and interaction. The important point is that both these qualities (altruism and spirituality) are related to specified individuals who publicly represent the church – a point discussed in detail in Pessi (2010).

In most of the towns in WREP, the majority of individuals who are working for the churches are volunteers. Generally this is regarded as a strength, largely because of the values and the personal commitment of the people concerned. As previously discussed, however, there is a potential (some would say inevitable) conflict between the importance of volunteers on the one hand, and the tendency toward professionalization and contractual arrangements on the other. Clearly the values of the church, as expressed by the volunteers, are seen as key factors in the delivery of high quality services. But when it comes to the capacities of volunteers not only to provide but to sustain an effective service, reactions are rather more mixed. In Thiva-Livadeia, for example, those who regard the church as generally more reliable than the state are balanced by a group who see the church's dependence on voluntary resources as a problem.

Individuals Matter!

A third finding is that individuals, both church workers and volunteers, are likely to have more than one role: they are representatives of the church as a whole, but at the same time they are personally responsible for what takes place in the local context. Many of the interviews reveal, moreover, that it is very important to distinguish between the church as an organization, and the individuals who represent it. For instance, when asked about the role of the church in public debate at least some local authority representatives in the English case make a clear distinction between the two. They consider the contributions of certain individuals to be very positive and mention with admiration those who have spoken out on social issues, but they are much more wary about the involvement of the church *as an institution* in public debate. One reason for this hesitation lies in the perceived tendency of the church to look inwards, and to focus on internal disagreements such as the long-running debate about the ordination of women to the priesthood. For many with little or no involvement in the church, this introspection is taken as proof that the church is out of touch with modern society. It is worth noting, however, that such criticisms of the church are sometimes grounded in extremely high expectations about what the church should be. For example, one of the welfare sector employees in Darlington asks, '[I]f we can't have high expectations of the church, what else can we have high expectations of?' (Middlemiss Lé Mon 2010: 127).

As major institutions with very deep cultural roots, the majority churches offer a variety of possibilities at the local level. What happens in practice, however, depends to a huge extent on particular individuals – i.e. on their abilities, vision, creativity and personal commitment to social issues. This was shown repeatedly in our material. An example from the Greek case can be found in the wide range of psychological and psychotherapy services provided by the diocese and parishes in Thiva-Livadeia. The establishment and development of these facilities is clearly related to existing local competence in the relevant fields among a number of priests within this diocese, and is not found elsewhere in Greece (Fokas 2006; Fokas and Molokotos-Liederman 2010).

Individuals in the churches contribute differently to the context of which they are part, for example as entrepreneurs, spokespersons, networkers, or simply as symbols of the church. Some are more effective in practical social work, others prefer public debate, yet others do both. An outstanding example of the dual role can be found in the leader of the Church City Mission (CCM) in Drammen,

Norway (Angell 2010). A close analysis of local newspapers reveals that the CCM leader is the only church-affiliated person in Drammen to act politically in the sense of trying to influence both public opinion and the decision-making of politicians. An important part of his 'message', which is clearly motivated by Christian values, is to encourage people (and indeed the political system as a whole) to acknowledge the dignity of all those who live in the community, whether they are 'straight' citizens or substance abusers. He says:

> We need to have two legs to stand on; we are obliged to help people in need; at the same time we must be outspoken about injustice. I am a columnist in the local paper every fourth week. We must confront the authorities. We must use the media and our political contacts. (Angell 2010: 70)

Despite its political overtones, the voice of the CCM leader is perceived as trustworthy and authoritative by the local population, and by the local authority representatives, because his words are congruent with the social activities organized by the local CCM. The frequency with which this individual appears in the local newspaper indicates that he is considered a reliable representative of the church in Drammen and an important contributor both to the care of disadvantaged people and to public debate.

Predictably, creative and entrepreneurial individuals are often involved in several different organizations in one locality, and at times their activities bridge the gap between the church and more secular groups. Potentially the crossing of boundaries can cause confusion between different areas of responsibility, but it can also become a resource. The latter is reflected in an interview from the Italian case. A former president of the Catholic welfare agency Caritas-Diakonia is now in charge of a local health authority. He says:

> This diocese is particularly enterprising … this is matched by the resourcefulness of certain executives in the public service … It is probably not irrelevant that I am director in a public service but also a Caritas volunteer. You can always trust Caritas; it is very easy to manage projects together. (Frisina 2006: 209)

As this quotation demonstrates, the contributions of particular individuals are often related to their personal links to the church and the positive values associated with this. At the same time, however, it is important to recall the tension between the individuals associated with the church and the institution itself – the latter, not least in Italy, is often criticized for being an old-fashioned, rigid and bureaucratic organization. The close connection between certain individuals in the community and the local church can therefore be interpreted in more ways than one.

Churches Provide Links between the Individual and the Wider Society

Looking at our work in this way reveals once again the links between the welfare functions of the church and its role in connecting individuals with the wider society. This relates in turn to the six tentative statements that were formulated above regarding the church's continuing role in European societies. It seems that the majority churches are still able to function as intermediate structures, and in general their capacities to link the individual to something bigger are regarded positively. As we have seen, many of our respondents considered this a contribution to welfare in the widest sense, including those who were critical of the activities of church representatives. Above all our interviewees appreciate that the majority churches are open to everyone and for this reason see them as the carriers of *collective* values.

Late modern societies, however, are often characterized by something rather different: by a growing pluralism (to the point of fragmentation) and by a tendency to focus on individual rather than collective needs, trends that are clearly visible in a number of large scale quantitative enquiries. Specifically, both the European Values Survey and its global equivalent (the World Values Survey) demonstrate a shift right across the Western world from what are called materialist values concerned largely with security and with society as a whole, to *post*-materialist, more individualistic values concerned primarily with personal freedom (De Moor 1995; Halman 2001). As part and parcel of this process, European societies have seen a weakening of the social bonds that exist between individuals (Inglehart 1977; 1990; Esmer and Pettersson 2007). It is equally clear that this movement towards a greater focus on the individual, and rather less attention to the collective, is seen by some observers as a threat to the values underpinning democracy and solidarity (see for example Putnam 2000; Bauman 2002). The role of Europe's majority churches as providers of links between the individual and the collective should be seen in this light. As our interviewees have noticed, they represent values of care, they encourage people to volunteer, to play a part in helping those less fortunate than themselves, and to act (and speak) for the common good. In short they are major contributors to social capital and thus – in the best case scenario – to the maintenance of social cohesion as well.

Religion in a Service Society: A Theoretical Perspective

The analyses above have all shown that there is a tendency for churches to increase their involvement in the provision of welfare, irrespective of their existing position in the welfare mix. How, then, can this increasing role as welfare agents best be understood, given the widespread view that the traditional churches have a diminishing influence in European societies? To grasp this question, the development of the majority churches as agents of welfare will be related to broader changes in society at large. The analysis will also reflect both traditional and more recent theories of religious change, and the growing visibility of religion and religious institutions in the public sphere.

From Enforcing Monopolies to Welfare Resources

Our case studies demonstrate unequivocally that religious change in the context of welfare must be seen as part of a more general transformation of society, appreciating that this is a long-term and not always predictable process. Europe's majority churches have been part of their respective contexts for centuries, and – it should be remembered – are continuously adapting their roles to accommodate new local, national and global pressures. Currently the majority churches are turning more and more to the voluntary sector as their natural sphere of action, at precisely the moment when this sector is increasingly recognized as a crucial social and economic resource.

A whole series of factors have come together to cause these shifts. On the one hand can be found a number of external pressures. These include the development of the European Union, which has led both to a growing convergence in the labour market (in order to increase labour mobility across Europe) and to more centralized forms of monetary control. The Economic and Monetary Union (EMU), moreover, has put pressure on member states to keep public expenditure low. Both these factors have encouraged a parallel process of convergence in the field of welfare – as the countries in question adapt to a rapidly changing labour market and struggle to reduce their overall expenditure. At precisely the same moment, however, the welfare systems of Europe have come under pressure from a different angle. As explained at the beginning of this chapter, new demands on welfare stem from a combination of demographic change, new forms of poverty and a marked increase in immigration. Taken together these shifts have led to renewed attention to the voluntary sector as an important societal resource. Religious organizations have always been part of this sector to some extent, but recent developments have prompted a widespread reappraisal of their potential to contribute specifically to welfare needs.

This reappraisal, moreover, has coincided with a change in the religious domain per se, as quasi-monopolies in the form of Europe's state churches mutate into religiously plural economies. This transformation should not be exaggerated – the historic churches remain important players in their own right (an important theme in WREP) – but religious institutions which previously functioned as part of the historic centre of society are now finding new roles, not least in the welfare sector. In short there has been an overall shift from a situation where churches are seen essentially as generalists at the core of society to one in which they become one form of specialist alongside others in the voluntary sector (compare Beyer 1994). As a result, churches increasingly function as distinctive service providers in specified areas of society, but – as we have seen – they must also keep *out* of certain fields, notably party politics. As our case studies have shown, however, these boundaries are inherently blurred: the ways in which the border between legitimate and illegitimate church involvement is drawn vary considerably, both between different localities and between different interviewees. There is no consensus about these matters.

Functional Differentiation as a Feature of Modern Societies

The new forms of religious presence in the delivery of welfare in twenty-first-century Europe can also be seen in terms of an accelerating process of functional differentiation, an approach which returns us more than once to the sociological classics. As Marx himself perceived, scientific and technological advance drive an unstoppable growth of rationalization, differentiation and specialization in the modern economy (Marx 1970; Morrison 1995), which leads in turn to a parallel change in societal structures – these too become increasingly plural and differentiated (Luhmann 1982). The shift in the status of religious organizations, and indeed of religion itself, from their position as a 'sacred canopy' at the centre of society to one in which they are responsible for much more specialized tasks, fits into this pattern. It is also the case that organizations as such, including the historic churches, are internally affected by this process – a fact with profound consequences for the ways in which they set about their mission (Dobbelaere 1981; Carroll 1991; van der Ven 1996; Diotavelli 2002). Instead of a standardized form of liturgy for Sunday service or a baptism, for example, different – even individualized – forms or worship are developed. Another illustration can be found in the churches' tendency to specialize in areas which are closer to their specific identity such as counselling or ethical issues, rather than political or financial questions.

There are, however, opposing forces at work which strive to keep society and its differentiated parts together. Here the sociological tradition reaches back to Emile Durkheim (1897/1987; 1912/1995), who saw the division of labour in society as having a primarily integrative function, in the sense that it created mutual dependency, thus strengthening the bonds between individuals. To an extent the same is true at the organizational level, where co-operative arrangements between different specialists help to keep the differentiated parts together. Once again our case studies offer clear examples of this process in the increasing co-operation between churches and local authorities in the delivery of welfare at local level. Indeed the evolving role of the churches in this field demonstrates *both* increasing specialization *and* its counterpoint – the attempt to maintain cohesion in an increasingly fragmented market. Unsurprisingly there is a certain amount of tension between the two (Martin 1978).

In pre-industrial society, the historic churches were perceived as significant for society as a whole partly, indeed largely, because they institutionalized the values which not only integrated but legitimated society itself (Durkheim 1912/1995). But when the forms of religion associated with these institutions became more specialized, what were previously 'total' values held in common became increasingly what Thomas Luckmann calls 'part-time norms' (1967: 39).

The result was an increasing segregation of the 'religious area' from other areas in society; the process that Max Weber termed 'secularization' (1920/1996). The consequence, according to Weber, is a disenchantment of society as a whole, as religion moves from being an all-embracing canopy to being one functional institution alongside many others (Swatos and Christiano 1999). This is often interpreted as an unequivocal loss for the churches: a loss of position or status, a loss in power and authority, and a loss in membership. That, however, is not the whole story. More recent contributions to the literature on secularization have understood the process rather differently – they have remarked for example on the increasing, and often more specialized, presence of religion in the public sphere and on the growing contribution of religious organizations in a variety of arenas, including welfare (Casanova 1994; Davie 2000; Hervieu-Leger 2000; Herbert 2003; Habermas 2006).

The significance of religion in modern European societies is, therefore, a complex matter. It is both increasing and decreasing at the same time, a process that can be discerned in changing social relationships at all three of the levels that have been introduced in this chapter: the societal, the organizational and the individual. At the societal level, religion and religious institutions have lost their dominant position as a single or dominant sacred canopy: nobody disputes this. This in turn means that institutions previously dominated by the churches – the legal system, education, medicine, the armed forces and so on – are now free to develop separately and lie outside the control of religion. A process of institutional separation has undoubtedly taken place, which has included the evolution of secular welfare systems with their own professional codes and institutions (Casanova 1994). At the same time, relationships between religious institutions (including the majority churches) and the wide variety of individuals or groups that make up a late modern society are changing in nature – they are increasingly based on choice rather than obligation (Davie 2006). In other words, people are free to choose their own modes of religious belonging and to decide for themselves whether or not to make use of the services offered by the churches. No longer can the latter coerce the populations of which they are part.

A great deal of debate in the sociology of religion concerns the extent to which the combination of all these factors should be interpreted as the reduced significance of religion as such, or whether it is more accurate to say that religion is not so much disappearing as changing – a process which enables it to discover new and different roles in late modern societies, even in Europe (Beckford 1989; Bruce 1996; Buckser 1996; Woodhead and Heelas 2000; Davie 2006). Broadly speaking, there are three clusters of scholars in this debate: those who maintain that the religious dimensions of society will continue to decrease and will eventually disappear altogether; those who think that religion and religious institutions are gradually discovering their proper, rightful place in society – i.e. as something distinct and separate from the mainstream; and those who see religion as a social phenomenon which is developing in new forms and who think that its impact on society is as likely to grow as it is to diminish. If the latter is the case, the reappearance of religiously-based agents in public social functions does not run counter to the historical logic of secularization. Rather, it stresses the definition of secularization as an *ongoing* process of functional differentiation driven by the rational division of labour, which takes on different forms in different times (Hervieu-Léger 1986).

A second, very important point follows from this. If the third view is even partially correct, it is clear that the social sciences must find new ways of analysing these issues. 'Traditional' views, overly based on unreconstructed views of secularization as the dominant paradigm, are no longer adequate – a need which is increasingly recognized by those who are working in the field (see for example Beckford 1989; Repstad 1996; Bäckström et al. 2004; Casanova 2006). These are questions to which we shall return in some detail in the conclusion to this book.

Churches Operating According to the Logic of Service Society

The shifts in the relationships between religion and society can be looked at from a different point of view – as part of the changes which occur when the dominant mode of economic organization, or dominant 'logic' of the society, alters. Much has been written in the economic and social scientific literature about the evolution of society from an agricultural base, via an industrial mode of production, to the logic of a global-service society (Normann and Ramirez 1994; Edvardsson et al. 2000; Lusch and Vargo 2006). Material from our case studies shows very clearly that the churches are highly affected by these changes – more specifically by the rhetoric of the service society which increasingly characterizes social relationships. No longer are they able to offer, still less to enforce, standardized religious 'packages' to the population as a whole. In a situation which increasingly resembles a market, the churches – just like any other organization – are obliged to compete with other 'providers' (Stark and Iannaccone 1994). As part of this process they have to ensure the quality of the services that they offer, a quality which will be judged not only from the church's point of view, but also (indeed primarily) from the perspective of the recipient or consumer (Slater 1997). The WREP material demonstrates that the majority churches have adapted themselves variously to this situation, both in general and as welfare service providers. Some have done better than others. Some in fact even use service management terminology in their language, referring to 'clients', 'quality' and so on. But even if they do not use these concepts overtly, the norms of the service economy are increasingly present in their approach.

A number of these points can now be brought together. According to the principles of both functional differentiation and the logic of the service society, churches as organizations must specialize in the areas where they have particular and acknowledged competence. The data from the WREP case studies indicates that the churches are at least moving in this direction in the sense that they are becoming 'distinctive' welfare providers. They, and the welfare services that they offer, are often associated with a holistic view of the human person; they are also able to provide a range of symbolic activities which is not found elsewhere.

The latter include symbolic acts, mostly in the form of ritual, which express the relationship of the individual to the transcendent, to society, to humanity as a whole and to the created order.

Paradoxically, the provision of services and worldviews that take particular account of the *wholeness* of the human person, and of his or her relationship to the cosmos can, indeed should, be regarded as a distinctive or *specialized* function. Who or what else is able to do this?[13] Such an approach was widely applauded by our respondents; it was seen as particularly important in relation to individuals who were deemed 'in need'.

There are other examples of distinctiveness or specialization. Almost no other institution in society, for example, is able to offer the liturgies or ceremonies that bring meaning to the turning points in life. This is most clearly the case at the time of a death when, as observed above, most Europeans still turn to the majority churches and welcome the liturgies that they provide.[14] Finally, even the continuing possibility of belonging, whether explicit or implicit, can be viewed as a 'specialist' facility. What other institutions in late modern societies offers the possibility of membership or attachment to everyone – men, women, old, young, and from every economic, social or ethnic background? Interestingly, this is exactly what Davie means by 'vicarious religion' (2000; 2006) – that is the understated but nonetheless important threads that connect European populations to their churches. When this is working well, the relationship is not only understood, but accepted by both parties. The idea was discussed in some detail in the final chapter of Volume 1.

Conclusion

In many ways our case studies demonstrate that the situation has moved full circle. From their dominant position at the centre of European society in the pre-industrial period, the churches were pushed bit by bit into a more narrowly defined and distinctively religious sphere – an important consequence of the process of functional differentiation associated with modernization. But as our interviewees have pointed out, the situation is now beginning to change again – gradually, and in a rather piecemeal way, the churches are seen once again as resources which are available to society as a whole. This is not, however, a return to the earlier situation. Rather the churches have become a particular kind of resource – as organizations that embody certain values and that bring certain qualities to the field of welfare, including a critical voice. We have seen that in some of our cases the churches offer important complementary services (for example in Norway

---

[13]   A secular parallel can be found in the holistic tendencies of alternative medicine and the growing popularity of the green movement.

[14]   Secular alternatives do exist (for example the rites of passage provided by Humanist organizations) – so far, however, they remain relatively limited.

and Finland); in others, however, they remain the major, sometimes the dominant provider (as in Greece and Germany). Bearing all this in mind, three brief points bring this chapter to a close.

Church–State Dynamics

When comparing the official positions of the churches (i.e. their constitutional status) with their roles at the local level, two rather different pictures emerge. Indeed in some cases (notably in France) these images are sharply contradictory. In general, however, our case studies reveal that the roles of the majority churches in the delivery of welfare at the local level cannot be related directly to the formal relationships between church and state. They are more likely to be related to the effectiveness of the state itself in the delivery of welfare. If the state is weak in this respect, the church is likely to have a high involvement in welfare. Conversely the stronger the welfare ambitions of the state, the more reduced is the role of the church – unless the state delegates these tasks to the church, as it does in Germany.

Our case studies also reveal that in some cases a separation between church and state can have a positive rather than a negative effect on the collaboration between the churches and the local authority in the field of welfare. When the church appears as an organization separate from the state, it becomes an available partner; it is no longer seen simply as an appendage to the state system. In other words it appears as one resource among others – to be used as the situation demands. This is certainly true in the Swedish case where the separation of church and state has occurred relatively recently and has been a largely harmonious process. It is less so in France where the much older separation between church and state was fiercely contested.

Organizations Seeking Identity

Broadly speaking, the majority churches in Europe are now situated 'side by side' with, rather than 'over and above', the secular organizations of modern societies. In this sense they constitute a natural part of the social economy or voluntary sector, with particular services to contribute to those who are in need. In terms of the WREP enquiry, this was expressed in a number of collaborative partnerships both with the local authorities as such and with other voluntary organizations. Such partnerships are highly valued. That said, they raise in turn important issues of identity, both internal and external, for the local churches. What is it that distinguishes them from other organizations? Such questions were raised in the English case as long ago as the *Faith in the City* report (Archbishop of Canterbury's Commission on Urban Priority Areas 1985); they also appeared in the discussions preceding the separation between church and state in Sweden (Persenius 1987; Bäckström et al. 2004).

Increasing Expectations versus Reduced Resources

A dominant expectation among our interviewees is that the state should have, and should keep, the primary responsibility for welfare in modern European societies. Expectations regarding the role of the churches are more varied, and – as we have seen – depend very largely on what the state itself can offer. That said, our case studies show pretty consistently that expectations regarding the churches as welfare agents have increased during the last decade – our interviewees expect more rather than less in the way of provision. At the same time, however, the churches are under pressure financially, sometimes very acutely. Shrinking membership, and a decline in public funding for welfare as a whole, narrows the churches' room for manoeuvre. Indeed from a financial perspective, the most sensible move might be to limit this kind of operation – either to stop it altogether or to refuse any further responsibilities. This tension (and the ambivalence associated with it) is expressed particularly clearly by the representatives of the church-related welfare organizations in Germany – it is developed at length in the German case study in Volume 1. On the one hand, the strongly positive expectations regarding the churches' contributions to welfare are noted with pride – these are a welcome change to more general assumptions about the declining role of religion and religious institutions in German society. On the other, it is this gradual process of decline, notably the diminishing membership base, which makes it impossible for the churches to respond adequately to these very high expectations – it is a classic Catch-22 (or no-win) situation (Leis-Peters 2010). In rather more modest terms, a similar dilemma is faced in all the eight countries included in WREP.

Hence a paradox, or rather a series of paradoxes. It is clear that the majority churches and their related organizations are involved in welfare in all the localities under review. At the same time the numbers of people attending services on a regular basis continue to fall; this is also true of statistics that relate to traditional beliefs (Pettersson 2006; Esmer and Pettersson 2007). That said, the role of the majority churches in individual lives continues in most of the countries in WREP, and in some of them it remains moderately strong. This is primarily revealed in two ways: in membership (or belonging), and in the continuing use of the churches by large sections of the population at key moments in the life cycle. It is in this sense that they can still claim to be 'majority churches', thus giving them a legitimate role in the public as well as the private sphere. As this chapter has made clear, these complex and seemingly contradictory developments emerge from the wider processes of economic, social and religious change in modern Europe which form the essential background to WREP.

Chapter 3

A Gendered Perspective on Welfare and Religion in Europe

Ninna Edgardh

Speaking for myself, I would not leave my grandmother in the hands of a man ... I find the idea of a male caregiver a bit funny! (Frisina 2010: 192)

This quotation from a male interviewee in the Italian case study gives a hint of how closely gender is embedded in the issues addressed by the WREP project. As will be shown, gender has an impact on the agency of churches both as welfare providers and as formers of public opinion. Gender influences the theological and ethical positions held by different churches, and leaves its imprint on the attitudes people hold on the role of the church in welfare. In daily life, however, this gendering is largely invisible. More often than not gendered divisions of labour, gender inequalities, and forms of commitment and neglect related to gender are taken for granted as something 'natural' and are thus 'beyond reflection'.

In recent years, scholarly interest in the gendering processes at work in many different aspects of society has developed fast, resulting in a growing literature on gender and religion, gender and welfare, gender and social care, and so on. Studies from all of these areas inform this chapter. The specific intersections between gender, welfare and religion in Europe, however, have rarely been properly explored. This means that we have had to start very much from the beginning in our studies, with relatively modest ambitions. The basic aim of this chapter is, therefore, to make explicit the gendered aspects of the social role of the churches and church-related organizations which are often rendered invisible. With this in mind we limit ourselves to exploring some of the gendered assumptions and structures that permeate our material, and to discussing what they might mean for the role of the churches in the ongoing restructuring of welfare.

The first section will give an overview of the fields of research to which our study relates, and some basic information highlighted by gender researchers in the areas of welfare and social care. The next section presents the results of the case studies viewed from a gender perspective. The third and final section discusses the sociological and theological implications of the gendered nature of the role of the majority churches in welfare.

Gender, Welfare and Religion

Welfare provision is a highly gendered field in all western European countries. Since the beginning of the 1990s an increasing amount of literature has been produced on the relationship between welfare regimes and gender (Daly 2000: 19–44). The literature points to the fact that the western European organization of welfare since the Second World War has been built on a family-based gender contract, presupposing a male bread-winner and a female care-giver (Morgan 2006). This contract is basically still at work, albeit in modified forms (Morgan 2009: 82). The majority of all care work, whether taking place within the family, in the voluntary sector or in salaried positions, is still performed by women (Daly and Rake 2003: 48–69; Abrahamsson, Boje and Greve 2005: 90). In some countries the majority of this work is organized on a voluntary or family basis. When professionalized in the public sector – as in Scandinavia – social care is likely, however, to contribute to an increase in female employment.[1]

Today, women in Sweden, Finland and Norway are almost as active in the paid labour force as their male counterparts (at around 70 per cent in all three countries, albeit slightly lower in Finland). The dominant spheres of working life in which women may be found are social care, health and education. Generally women in the Nordic countries are paid less than men; in Sweden in particular, women seek solutions in the form of part-time employment to a much higher degree than men, in order to reconcile demands from the labour market and the needs of the family. Finland is an exception in this respect, with considerably fewer women engaged in part-time work. Women in England, Germany and France work outside the home to a significantly higher degree than ten or 20 years ago, but still less than in most of the Nordic countries (at around 60 per cent, with England approaching the figures of Finland, the Nordic exception). In England and Germany in particular, the proportion of women in part-time work is very high. Women in Italy and Greece participate in the labour market to a much lower degree (around 45 per cent), which may result from the fact that opportunities for part-time work are rare in these countries. Women who do take up paid employment in Greece and Italy generally work full-time. As we will see, these variations have considerable

---

[1]   The figures presented here are from 2005. It is worth observing that they include all paid work, even if it is only one hour per week. However, they do not take account of the degree to which women are employed in part-time or flexible work, which is generally more common among women than men, even if the frequency varies considerably between countries. Exact figures are difficult to provide, because the number of working hours per week counted as 'full-time' also varies between countries. Figures from Eurostat on part-time work build on people's own estimations, and show that part-time work is most common among women in Germany and England, closely followed by Sweden (around 40 per cent of employed women), while it is much lower in Finland and Greece (Eurostat 2007: 135, 138).

implications for the roles of the churches in welfare, and for the roles it is possible for women to adopt within these institutions.

While the gendered aspects of welfare provision seem obvious when considered through figures like these, it was not in fact until the beginning of the 1990s that a debate arose concerning the inclusion of gender as a relevant variable in the study of the welfare regimes constructed by Esping-Andersen and others. Earlier research was criticized for not taking enough account of either the dimension of care or the role of the family in welfare provision. A pioneering effort to theorize the gendered nature of welfare regimes was introduced in 1992 by Jane Lewis, when she presented the idea that different types of welfare regimes adhere to varying degrees to a 'male-as-bread-winner' ideology, prescribing wage-earning for men, and caring and homemaking for women. Lewis operationalizes such an ideology in terms of the norms and assumptions about women's roles that are encoded in social policies. According to her model, European welfare states may be grouped on a continuum formed by strong, modified and weak male bread-winner models (Lewis 1992), exemplified by Britain (strong), France (modified) and Sweden (weak). The strength of Lewis's contribution lies primarily in highlighting how welfare regimes could by typified according to gendered divisions of labour, in parallel with other relevant criteria.

The discussion concerning the relative prevalence of the male bread-winner model in different countries, and how the model may be combined with other theoretical perspectives has continued (Trifiletti 1999). In different ways, gender specialists have highlighted the importance of including family-based responsibility in any analysis of welfare systems. Such inclusions must, however, acknowledge that the family is not a gender-neutral reality: family-based responsibility for care normally presupposes a female caregiver, who works without pay within the context of the family. Some scholars have used comparative methodology to show the effects of gender on, for example, different income support policies (Sainsbury 1994; 1999a). Based on her comparative research, Diane Sainsbury has introduced the concept of gender regimes, as a parallel to the welfare regimes suggested by Esping-Andersen. A regime is, according to Sainsbury, 'a complex of rules and norms that create established expectations'. A gender regime thus 'consists of the rules and norms about gender relations, allocating tasks and rights to the two sexes' (Sainsbury 1999b: 5). Worth observing from our perspective is the fact that the churches have traditionally been major providers of such rules and norms about gender relations.

Among the more recent studies of gender and welfare in a comparative perspective we find a study of seven European countries and the United States by the sociologists Mary Daly and Katherine Rake (2003). They argue that a feminist approach which stays within the framework of welfare regimes does not take enough account of differences between groups of women, or of how policies differentiate between lone mothers, older women and other groups. Daly and Rake also criticize approaches to welfare studies that remain within the framework of economic redistribution. Consequently, they take a comprehensive approach trying to integrate the three aspects of welfare, care and work. Several interesting observations emerge from their analysis. Data about female employment reveal that women's life-courses have changed dramatically over a couple of decades, and today are significantly more like those of men. However, a similar change has not occurred in the lives of men, who have not increased their engagement in informal caring in a comparable way. Women in Europe are, in fact, twice as likely as men to be involved in providing unpaid child care, as well as caring for ill or elderly adults (Daly and Rake 2003: 55).

This situation is not, apparently, in accordance with how people wish things to be: Daly and Rake point to figures from the OECD that show a wide divergence between actual arrangements of employment and family, and what might be termed 'preferred outcomes' (OECD 2001; Daly and Rake 2003: 169). The general finding from this study is that families feel that they experience too much of a male bread-winner model, and too little of other solutions to the combination of caring and earning. Daly and Rake identify several reasons for this, which in turn call for reforms in working life, in order that both women and men may assume their roles as carers. Until then, they argue, the changing nature of the family means that welfare states can no longer assume that caring will be automatically provided by the family. This becomes all the more problematic as the demand for care grows. The preferred solution to the problem has thus far been an individualization of policies, even with regard to children, who are increasingly granted social rights as individuals rather than as members of a family. Daly and Rake observe a tendency across Europe today to forge a new contract between the welfare state and individuals, in which the latter are encouraged to take on greater responsibility for their own welfare as well as for that of their families (Daly and Rake 2003: 168–71).

Daly and Rake point to important gender implications of this development: generally speaking, they argue that women will suffer disproportionately from any diminution in the role of the state as responsible for the welfare of the citizens. Individualized solutions do not sufficiently protect women, who are still the major bearers of unpaid care work within the family. When risks are to be taken by individuals rather than by the state it is the poorest – among whom women are over-represented – who are the least able to bear them. Individualization also threatens the elements of familial protection still common to many social security systems. Increasingly women have to make claims in their own right and on behalf of their children. It is questionable, Daly and Rake state, whether women have access to the power necessary to press their claims successfully (Daly and Rake 2003: 175–8).

Male scholars have joined the critique of the gender-blindness of previous welfare typologies. Jeff Hearn and Keith Pringle observe that gendered categorizations of welfare states need to be developed in order to take account not only of the situation of women, but also of differences amongst men and men's practice in the various cases (Hearn and Pringle 2006: 10). Models sensitive to gender differences, including details relating to the situations of both women and men, are needed.

Although no feminist typology has gained absolute precedence, the literature on gender and welfare regimes has expanded and the theme is frequently discussed. One result of this debate is that dominant scholars in the field of welfare typology have had to reconsider their work in terms of gender. Gøsta Esping-Andersen, for example, has reconsidered his typology in order to include the role of welfare provision by the family among his parameters. The concepts he uses are 'familialism' and 'de-familialization', with 'familialism' referring to the ideology that states that the household is responsible for the welfare of its constituents, and 'de-familialization' referring to the degree to which the responsibility of the household for welfare is relaxed either by the state or the market (Esping-Andersen 1999: 5).

Gender and the Deficit in Care

It is clear from several of the comparative studies on gender and welfare cited above that many of the challenges facing the organization of welfare in Europe have to do with changing life and family patterns for women and men. A traditional economic dependence on a male breadwinner is losing its dominance all over Europe, even if not always at the pace families would want. Increasingly – though to varying degrees in different countries – women are expected to follow the life pattern of the male worker. As a result, the traditional dependence on the female care-giver is also threatened, at least if she is expected to do unpaid work within the family. In the words of Daly and Rake, the problem lies in the fact that 'the demand for care is growing at the same time as the supply of private care within the family is contracting' (Daly and Rake 2003: 168). As suggested by Arlie Russell Hochschild (1995) this points to the problem of an increasing 'care deficit'.

It would be wrong, however, to say that the problem of a deficit in care is wholly caused by women entering the labour market to a new extent. Such a statement would, in any case, take for granted the presupposition that responsibility for care rests more on women than on men. In fact, many of the changes in women's life patterns are positive, allowing new freedom for women as individuals at a time when family bonds are dissolving. The problem is that the changes presuppose new arrangements of care involving society as a whole, and – as shown by the Swedish economist Agneta Stark – European politicians have been reluctant to recognize this need (Stark and Regnér 2002). The assumption that women are to provide care for the members of the household is not an agreement based on a formalized contract, adopted as a result of political decisions, but rather on an informal agreement related to ideas of caring as a 'natural' feminine trait. This means that there is no formal requirement for the contract to be renegotiated when the circumstances on which it has been based are changed. Instead, the tendency is to individualize the problem and its solutions.

One solution of this nature is for young people to postpone having children. As discussed in the previous chapter, women in Europe today give birth to significantly fewer children than in earlier generations, and are older when their first child is born. Together with the increase in average life expectancies, the effect is that the population is ageing. Dwindling numbers of working people have to support growing numbers of elderly people, and thus the need for care increases.

Another solution that has become increasingly common across Europe, particularly in the south, is to employ an immigrant woman to fill the gap in the home (Ehrenreich and Hochschild 2003; Lyon and Glucksmann 2008). Although the choice to hire such a woman as an alternative carer is made on an individual basis, the effects are political: the gendered character of care is ethnicized, and the burden of the care deficit is moved from western Europe to 'the others', in the migrant woman's home country. This trend shows clearly in the Italian and Greek case studies. In contrast, the Nordic political solution has for a long time been to organize care publicly, still primarily provided by women, but as salaried work. This solution, however, increasingly collides with financial strains and pressure on cost reductions. In recent years, therefore, efforts have been made to move responsibility back to the family, and primarily to women (Szebehely 2005).

The tensions involved in this field have led researchers to look in more depth at the whole area of social care, which has previously been neglected by theorists. A basic assumption in the recent literature is that the provision of care is a crucial element in welfare production and the institutional framework of welfare states (Pfau-Effinger and Geissler 2005: 4), and that provision of care is thus a key element in the present restructuring of welfare (Daly and Lewis 1998; 2000). In short, it is impossible to understand the form and nature of contemporary welfare states without a concept like 'care'.

Efforts to define what is meant by the concept are often quite straightforward, stating that care involves 'the physical, mental, and emotional activities and effort involved in looking after, responding to, and supporting others' (Baines et al. 1998: 3). Other scholars stress that there rather are more dimensions to this labour, as it occurs in a context of strong norms of obligation, responsibility and feelings of affection and resentment (Baines et al. 1998: 4). Daly and Lewis, in their pioneering effort to make care work an analytical tool in the discussion of welfare states, have presented a multi-dimensional definition of social care as 'the activities and relations involved in meeting the physical and emotional requirements of dependent adults and children and the normative, economic and social frameworks within which these are assigned and carried out' (Daly and Lewis 2000: 285). This definition underlines the idea that caring *is* a type of labour, combined with certain costs, but also occurring within certain normative frameworks. These frameworks are closely linked to ideas about femininity and subordination. As noted by Daly and Rake, 'care has been identified as work with a woman's face' (Daly and Rake 2003: 49). Caring is seldom professionalized, is usually poorly paid, and often deemed to be of low status (Pfau-Effinger and Geissler 2005: 5).

In relation to this normative framework it is interesting to point to the role of religion. Renita Sörensdotter concludes in a Swedish discussion of social care that 'to be born with a woman's body is to be a potential caregiver' (Sörensdotter 2004: 50). Interestingly, a religious image, the Madonna with her child, has become paradigmatic for illustrating the link between care and femininity, as shown by the plentiful illustrations in the volume by Sörensdotter and Mikaeli (2004). We might, therefore, expect a connection between Christian ideals of femininity and the role of the churches in social care to be revealed in the case studies. This connection is highly relevant, as shown in a significant British debate initiated by Alison Wolf, professor of public sector management at King's College London. In the cover-story of *Prospect Magazine* in April 2006, Wolf reflects on the possible future of female voluntary caring, which has been deeply anchored in religion, saying, 'The 19th and early 20th centuries saw the development of myriad charities with religious links, many of them aimed at women and almost all relying heavily on female volunteers' (Wolf 2006). Wolf argues that today we are facing 'the end of female altruism', emptying families and the voluntary sector of their major resource. This emptying, contends Wolf, is caused by the 'rupture in human history' created through the opening up of all sectors of the labour market for women.

Wolf's article was rapidly echoed in British daily papers. *The Times* published her story under the provocative heading 'The Egoistic Sex?', accompanied by a full page photo of an elderly woman (Henery 2006). Whether she was supposed to be the victim or the villain of the egoistic treason against her sex was left for the reader to judge. Wolf, and *The Times'* piece in a less attractive way, seem to take advantage of the situation in order to impose guilt on women who do not live up to the expectations imposed on their sex. Nevertheless, the articles reveal important dimensions of what is at stake with respect to values and traditions relating to religion, gender and care. While women's voluntary caring, according to Wolf, has been imbued with idealistic religious language and values of self-sacrifice, the female ideal of our time is expressed in the iconic image of the advertisement, arguing that you should invest in your beauty 'because you are worth it' (Wolf 2006).

As we have shown, most solutions introduced to solve the 'care deficit' still rest on the perception of women as primary carers – a tendency of which Wolf's argument seems to be a good illustration. Along with several of his colleagues among welfare researchers, however, Gøsta Esping-Andersen argues that the only way forward for the European welfare state is for similar changes to take place in the life-course of men to those which have already happened for women (Esping-Andersen 2002: 70). As women have increasingly become breadwinners along with men, so men have to become carers along with women if the welfare of present and future generations is to be secured.

The Role of Religion

While gender and care have been effectively, though somewhat recently, introduced as relevant factors in the study of welfare regimes in Europe, the same cannot be said of religion, which remains significantly absent from much of the discussion. In many ways, this is not surprising, as religion is – according to theories of secularization – expected to play a diminishing role in European public life. That said, one specific connection between gender, religion and welfare is frequently commented on in the welfare literature, even if it is seldom examined in depth: the role of religion as a creator of the familialist ideology present in the welfare systems of central and southern Europe in particular. This ideology is strongly influenced by the Catholic Church and its social teaching, especially the principle of subsidiarity (Esping-Andersen 1990: 61; Borchorst 1994: 34). The theological foundations of this teaching are explained at greater length in the following chapter. Here it suffices to say that the principle of subsidiarity states that no social undertakings shall be made by larger and more complex social organizations, which could be performed by smaller and simpler units. In practice the principle has led to a strong emphasis on the role of the (extended) family and of voluntary organizations within welfare in countries like Italy and Germany. The role of the family has been closely connected to ideals stressing the caring role of women, repeatedly underlined by Catholic authorities. This, in turn, is perceived as a problem from the perspective of gender equality, as it contributes to preserving legal and financial inequalities. Consequently, when religion does appear in literature on welfare, it is most often cited as a negative factor.

The Scandinavian countries are very different: they have displayed noticeably high scores on comparative measures of welfare states, from Helga Hernes's characterization of the Scandinavian states as 'women-friendly' onwards (Hernes 1987). For example, in their eight-nation comparison, Daly and Rake find Sweden to be a particular case marked by 'a diversity of opportunities available to Swedish women, which, while they do not equal those available to men, are richer in their range than elsewhere' (Daly and Rake 2003: 161). Predictably, Scandinavia's positive image is sometimes interpreted as a result of its high degree of secularization, and is thus inversely connected to religion, since secularization is seen as an important prerequisite for women's emancipation (Inglehart and Norris 2003).

One of the few studies to dig deeper into questions about gender, religion and welfare is that of the political scientist Kimberly J. Morgan, a member of a European research group (led by Philip Manow and Kees van Kersbergen) concerned with the historical influence of religion on the Western welfare state. Morgan's special interest has been the interaction between religion and family policies. Accepting the general assumption that a strong religious influence implies traditional divisions of gender roles and a traditional role for the family, she argues that it was not the different church traditions as such, but the divergences in types of relation between state and church in the different countries, that came to be decisive for the gendering of the welfare regimes during the twentieth century (Morgan 2002; 2006; 2009). Through the lens of policies for working mothers Morgan traces the pathways taken by different clusters of European countries (Morgan 2009). As it happens, all the countries involved in the WREP project, except for Greece and England, are included in her analysis, which concentrates on two decisive periods: the decades around the turn of the century (1900), and the decades after the Second World War. Morgan distinguishes between three different paths: the Nordic model, with religious homogeneity, church–state fusion and a resulting lack of religiously-based political conflicts; a clerical–anticlerical model of contestation, found in Catholic countries with strong anticlerical forces; and an accomodationist model in countries where the religious forces were more successful in asserting their interests (Morgan 2009: 57).

These different patterns, contends Morgan, influenced law and early public policies for women, children and families, and were perhaps most clearly expressed in how control over education evolved. In turn, the same variety in policy approaches laid the basis for later developments during the 'golden age' of welfare state expansion. In the Nordic countries, for example, a statist family policy tradition – reflecting the early fusion between church and state established during the Reformation period – implied that responsibility for education could easily be transferred from the church to secular authorities. Secularization spurred on the legal individualization of women, constituting the background to present-day gender equality policies. France and Italy, in contrast, have a long history of conflict between clerical and anticlerical forces. Where the state gained the upper hand in these conflicts, as in France, the role of the state expanded and familialism weakened. In Italy, conversely, the church and related voluntary organizations kept control over education. Germany, finally, experienced religious conflicts similar to those in France and Italy, but the conflicts developed somewhat differently as they were combined with a Catholic–Protestant division. Protestants and Catholics were, however, united around the goal of preserving control over social and educational services. Consequently, the principle of subsidiarity was institutionalized in the welfare state: welfare provision, including some educational functions, was delegated to religious and voluntary organizations. This left Germany with strong conservative forces (which – unlike in France – lacked contestation from the left) with regard to gender roles and the family.

Morgan argues that the deep historical factors which shaped party ideology and public policy in Europe during the twentieth century have continued to influence beliefs, practices and policies in Europe until today, and that they largely explain the continuous influence of modified versions of the male bread-winner model, despite efforts on many levels to realize a more radical shift to a gender-neutral model. It will be the task of the following analysis to see how these patterns are expressed at the local level in the case studies included in WREP.

Theoretical Starting Points

Before turning to the case studies themselves, a number of theoretical points need clarification. The first concerns the concept of gender, which will be used as an analytical tool throughout the chapter. Religious contexts often presuppose a 'givenness' of gender roles that stands in sharp contrast with the social-scientific approach used in this chapter, where gender is analysed as a dynamic and continuing process, rather than as a pattern of given and stable binary categories. So used, the concept has its roots in the 1960s, when the grammatical term 'gender' was adopted by social scientists who needed a word to capture the social organization of women and men. The new usage has since made its way rapidly into both daily speech and academic terminology. Gender is understood here as being continuously created and recreated on the individual level through the activities of women and men, as well as on the societal level by institutions such as the family, the welfare state, the labour market and religion (compare Daly and Rake 2003: 37).

A useful definition of gender is that presented by Amy S. Wharton, who defines gender as a 'multilevel system of social practices that produces distinctions between women and men, and organizes inequality on the basis of those distinctions' (Wharton 2005: 217). As suggested in this definition, gender not only refers to the distinction between the categories 'women' and 'men', but also to the very processes whereby these categories are produced. Wharton's definition also includes the important concept of power, noting that the distinctions are created in a hierarchical order, which may vary in content, but is surprisingly stable in continuously ordering female under male. Wharton identifies two major ways in which gender inequalities are created, namely *institutionalization* and *legitimation*. Institutions comprise social structures and practices, including symbols and beliefs. When structures and practices are institutionalized, they become so regular that they are accepted as 'the way things are'. Thus they tend to reproduce themselves. This also goes for social inequalities based on gender, class or race. Long-term institutionalized inequalities of this type affect all people, irrespective of whether they belong to the dominant or subordinate group in the hierarchy (Wharton 2005: 220). At the same time, Wharton underlines that inequalities persist because people view them as legitimate. Legitimation is thus a process through which inequalities are justified. A major factor in this respect is ideology, by which Wharton means 'a widely shared worldview that reflects people's understanding of the world around them' (Wharton 2005: 222).

A consideration of how gender is institutionalized and legitimated will be an important dimension of the following analysis. It is worth observing that religion is given a special role in both processes, since it claims to represent something eternal and stable. In Christian traditions, concepts like *God* and *creation* are regularly used to legitimate these claims – but ideas about *sexuality*, *family* and *gender roles* are also woven into this fabric of understanding. In this way a specific type of sexuality, a certain type of family formation, or a particular division of male and female roles is considered more in line with divine creation or the will of

God. Thus the practices of religious institutions in welfare provision are integrated into a framework of religious interpretation which legitimates the practice on an existential level. Religious language is a powerful instrument regulating social relations. It is for this reason that feminist theologians have put so much effort into the critique of male language for God, and of theologies that legitimate the subordination of women under men (Radford Ruether 1983; McFague 1987; Chopp 1989).

The following analysis of the WREP findings concerns the social construction of gender in religious practice. The decision to focus on gender does not mean that we see this as isolated from other aspects of social life. On the contrary, gender always comes together with a whole range of factors which are important for social organizations, such as class, race/ethnicity, and sexuality (Phoenix and Pattynama 2006). As discussed at greater length in the Welfare and Values in Europe (WaVE) project, religion is also closely intertwined with many different aspects of social life. In what follows, however, the primary focus will be on the connections between gender, family and sexuality.

It is worth observing that an approach to 'gender as a social construction' does not, as some might expect, imply an understanding of gender as flexible. Quite the reverse in fact – a social practice may be even more stable than a material 'given'. Indeed the institutionalization and legitimation of worldviews takes place at several levels. As shown in the previous chapter, religion works at the individual level, in shaping individuals' understandings of themselves and the world they live in; at the organizational level, in religious institutions; and at the societal level in the wider construction of religion in society. A notion of gender as a continuously-changing but in many ways stable social practice involves all of these levels. For example, the individual believer who takes part in a religious service is invited to identify with a whole range of images, which are imprinted with religious symbolism but also with gendered meanings. Religious organizations function like most other organizations with regard to how gender influences, and is influenced by, divisions of labour and decision-making. On the societal level, religions may be more or less influential in the public (and traditionally male-dominated) sphere or in the private (and traditionally female-dominated) one.

The second point to be clarified before approaching the case studies concerns the nature of the data used in the analysis – indeed the nature of the text as such. When gender is discussed in daily speech, personal experience is mixed with presuppositions about other people's experiences, given ideals as to what gender relations ought to be like, and expectations about the nature of other people's ideals. This mixture is quite natural when we speak to friends, and occurs frequently in replies from interviewees. In our analysis, however, we require greater clarity. It is especially important to distinguish between a descriptive discussion and a normative one (compare Blennberger 2004).

Part of the analysis in the following section concerns descriptive issues, supported by observations about the ordering of women and men and the factors that lie behind this ordering. For example: to what extent do women and men respectively represent the local churches as providers of welfare services and as formers of public opinion? Which roles do women and men play in the practice of the parishes and church-related organizations? Which ministries exist, and which of them require ordination, in the respective churches, and are these equally available to women and men? What are the conditions in which the respective roles of women and men are played out? Are welfare services provided primarily with the help of paid personnel, or volunteers, and what does the gender distribution look like in the different categories? To what degree do different roles imply access to – or exclusion from – positions of power and influence within the church? It is important to remember, however, that first-hand data has not always been available to the researchers. In these cases, it has been necessary to rely on information from the interviewees, which has then to be critically assessed.

A second category of questions concerns the ways in which people perceive the existing gender order, and how they explain its existence. As will be shown below, the boundary between how a respondent comprehends a situation as such and how it is described – for example, with reference to the perceived natural roles for women and men – is quite often blurred. Close on the heels of people's descriptions of the present situation come their perceptions about what would constitute an ideal gender order. However, even if the *issues* discussed are of a normative kind – such as statements about ideals as uttered by interviewees or by a church organization – the *data* as such are descriptive. Many interviews in our material touch upon issues related to gender roles and gender equality that are in flux in Europe today. Some of these issues surface in debates within local churches, and also in our respondents' perceptions of the role of the church in welfare. They may, for example, be related to reproduction and sexuality (like abortion, the use of contraceptives, or the acceptance of pre-marital sexual relations), or to family and personal relations (like the possibility of same-sex marriages, or the legitimacy of divorce). Another area of relevance might be the widening of options available for women, for instance the ordination of women to the priesthood.

An additional point follows from this. Even if the questions discussed are of a descriptive kind, ideals concerning gender equality and presuppositions about present inequalities have, of course, influenced our way of posing questions and how we have framed the discussion both in the interviews and in the analysis in this book. It is, finally, a crucial characteristic of a comparative project that similar questions posed in diverse cultural settings may be very differently interpreted. The analysis of the qualitative material must take this into account.

Normally social scientists limit themselves to descriptive and analytical work. For an ethicist or a theologian, however, a normative discussion of an ideal gender order – and good methods for achieving such an order – may be equally relevant. In this chapter, such issues will be considered in the concluding section, where the implications of our results for the possible role of churches and church-related organizations in the structuring of welfare are discussed. Examples of feminist theology will inform this discussion, but will be critically evaluated and placed firmly in the context of the WREP project.

Churches as Gendered Agents of Welfare

Against this background, we will now turn to the data themselves. These will be organized according to four major themes:

- the uneven representation of women and men in the activities covered by the case studies;
- the unequal influence of women and men in relation to these activities;
- how inequalities in representation and influence are explained and legitimized;
- contested standpoints with regard to family, gender and sexuality.

The themes will be discussed in sequence, in order to make clear what conclusions may be drawn from which type of data. The discussion of the first theme will also give a more general introduction to the most significant gender-specific aspects of the national and local particularities of each case.

The Uneven Representation of Women and Men in Welfare Activities

Women predominate in the hands-on provision of welfare services by the parishes and church-related organizations in all the towns we have studied, and there is a clear divide between the type of tasks undertaken by women and men respectively. This is the most basic finding of our studies, and is unsurprising in light of what has already been said about the gendered nature of care. However, we have not found any previous studies documenting this aspect of church life in different church settings across Europe. Indeed the comparative perspective renders the results even more striking: the predominance of women in these types of church-related activities seems to be very similar across different theological traditions, different types of church organization and different ways of gendering the societal organization of welfare. As the following discussion will show, however, the variations themselves affect both the ways in which the situation is perceived and how social care is carried out.

We will start with the cases representing the strongest familialist organization of welfare provision, among which we find Greece, Italy and Germany. Interestingly, the three cases represent three different church traditions, namely Orthodox, Catholic and Protestant (our German case took place in a town dominated by the Protestant church).

Greece   Greek welfare provision relies heavily on the family and – to a lesser extent – on voluntary contributions, often inspired by religious faith though not always institutionally related to the church. This reliance on the family is built on the premise that women are available at home, caring for an extended family including young and elderly people. At the turn of the millennium, for example, only 5 per cent of elderly people in Greece lived in a nursing home, and only

3 per cent of the care of children under the age of three was provided by the state (Molokotos-Liederman and Fokas 2004: 327). It is also clear that the gap in domestic help and nursing, created when women leave home for paid work while no other provision of care is available, has to some extent been filled by immigrant female labour (Molokotos-Liederman and Fokas 2004: 290; Fokas 2006: 260).

Despite their increasing participation in the labour market, it is still women who provide the majority of social care, either as employed social workers or as volunteers. The Greek Orthodox Church relies for its welfare activities on a large network of approximately 23,000 volunteers (Molokotos-Liederman and Fokas 2004: 319), among which about 80 per cent of those active in welfare services are women (Fokas 2006: 229). And even where men are engaged in welfare related activities, their role is significantly different from that of women. Based on information from the interviewees in Thiva and Livadeia our researcher concludes:

> Male activities include (but are not limited to): offering part of a crop to the soup kitchen (which entails physically carrying crops which they have tended); gardening at the newly-established home for elderly people; and helping with technological or electrical problems in a given institution, etc. Meanwhile, women visit and help care for the residents in church care homes; volunteer to clean and decorate church institutions; and cook for the soup kitchen (amongst other activities). (Fokas and Molokotos-Liederman 2010: 180)

Social work, or *diakonia*, is highly valued by the church, and is theologically interpreted as the 'liturgy after the liturgy' – that is, as Christian worship expressed in committed engagement with society and culture. The church does not, however, want to promote its welfare work publicly, because – as one interviewee notes – this could be seen as contrary to basic principles of philanthropy and the Orthodox ethos. The church, it is felt, should not seek praise for its good works, but should simply perform them. This will ensure that the church does good works because they are good in themselves, rather than for any praise it may gain from making them publicly known (Molokotos-Liederman and Fokas 2004: 318).

The Mother of God (*Theotokos*) image has an important role in Greek Orthodox theology and spirituality, and is seen as a role model of the 'pure mother' and an example for women in the church. Women are encouraged to participate actively in church life, and in the workplace, but without allowing their career development to undermine their vocation to motherhood. Marriage, motherhood and family are seen as liturgical events – ways for women to become true partners of God (Molokotos-Liederman and Fokas 2004: 314). In this way, the Greek case clearly exemplifies how theology legitimates the role of women as carers.

Italy   Vicenza in Italy is our second case characterized by a strong familialism, especially so as the Veneto region is among the most traditional in Italy. But even in the Italian welfare system more broadly, the traditional extended family is socially and politically taken for granted. Female employment in Italy is regarded as a private rather than a public matter, which means that public services facilitating women's participation in working life are not provided. Half of all married women aged between 20 and 50 in Italy are housewives, and women with paid jobs still usually take on the full responsibility for housework as well (Frisina 2004: 279–80). Social insurance is designed to protect the family, through the head of the household, who is normally the male bread-winner (Frisina 2004: 270). Other factors are, however, important. Responsibility for the poor may rest primarily with their families, but private initiatives and charity organizations 'fill in' when the family fails. And as in Greece, the deficit in caring resources created by the lack of alternative forms of care, when women increasingly take up paid work, is to a large extent compensated for by the 'undocumented women' employed as domestic workers. Indeed, our researcher observes that immigrant women are today the main providers of care for elderly people in Italy. This situation has increasingly been acknowledged by the Catholic Church. With its long history of defending the traditional family, it has been among the first to voice concern over the consequences of this 'silent revolution' – not least for the families these women leave behind in their home countries (Frisina 2004: 274).

As shown in the previous chapter, the Catholic Church is present in the Vicenza welfare sector by means of a broad variety of actors: the parishes, with various charitable practices; the religious institutions, operating mainly in the field of education; and finally a heterogeneous world of Catholic associations, of which by far the largest is Caritas-Diakonia. All of these rely to a large extent on volunteers. A national survey in 2002 showed that 65.5 per cent of the personnel involved in church related social assistance are unpaid volunteers. Women make up 62.7 per cent of the lay and 65.7 per cent of the religious personnel in this type of assistance (Frisina 2004: 278).[2] No exact figures are available showing the corresponding gender distribution in Vicenza itself, but answers from the interviewees confirm the general picture of female dominance.

Germany   The third case is the German one. Here the organization of welfare is much more developed than in Greece or Italy. 'Family' in this case tends to mean the nuclear family, in contrast to the extended families still dominating in the Greek and Italian situations. Nonetheless, there are important similarities between the systems, in that they presuppose that the basic responsibility for the welfare of the individual rests with his or her closest relatives. Parents, children and spouses, for example, are economically responsible for each other throughout their lives. The insurance system, too, focuses on the individual within a family context. It is job-centred, in that citizens become independent members of the insurance system when taking a job, which is subject to compulsory insurance. For women it is still difficult to combine family responsibilities with full-time professional activity, as

---

[2]   'Lay' is here understood in contrast to 'religious', which in this context means ordained or belonging to a religious order.

care services for elderly people and children are insufficient. In reality, this means that many women and children are dependent members of an insurance system through their husbands and fathers. Part-time work is a solution for many mothers and, as in Italy and Greece, it is not uncommon to employ women from abroad (primarily from eastern Europe) to care for elderly relatives.

The significant family orientation of the German system, and its reliance on the active participation of professional welfare organizations, has its roots in the strong impact of the two major 'folk' churches, Catholic and Protestant. Historically it has also been influenced politically by the former Zentrum Party, which represented a major social Catholic interest. The state's reliance on voluntary organizations, and therefore on women, in the German case is evident when examining the ample statistics available. For example, 57 per cent of members in the Protestant churches are women (Leis-Peters 2006: 77). The Bruderhaus Diakonie, which is the major Protestant welfare provider in Reutlingen, has about 1,500 employees in the district, of whom around 80 per cent are women (Leis-Peters 2006: 65). In 2002 the Evangelische Landeskirche in Württemberg had 4,000 paid employees, but as many as 131,000 volunteers, 70 per cent of them women (Leis 2004: 221). The tasks of these volunteers vary widely, from editing the parish newspaper to singing in choirs. The case study shows clear signs of a female majority among the volunteers in church-related social projects like the Vesperkirche and in parish-related work such as visiting services. It is also clear that women and men take on different tasks in these activities: women who are active in the Vesperkirche enjoy meeting people from different social backgrounds, while the men prefer organizational or practical tasks (like fetching food or making rotas) (Leis-Peters 2006: 78).

France　In terms of a gender perspective, some of the specificities of the French case have already been mentioned. France is a country with a Catholic majority church, whose direct influence on the organization and provision of welfare has been restricted for reasons that date from the nineteenth century. In contrast to the previous three countries, the French system of social protection has been built on a strong, highly centralized state and is organized around work. The French welfare model has been referred to as a 'modified male bread-winner regime', which might still be an apt characterization in that the social security system tries to strike a balance between different types of families (Mabille and Valasik 2004: 258). The rate of female employment is higher in France than in Greece and Italy, but about one-third of the women work part-time. Women are generally lower-paid, and spend two hours more per day on household tasks than men (Mabille and Valasik 2004: 258). A distinctive feature of the French case is the 'gender-biased universalism of French political culture' (Reuter and Mazur 2003: 48), which takes gender complementarity as a given, but sets this in a framework of universal rights that does not permit the articulation of group interests. As 'rights' have often been understood as relating to citizenship and nothing else, feminist demands have been looked upon with suspicion until relatively recently.

A second factor characterizing the French case is the strict separation of the religious and secular spheres. When examined more closely, however, the system does include an important role for religious associations, which are sometimes more open to women's leadership. A further factor influencing the French results is the struggle over questions of authority within the Catholic Church, revealed amongst other places in ambiguous standpoints with respect to hierarchy and religious freedom – a point to be developed below.

The formal absence of church-related welfare activities in France means that it is hard to access data on the involvement of women and men in this kind of welfare provision at the local level. Nonetheless, a striking feature of the Evreux case is that the increasing lay involvement in church activities, due among other things to a lack of priests, permits more room for women's participation. This space is, however, constructed according to a logic that still keeps male and female activities apart. When women hold positions of responsibility within the church, according to our researcher, 'they have posts corresponding to typically "feminine" qualities: listening to people sympathetically, communicating, being open, helping the sick, etc.' (Valasik 2006: 175). In concrete terms this means that women have taken charge of pastoral work linked with health, communication and dealings with lay people, while men still retain the management of press relations, pastoral care for young people, training and accounts.

England   The British situation[3] has been characterized both as a liberal welfare regime, and as a male bread-winner model. The male bread-winner model has, paradoxically, been both strengthened and weakened in recent years. On the one hand dependence on female care-givers has increased due to cuts in welfare budgets, moving care that formerly took place in hospitals and institutions back into families. On the other, 'welfare to work' policies have meant an increase in female employment, with equality for women understood by the government to be a catalyst for economic growth. The British welfare mix comprises a state-controlled system, which leaves much of the actual provision in the hands of private and voluntary actors and the family (many women hold part-time jobs, and spend more than double the time that men do on household chores) (Middlemiss 2004: 186).

In Britain, a large number of key institutions depend on the contributions of lay men and women, who are not reimbursed for their work. This is very true of the parishes in the Church of England, and their related welfare activities, which are completely reliant on volunteers. No official figures are available, but the researcher notes a consensus among the interviewees that there are more women than men engaged in this type of work: 'I think women have always been greater in numbers, not only numerically in the congregation, but also in the participation

---

[3]   See Chapter 2, note 9. Once again, the references here are to the British state, though the case study in itself concerns England and the role of the Church of England in welfare activities.

in the life of the church' (Middlemiss 2006: 24). There is also a clear gender divide in the types of work that male and female volunteers do within the context of church welfare activity, as observed in the case study: men tend to take on practical tasks connected to care of the buildings or churchyards, providing a taxi service to and from lunch clubs and other events, and fund raising, whereas women are more involved in work with children, and visiting elderly and bereaved people: 'We have a good stalwart group of men, but they are in the minority still and many of the men act as taxi drivers for the women ... the men are often in the background actually' (Middlemiss 2006: 24). Quite apart from this, some interviewees comment that women are more proactive in *seeking* help both in general and from the church.

Sweden, Norway and Finland   The Nordic cases will be presented together, as they are all characterized by a universalist model of welfare provision, with high state involvement and a high proportion of women in salaried work. This involvement is facilitated by active gender-equality policies, including well-organized public child care and good opportunities for parental leave. Finland and Norway share many of these traits with Sweden, but family policies in the former have not been as encouraging towards women's employment. The Norwegian system, for example, has been criticized for the gender-segregating effects of its 'cash-for-care' system, encouraging parents to stay at home with their small children after the first period of parental leave. In practice the system is primarily used by women, who then postpone their return to the labour market. All that said, and while recognizing the relative advancements of gender equality in the Nordic countries, gendered patterns similar to those in other countries continue to divide the welfare sector. This can be seen, for example, in the very segregated labour markets, with social and educational services highly dominated by women. It should also be noted that the Nordic countries share the dominance of Lutheran folk churches which, as already noted, still gather most of the population.

Let us, then, turn to the specificities of the different Nordic cases. Sweden was characterized by Jane Lewis (1992) as a weak male bread-winner model, and is, according to other researchers, the country that has most clearly broken with this approach, paving the way for a universal bread-winner model in the 1970s by introducing paternal leave and individual taxation. That this break with the male bread-winner model has taken place with the help of a huge expansion in public sector services is clearly shown in Gävle, where 90 per cent of the employees in health and social care are women, of whom about one-third work part time. Swedish women still spend considerably more time each week on household chores than men, and have therefore fewer hours to spend on paid work.

The Swedish church is relatively rich and can afford a high number of employees. The parishes in Gävle employ several hundred people, about 75 per cent of whom are women. The highest proportion of women is to be found among those engaged in education and children's and youth work. No exact figures are available, but the number of volunteers in social care is modest, due to the high ratio of paid personnel and to the relatively marginal role of the church in the provision of welfare services. About 4 per cent of the population is involved in church-related voluntary work, according to national surveys on volunteering. The 'typical' volunteer in this sector is an older woman. The situation in Gävle is nicely illustrated by the fact that in one parish two groups of volunteers comprise 33 women, but no men. A few men are engaged in voluntary work, but without being involved in a group. Again, clear differences are observed concerning the tasks women and men undertake. Female volunteers are, for example, said to be enthusiastic about preparing an act of worship, but when it finally occurs, do not want to be seen 'on stage'. Men do not want to be seen participating in social aid, but this does not mean they do not want to help. They find less visible ways of doing it, as explained by a male interviewee: 'A man doesn't like to stand there and show that he is helping, but nevertheless he is prepared to pitch in' (Edgardh Beckman et al. 2006: 57). These stories seem to exemplify how women and men may feel awkward about being visible in each other's arenas: men do not want to be seen doing caring work while women do not want to be visible in a 'public' place.

Interesting in the Swedish case is the fact that several interviewees observe a predominance of women not only on the 'supply' side, but also among the beneficiaries of church-related welfare. Services for elderly women and lone mothers are specifically mentioned, but even in services explicitly meant for both men and women, the latter tend to be the ones to seek help, sometimes on behalf of the wider family. As explained by a male priest, even in the case of baptism, the relationship with the church tends to be a woman's matter: 'You call the family in making preparations for baptism and the man answers: "Yes, hold on a sec and you can talk to her ..." This is interesting. Matters like these belong to her' (Edgardh Beckman et al. 2006: 57).

The rise in the social contribution of the Finnish church since the beginning of the 1990s is clearly reflected in Lahti. As of 2003, the local church provides jobs for 351 employees, more than 70 per cent of whom are women. Included in these figures are 37 parish priests and 35 social workers (deacons). In addition, 2,300 volunteers are engaged in the work of the parishes, one third in social work (Yeung 2006: 157). Unfortunately no figures on gender are provided for the Lahti parishes as such, even if the observations of the researcher confirm the general image of a predominance of women among both volunteers and employed personnel in social work (Yeung 2006: 194–5). Figures for the Finnish church as a whole support this picture: about 70 per cent of its employees are women, and in social and children's work the share of women exceeds 90 per cent (Yeung 2004: 124).

Church social work in Norway is less frequent than in Finland, and in this respect is more similar to Sweden. Gender segregation seems, however, to be as evident in Drammen as it is in the other cases. The church representatives who were interviewed perceive the majority of volunteers in churches to be women; and, while only three out of 11 parish priests are women, four out of six deacons are female (Angell and Wyller 2006: 133–5). Several interviewees observed that 'traditional' forms of welfare activities appeal more to female than to male volunteers: for instance, groups for the bereaved, visiting services and traditional household-centred activities. It is, however, interesting to note the central role played by the Church City Mission in Drammen, not least its male leader who is very outspoken on social issues in the media. His role is rather similar to that of two male priests in the Swedish case, who resigned before the fieldwork was carried out, but who had both for many years had a very visible media-related role as spokespersons for the church and were often referred to by interviewees. These are all examples of a public 'prophetic' role related to Christian social work, seldom taken on by the churches as institutions, but apparently open to individuals. In our case studies, this kind of role is more frequently taken by men than by women.

The Unequal Influence of Women and Men in Welfare Activities

A second common feature in all of the case studies is the dominance of men among the decision-makers in both churches and church-related organizations. The combination of female predominance among the 'doers', and male dominance at the top, is surprisingly consistent from south to north in Europe, with a number of variations depending on particular church traditions.

An important aspect of this male dominance relates to the ordained ministry of bishops, priests and deacons, the shape of which differs significantly between the churches in question. While the Protestant cases include women in their ordained ministries, the Catholic and Greek Orthodox churches do not. The proportion of women among the priests varies in the Protestant churches, but has still not reached 40 per cent in any church. In modern Europe in general, it is perceived as a curiosity that a profession can be reserved only for one sex. Despite this, the decision to allow women into ordained ministry has been controversial in most churches, and attitudes concerning ordination of women to official church ministries have been hotly debated in most countries. Unsurprisingly, therefore, several of the case studies reveal a lingering suspicion, not to say discontent, among both the representatives of public authorities and of the population as a whole regarding how the churches have handled this situation. Even if the churches now ordain women there is still a feeling that one cannot rely on the church to champion women's rights.

Less debated, but particularly interesting in relation to this study, is the position of the diaconate. The topic concerns access to the ministry for both genders, and the place of the diaconate itself within church hierarchies. While the church traditions included in WREP all ordain bishops and priests, not all of them ordain deacons. Quite apart from this, the position of deacon has very different meanings across the traditions, as a result of the historic development in the Protestant as opposed to the Catholic and Orthodox churches. The three Nordic churches all have deacons: in Norway and Finland they have tasks relating to social issues in the parishes, but their roles are not seen as part of the ordained ministry in the same way as that of priests and bishops. Only the Swedish church fully includes deacons in the ordained ministry of the church, and has only done so since 2000. Despite the formal parity of bishops, priests and deacons within the threefold ministry in the Church of Sweden, in reality inequalities still persist.

The traditions in the German Protestant churches vary, but in the Evangelische Landeskirche in Württemberg, deacons are not ordained (Leis 2004: 221). In the Catholic and Anglican churches the diaconate is traditionally seen as a step on the way to priesthood. The role of the deacon is liturgical, but may also include social tasks. In the present situation in the Catholic Church, where priests are scarce, the role of deacon has become more important. A greater proportion of deacons now consider the role as a permanent rather than an interim position, which may be because deacons, in contrast to priests, are able to marry and have children. The Catholic diaconate is, however, still reserved for men. Orthodox deacons have a liturgical role and in recent years there has been intense debate concerning the possibility of opening this ministry up to women – a major argument in favour of this being that women served as deacons at earlier stages in the church's history – but so far no firm decisions have been taken in this direction (Molokotos-Liederman and Fokas 2004: 313).

All in all, the ordained ministries of the church traditions included in the project are still male-dominated. The diaconate is the part of the ministry which has historically been more open to women and oriented towards social issues. The ongoing debates concerning the role of deacons may be a reflection of the lower status granted by the churches themselves to this ministry relative to that of priests and bishops. This value-hierarchy is sometimes reflected in the attitudes of the interviewees towards different types of ministry. In England, for example, the priest is normally the only individual employed by the parish, and is thus seen as the one who symbolically represents the church. In the French case study, a number of lay people expressed scepticism towards the idea of people other than the priest representing the church. A religious sister working as a health worker says that the people she meets prefer priests to nuns, but also prefer nuns to laypersons – especially if the nuns are dressed in their habits: 'I can see it with the chaplain in the hospital, people always ask for a priest. When I say I am a nun, things are easier but it would be better if I had a uniform' (Valasik 2006: 175).

A second aspect of the dominance of men as decision-makers in churches and church-related organizations, which may in fact modify the general image of a vertical segregation with men at the top and women at the bottom, has to do with the diversity of possible ministries in the churches and the multiple forms that church-related social work takes. Several case studies show a general increase in the roles played by lay people and volunteers, and a more visible leadership role for women in organizations that complement the traditional parish.

Religious orders of various kinds comprise a special category in this respect – alongside both ordained ministries and lay organizations. These orders are most frequent in the Catholic and Orthodox churches, and are strictly divided by sex. Some religious orders play very active social roles, and a female religious order can, because of its particular position within the church, offer space for women to exercise a great deal of influence. It must, however, be observed that these orders are always integrated into a wider church order with a specific place in the church's hierarchy. Religious orders are therefore never completely free in relation to the church tradition to which they belong.

Concerning the role of lay people, the Greek researcher comments that most of the church's social contributions are organized outside the traditional parish structure. Even at parish level, however, women are increasingly involved in educational, administrative and charitable tasks, though their roles are not always official. In specific institutions, such as care homes for elderly people, women are found in leadership (Fokas 2006: 232). Women also provide welfare through dedicated women's organizations: one example is a soup kitchen (*sisitio*) in Thiva, run primarily by the Women's Association of Love, which provides food for the poor in the parish. Smaller soup kitchens, also operated by women, appear at the local level in Thiva and Livadeia (Fokas 2006: 229). In this connection, the researcher specifically notes that while more women are engaged as volunteers than as paid workers, there is no perceptible difference between the access to influence and decision-making power which volunteers and paid workers enjoy (Fokas 2006: 233). In short, the Greek Orthodox Church as an institutional body is clearly male-dominated, but the shape and nature of its social activities reflect an increasingly important role played by women (Molokotos-Liederman and Fokas 2004: 315).

The Italian situation is characterized to an even higher degree by a diversity of organizational forms, varying from traditional and hierarchical organizations to activist groups consciously trying to break with old patterns (both within their own associations and towards their beneficiaries). According to several interviewees, women generally find that the most favourable environment is in co-operatives, where they can have greater responsibility and where social care is more equally shared with men (Frisina 2006: 206).

The German report describes a new situation, in which the church is becoming much more dependent on the work of volunteers than before. This opens up more room for volunteers – and, accordingly, for women – in positions of power. All parish kindergartens in Reutlingen, for example, are supervised by a lay member of the church council and not by a priest. An interviewee says: 'People think less hierarchical in the church than before. The ministers are much more open and human ... and they are thankful for ideas and impulses. They say: "If you think this is a good thing to do and if you are willing to engage in it you have my support"' (Leis-Peters 2006: 95).

The same phenomenon is seen in the quite different French case, where a scarcity of priests has resulted in an increasing role for lay people and deacons. The physical impossibility for a priest to be permanently present in his parish (and even more so in the local community) has led the diocese to develop the concept of *co-responsibility* of the priest and the lay person in charge. This means that the lay person takes charge of certain activities, while formally remaining under the priest's authority (Mabille and Valasik 2004: 141). Women also play an important role in the pastoral councils of the parishes. The impression of the researcher concerning the role of women in the church is that, in practice, 'the absence of priests leaves them with almost total freedom of action' (Mabille and Valasik 2004: 266). The French case also illustrates the importance of religious orders and religious associations as providers of welfare services. In the diocese of Evreux alone there are six different religious orders, five contemplative monasteries and 15 apostolic congregations existing alongside the parish structure.

Interestingly, the situation in the Nordic countries parallels central and southern Europe in many respects. While women represent only 12 per cent of parish priests in Norway, they are in a majority among the leaders of parish councils. In Sweden, too, electoral bodies have provided a space for women within the church to exert leadership and power. Women are also much more frequently found in lay structures such as the sewing circle, a major movement through much of the twentieth century which has played an important role both for the women concerned and through the collection of money for local and international projects.

How Gender Inequality is Explained and Legitimized

The third common theme that emerges from our data has to do with how the gender-segregated practice of church social work is explained and legitimized by interviewees. To help us analyse the responses in this area, we will turn to the American feminist philosopher Nancy Fraser, who in the article 'After the Family Wage' (1997) discusses a possible solution to the dilemma of how to establish a post-industrial welfare state that is able to combine welfare for all citizens with gender equity. Fraser argues against the polarized dichotomy between 'equality' and 'difference' that characterizes much feminist debate. 'Equality', in her use, stands for the position that women should be treated exactly like men, while 'difference' implies treating women differently insofar as they differ from men. Fraser observes that feminist debates have often ended in a stalemate between these two positions, and suggests that the aimed-for gender equity needs instead to be treated as a complex notion of distinct normative principles that will include elements from *both* the 'equality' and the 'difference' poles of the debate. She demonstrates the consequences of her theoretical approach by presenting feminist visions of post-industrial welfare as alternatives to the existing welfare regimes described by Esping-Andersen and others. The first is the 'universal bread-winner' model, building on the equality principle with paid employment being the norm for both women and men, while the second is the 'caregiver-parity' model, building on the principle of difference, with informal care work being provided by women and financial resources being provided by men. Fraser stresses that both visions are utopian, far from current realities in the United States. But even in their visionary form, she argues, both models fail to achieve real equity. Neither manages to overcome all forms of the marginalization of women and women's work, and both fail to demand any change on the part of men.

We will return in due course to Fraser's own vision of the future welfare state, but at this stage it is helpful to look further at the dichotomy she tries to overcome and see to what extent its traits can be recognized in our material. With Fraser, we state that gender equity can – at least theoretically – be achieved in two ways:

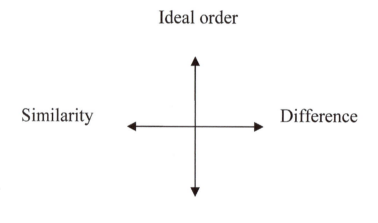

Figure 3.1   The existing and the ideal regarding gender roles in church-related social work

either by stressing the *difference* between women and men, who are understood as complementary but of equal value, or by stressing the *similarity* of women and men, with their equal value being rooted in their common humanity. The two extremes of difference and similarity can be illustrated as poles on an axis. (*Similarity* will here be used instead of Fraser's word *equality*, in order to avoid confusion concerning the double meaning of the latter word.) Our main question to the material, then, is how and to what extent our interviewees argue for difference or similarity in their descriptions of, and visions for, the relationship between women and men in church-related social work.

A second question follows from this and concerns the ways in which the respondents relate their descriptions of the present situation to their ideals of how things ought to be. In order to discuss this, we will, in addition to the axis ranging from *similarity* to *difference*, introduce a second axis, reaching from the *existing order* to the *ideal order* (see Figure 3.1).

Looking at the similarity–difference axis first, it is clear that the material is mostly imbued with the second attitude, understanding male and female as radically different. This understanding very often seems unreflective, and is more like an observation of the surrounding reality – an approach nicely exemplified by a Norwegian deacon:

> [The tasks for the volunteers] are most suitable for women, I think. There is much coffee making, baking, kitchen service, and visiting service. Only women are involved in it [in our parish]. Men are not interested, and women may be

more social. Diaconal activities are care work; typically women things. (Angell and Wyller 2006: 122)

Attitudes concerning gender are, however, clearly embedded in a cultural context, which differs significantly between the cases. The English researcher, for example, observes that in Britain the discussion about gender equality is normally included within a more general discourse about equalities referring also to race and class, and cannot be discussed separately from these. Still, a paradox exists, in that most respondents insist that 'gender equality' should not be understood to mean 'sameness'. Space needs to be given for natural difference, in a way that is less often presupposed with regard to class or race. Men and women 'offer something different just by their nature' (Middlemiss 2006: 52). This attitude is even more explicit among the French interviewees, where even the possibility of equality with regard to gender is sometimes questioned:

> It is said that there is equality between men and women, but what equality is there? I think equality for salaries and for some other things is a good thing but men and women are not equal, they are complementary by essence, by nature itself. It's a bit of a pity; a woman does not have the same equality, as she is lucky because she can carry a child while a man cannot. (Valasik 2006: 152)

This kind of remark is much less likely to be made in Sweden, where public policies regarding gender equality are explicitly based on ideals of treating women and men the same, presupposing similarity. Indeed the Swedish study stands out in relation to the others in one notable respect: many of the church interviewees regard the predominance of women in church-related activities as a 'problem'. Interviewees tend to see their own workplaces as gender-equal, but stress that there is a more general problem of gender imbalance. Men do not apply for jobs involving care in the church very often: a female interviewee says, '[W]e are happy when men take up positions. We have been short of men. And that is not good. Much better with a balance' (Edgardh Beckman et al. 2006: 59). However, it is not always clear whether the balance referred to is desired in order to achieve a just gender representation – as Swedish policies require – or because of presupposed differences between men and women. The latter attitude is quite clearly expressed in arguments which say that the sexes 'complement each other' and that men are needed 'for another point of view'. In this respect, the Swedish responses imply a difference between women and men very similar to most other cases. Sometimes the felt need for 'balance' is even given divine legitimacy: 'If you imagine … that the human being reflects the divine, then both men and women are needed' (Edgardh and Pettersson 2010: 53).

This response leads us to the other axis, which shows how reactions vary from descriptions of gender-segregated practice in the existing order, to aspirations to be realized in an ideal order. Gender imbalances seem to crave explanation: for this reason many quotations in the case studies start with a descriptive statement, which almost invisibly turns into an explanatory statement, which in turn slips into a normative statement: that things are just as they ought to be. An illustration of this process can be found in the English study, when it is said that the church can be seen as an extension of the domestic area of the home, which is perceived as a female sphere. This, in turn, is connected to the fact that more women than men remain within the geographical area of the parish, as they spend more time at home (Middlemiss 2006: 24). Very often, moreover, explanations of this kind are complemented by comments to the effect that the gendering of the social situation is 'natural'. Understanding women and men as *by nature* radically different seems to help interviewees explain the gender order they see around them. In other words, the explanation legitimates perceived inequalities, turning them into positive differences.

A quotation from a female interviewee in the Greek case study illustrates this point perfectly. She starts by observing that 'usually women are the ones who help. Men do different things.' This is a descriptive statement about the situation in the home for elderly people where she works, but then she continues:

> Someone [a man] came to help in the garden. This too is significant work, and also an expression of love. But a man will not come to wash the elderly. The woman will: she has washed her mother, her grandmother, her children. The woman is more familiar with this type of work. And I think this is the *diakonia* of the woman in the Church. (Fokas 2006: 248)

Here the observation that men do different things from women turns into a statement that this does not mean any difference in value. Women have their role and men their role due to deep-seated traditions. The interviewee then adds the religious statement that this is *diakonia*, implying that washing or cleaning is women's way of serving God – a statement that she later develops into a somewhat surprising suggestion seeming to imply that men tend to serve God best by socializing over a cup of coffee:

> Imagine a man going to wash an older woman. It won't happen. But it's more natural for them to come and work in the garden, to play backgammon with the elderly. This too is *diakonia*. To drink his coffee here instead of at a café. This is an expression of love. (Fokas 2006: 249)

The Greek case study is especially useful for illustrating the tendency to jump from description to value statement, as all categories of interviewees without hesitation uttered generalized statements about the 'natural roles' of women and men, about 'women's nature' as caring beings who are 'better-suited' to welfare activity, or about men as 'ill-suited' to welfare activity and simply less capable of handling such work. Examples of the same tendency (to slide from descriptive to explanatory and then on to normative statements) can be found, however, in most of our case studies. For instance, a very similar type of argument emerges from the

Italian case, this time in the words of a male participant in a focus group, already quoted in the introduction to the chapter:

> Welfare is supported by women ... Also because they are more predisposed to care giving ... Perhaps because of motherhood, perhaps because of culture ... We are talking thousands of years here! You cannot change everything that easily! I think it is very difficult that certain kinds of work will be carried out by men ... In the end, speaking for myself I would not leave my grandmother in the hands of a man ... I find the idea of a male caregiver a bit funny! (Frisina 2006: 200)

This interviewee does not use religious rhetoric as did the previous one, but the way of arguing from the level of description to the level of norms and values is very similar.

Not every statement about the 'natural' differences between women and men, however, is used to legitimate the present order of things. As Nancy Fraser argues, perceived difference may also be used in favour of a more equal order of things. It is precisely *because* women are perceived as being different that they may have something additional to contribute. In the English case, for example, the supposed difference between women and men is used by one interviewee as an argument in favour of employing both women and men: 'I would want to say ideally to have a man and woman in a parish would be perfect because they both offer something different just by their nature' (Middlemiss 2006: 52). In a similar vein, a French interviewee argues for more influence on the part of women. Unlike men, runs the argument, women would not give dubious candidates admission to the seminary:

> I'm sure that a woman would have had more sensitivity and could have said: 'No, this isn't right'. And we would avoid making mistakes. I don't know if I have the right impression about women but I think they are more sensitive, intuitive, there's complementarity. (Valasik 2006: 152)

A final reflection on the attitudes towards the gendered social practice of the churches concerns the fact that, in some cases, interviewees appear reluctant to reflect upon gender issues at all. The Finnish, Norwegian and German researchers all report that gender questions were difficult to raise, and were received as either too sensitive or simply uninteresting. The Norwegian researcher experienced a general pride on the part of the interviewees in relation to Norwegian achievements in gender equality, both within the church and in society as a whole. Norwegian respondents also expressed optimism that gender roles are changing and that today more men participate in activities that previously were coded as 'female'. Norway, however, is the only place where such optimism was registered. In most other countries, a pessimistic attitude dominates. In the German case, for example, hope for change is linked with the market: when market forces need gender roles to change, they will change, but not before (Leis-Peters 2006: 117).

The Finnish case is particularly interesting in that the researcher detected a clear tension between – on the one hand – an attitude from the interviewees that gender issues had been dealt with and were no longer particularly relevant, and – on the other – a reality where gender still seemed to be a structuring principle in church social work. The researcher explains this as follows: while national-level documents in Finland present the ideal picture of gender equality, the local reality might look otherwise, which may be difficult for people who are active on this level to admit (Yeung 2006: 193). The fact that a substantial majority of welfare workers and volunteers are women, for example, is not commented on by the interviewees as a problem or a challenge. Nor are a range of different issues relating to the well-being of women and men considered in gender terms. Rather, the same mechanism (i.e. explaining the gendered reality as 'natural') seems to be at work among the Finnish interviewees: a family counsellor observes that only one third of the clients are men and explains this as a natural outcome of the fact that women express themselves better verbally. He suggests, for instance, that 'marriage means a human relationship', and that this matters more to women than to men (Yeung 2006: 194). Like many of the examples given above, this demonstrates how the processes of institutionalization and legitimation work – in the sense that they make gendered phenomena seem natural. They are, therefore, taken for granted, as 'the way things are', in the church as well as in society at large.

Contested Standpoints Regarding Family, Gender and Sexuality

While the processes discussed above serve to stabilize established gender orders in church-related social work, the fourth common feature does the opposite; it involves *de*stabilizing elements and reflects the fact that issues of gender, family and sexuality are contested areas in the churches today. This reality is also visible at local level and is apparent in the case studies, bearing in mind that the examples may be somewhat random due to the particularities of the selected towns. Our starting point for the discussion is, however, very clear and echoes the connections set out in the introduction to this chapter: it assumes that issues of gender, family and sexuality are inextricably linked to the role of the churches in welfare.

This feature of the case studies also relates to the issues of power and influence already considered, but the focus for the following discussion will be different: it will ask how structures and positions come into conflict. The timing is important. It is clear, for example, that the major church traditions in Europe have lost their former authority in society. The following conflicts should therefore be seen in the context of the changing relationships between church and state. They should also be related to broader theological currents, in so far as the theological traditions, at least on a formal level, have led to widely differing attitudes toward the issues at stake.

For example, the Greek Orthodox Church retains a strong position in Greek society and 'officially' has taken a clear position against Western feminism, which is seen as an attempt to overturn the 'natural' order of things. Men and women are regarded as equal and mutually interdependent, but not as identical, since they are supposed to have distinct and complementary roles in life (Molokotos-Liederman and Fokas 2004: 313). Since the 1980s, however, women have gathered for conferences concerned with the situation of women in the church and with the possibility of ordaining women as deacons or even priests (Liveris 2005). The Catholic Church has repeatedly stated that women and men have different God-given roles, as in a letter from the Congregation for the Doctrine of the Faith (2004) entitled 'On the Collaboration of Men and Women in the Church and in the World'. The issue of women's ordination is contested, but the official position opposes even the discussion of this question. The Protestant churches, conversely, have been less willing to make wide-ranging claims concerning gender, in line with a reluctance to make official theological statements overall (see Chapter 4). They have also been more open to changes in practice with regard to gender roles – for instance, by permitting the ordination of women. The Nordic churches have also taken an explicitly positive stance toward national policies promoting gender equality.

From what has been said so far we might conclude that there are significant differences between the church traditions involved in the project. That is true. The major ruptures, however, seem to run through the churches, rather than between them, or between church and society. The controversial issues – from contraception to same-sex unions – cause internal conflicts within most churches. In several cases, moreover, there are major differences regarding gender and family issues between the standpoints taken 'officially' and those assumed both by ordained representatives at the local level and by active lay people. As this varies between the cases, we will discuss each of them in turn in order to get a better picture of what issues have appeared as controversial in which places.

The case study in Thiva and Livadeia in Greece shows two clear and partially contradictory tendencies. The first is a deep respect for the church as a social actor, including its ability to modernize and adapt to changes in need (Fokas 2006: 240). The second is considerable evidence of criticism and anxiety about the situation in the church. These feelings were prompted by the extraordinarily turbulent situation at the time of the field work, when a scandal was revealed involving the senior leadership of the church in financial irregularities, not to mention sex, drugs and human trafficking. For these reasons, and despite the relatively strong position of the Church in Greek society, the Greek case study showed distinct signs of the traditional structures of the church being shaken by new challenges.

In contrast, the two Catholic cases reveal that the most obvious examples of conflict involve issues of gender and family. In Italy in general, gender issues are not high on the public agenda, even if the debate is advancing with regard to welfare issues. According to the Italian researcher, 'It is hardly possible to relegate gender issues to the shadows much longer, for they are … closely bound to the contradictions of the Italian welfare state' (Frisina 2004: 282). Precisely this comes through in the responses from interviewees, who often become quite engaged when the role of the church in welfare is discussed. The researcher also underlines that Catholicism in Italy is now very heterogeneous, a fact displayed admirably in the diverse types of church-related agents active in Vicenza. Historically the Catholic Church has played a conservative role in politics, defending the traditional family model. One example debated during the field work was the proposal to introduce a law recognizing civil unions, after the model of the French civil pact. The Italian Council of Bishops (CEI) publicly intervened in this debate, stating that a juridical recognition of *de facto* couples would be 'morally unacceptable' (Frisina 2010: 151). At the same time, however, movements for democracy and change in the church are evolving. There is, for example, an Italian section of the international movement We Are Church, which argues cogently in favour of a church 'from below'.[4]

In the course of the fieldwork, church interviewees were found to represent many dissident voices within the Catholic Church – they were concerned not only with issues of democracy and feminist demands, but also with the social teaching of the church (subsidiarity, for example). Interestingly Catholic sisters sometimes adopt more radical positions than other groups. This may have to do with their vocation, expressed in their vows, or their 'in-between' position as well-educated women but without access to positions as priests or deacons. It is not surprising, therefore, that the most outspoken criticism heard in the Italian case was articulated by an Ursuline nun, who has created a centre for gender studies within her religious institution and has published a series of books in order to initiate a debate on the role of women within the church. This very enterprising individual has also created a working group of women who operate within lay-led private social organizations. The group reflects on the social situation from a feminist perspective and organizes cultural events for citizens (Frisina 2010: 163).

In the course of their interviews, representatives of these lay-led organizations, social workers and nuns were noticeably critical of the possibly negative consequences of placing practical social work under the authority of the church, particularly if this means that the church simply tries to fill the gaps in the already inadequate Italian welfare system and thus to perpetuate a system unfair toward women. Observing a tendency to push responsibility back onto women by arguing for the importance of families, one interviewee comments:

> Nowadays the government is telling families that they are very important and there is a vast acknowledgment of the educational task of parents … But it is a trap, because by doing this public authorities are dumping problems on families, that is to say on the women in the families. (Frisina 2006: 206)

This criticism is particularly strong in the case of migrant caregivers. Here some Italian interviewees express a sense of social responsibility and solidarity stretching

---

4   See http://www.we-are-church.org for more details.

beyond national borders: '[T]his other woman also has a family ... it is a chain reaction ... can we break it?' (Frisina 2006: 212).

Similar criticism is detected in the French case study. The researcher observes that historically the church in France has played an ambiguous role in relation to the place of women in society. After the Revolution, the church encouraged women's involvement in social action, in the hope that this would reinforce the power of Catholicism. The second half of the nineteenth century marked the apotheosis of this relationship, with the revival of the Marian cult including pilgrimages and places of devotion. Women involved in charitable work and education were seen as pursuing their maternal vocation to nourish and nurture. From the middle of the twentieth century, however, this situation changed, as the church lost its hold and the role of women in society became more and more estranged from Catholic ideals (Mabille and Valasik 2004: 263). Nonetheless, through its youth movements the church could still offer young women new modes of action and reflection, and in the philanthropic sector they still enjoyed relative freedom (Mabille and Valasik 2004: 264).

The current situation is contradictory; gender issues are debated to some extent and today they mainly concern issues of sexuality. The Social Commission of the French Bishops firmly supported the law on male/female parity in political elections (Mabille and Valasik 2004: 265), and French bishops have implicitly broken free from the 1968 papal encyclical *Humanae Vitae* by making it clear to couples that the decision concerning contraception is theirs to make. At the same time the bishops encourage women to raise their voices concerning the need for a reduction of working hours, arguing that society today reduces social identity to professional identity to an exaggerated extent (Mabille and Valasik 2004: 264). Among more dissident voices are lay movements like Femmes et Hommes en Eglise (Women and Men in Church), which works explicitly for gender equality in the church, or the association Plein Jour (Full Daylight) which brings together women who share their lives with priests. A sign of the public support for such dissident voices was seen in a poll published in June 2000 in the weekly magazine *La Vie*, showing that 90 per cent of French church-going Catholics are in favour of a third Vatican Council dealing particularly with the place of women in Catholicism, the place of the laity (women and men), the ordination of married men, and the dialogue between religions (Mabille and Valasik 2004: 266).

At the local level Evreux has its own examples of ongoing power struggles. One is Carrefour Rural (Rural Crossroads). Given the particular difficulties faced by rural areas in recent decades, a Catholic movement known as the Rural Mission was created. It permitted Catholics to come together to discuss their thoughts and propose solutions. The Carrefour Rural emerged out of this movement. Amongst other things, Carrefour Rural addresses questions involving the life of the church that are not taken into consideration by the diocese. For example, people who have had a religious wedding and are then divorced cannot re-marry in the Catholic Church; Carrefour Rural offers these people an alternative ritual so that they may 'still feel that God loves them'. Couples are invited a number of times in order to organize a celebration, in which each of them will take an active part – for example, by reading a text aloud. This event takes place not in a church building, but in an alternative venue with a priest present. All the priests in the diocese are familiar with this initiative and provide information to anyone requesting it. In fact, even some priests who oppose the celebration will refer people to Carrefour Rural (Valasik 2006: 166).

A second example from Evreux is found in the case of the former bishop, Mgr Gaillot, who attracted national attention when he was removed by the Pope in 1995 because of disagreements with the hierarchy. His removal was widely criticized in France by Catholics and others. During his last mass on 22 January 1995, 20,000 supporters protesting against his removal gathered in Evreux (Valasik 2006: 136). The aftermath of this conflict is still evident in comments made by our respondents. For instance, one man in a focus group became very agitated when reflecting on the case, saying, 'The Roman Catholic Church is against everything: condoms, sexual relationships … It's not concerned by the fact that AIDS is rampant in Africa! And when there's a good one, he gets fired!' (Valasik 2006: 153).

A strong scepticism about the church hierarchy in general is voiced in the interviews with representatives of the population. Despite admitting that they know little about church politics, people are still highly cynical about the church's official 'face': 'Me, I had an abortion so when I see a priest on TV I change the channel immediately. I won't even listen. They have no right to talk about my way of life' (Valasik 2006: 154). However, there is more trust demonstrated toward Catholic welfare associations and the individuals involved in them: 'The congregation is not the same thing as the church, you see members helping homeless people. Those are the real Catholics' (Valasik 2006: 154). Respondents from within the church itself, however, recognize that the church's voice is seldom heeded any more:

> This comes from internal causes: the decrease in the number of priests, a quite strong separation from a society that has developed its own private views on sexuality, etc. and which does not accept that an organization like the church should have a word to say on people's private lives. There's a gap that has been there for about forty years. (Valasik 2006: 149)

These conflicting positions stem from internal issues as well, since the attitudes of people used to a hierarchical organization tend to change slowly. French Catholicism has always been based on a strongly hierarchical model, in which the words of a priest are given more weight than those of lay people. While lay people are given far more responsibility in parishes today, not all are enthusiastic about this. Currently the clergy expect laypersons to take on more responsibilities and propose innovations in the parishes, while the laity tend to await instructions from priests, but question these directives when they are considered too direct

(Valasik 2006: 169). Hierarchies live on in people's memories even when efforts are made both formally and in practice to leave them behind.

The strengthening position of lay people has already been discussed in relation to the German Protestant case. On the whole things seem to go more smoothly here – but the interviewees were clearly divided with regard to the changing nature of the family and gender. While many of them want the church to support women in combining family and work, others express a longing for the 'traditional' family with its associated role models which are perceived as related to Christian values. Such values are once again closely guarded – as much by ordinary church people as from above.

That said, ongoing changes within the Protestant churches in Germany are clearly visible, both in the increasing role of the laity and in the simultaneous increase in the number of female clergy following the 1970 decision to ordain women as priests. Even if these women do not yet hold positions of authority to the same extent as men, the shift is obvious. The clearest example of a conflict concerning gender in the German case concerns, however, the different perceptions of the role of the church held, on the one hand by those who are most involved (interviewed as representatives of the church), and on the other by representatives of public authorities and the population. While the former quite clearly believe that the church has done away with its previous discrimination against women, especially in comparison with the Catholic Church, the latter more frequently hold the Protestant churches responsible for the persistence of traditional roles in German society. One reason could be that these interviewees do not always distinguish between the different church traditions (Protestant and Catholic); but they could also find evidence that the Protestant churches do not promote women's emancipation as actively as they would like. One example cited at the time of the fieldwork concerned church-run kindergartens, which maintained the traditional model of care for only part of the day, instead of introducing an innovative whole-day model which would allow women to work longer hours (Leis-Peters 2006: 117).

The English case is rather different. Here conflicting views are not so much linked with the church's authority, but with the diversity of theological positions represented by the ten parishes in Darlington. On the national level the church has said very little about gender. However, conflicts regarding attitudes towards homosexuality became increasingly ardent at the time of the fieldwork – not only did these involve other parts of the Anglican Communion, they also challenged the notion of the Church of England as a theological 'middle way'. Locally the issue was raised by the presence of a priest in one of the parishes, who was outspoken in favour of the acceptance of homosexuals by the church. At the other end of the spectrum, a second parish stood out because its priest belonged to Forward in Faith, a movement which rejects the ordination of women to priesthood. This parish is ruled by a Provincial Episcopal Visitor (the proverbial 'flying bishop'), part of the Church of England's strategy for dealing with the conflicts between those for and those against the ordination of women.[5]

These two parish priests represent very different theological positions and traditions – but so do all the other parish priests who took part in the WREP enquiry. In fact, the researcher found it quite easy to place the different parishes, represented through their clergy, on a 'map' indicating different types of churchmanship and associated theologies. Allowing this diversity to be expressed territorially, as in Darlington, may be one way of dealing with the conflicts present in most of the cases in our study. However, this 'solution' does not prevent the legitimacy of the church's authority being questioned in relation to matters of gender, family and sexuality. Specifically, the church representatives who were interviewed feel that the church has credibility problems, because of well-known scandals and the fact that it is increasingly seen as out of touch with society on issues of human sexuality and the role of women in the church. Interviewees representing the public authorities think that the church ought in principle to have input into public debates on gender equality, but a number of them feel that the church needs first to address internal issues and to reform its own hierarchical structures.

Once again the three Scandinavian cases represent a quite different situation regarding gender, family and sexuality. All three Nordic churches have officially acknowledged that they support policies of equality of women and men, and have pledged to work for a more gender-equal situation within the church. All three, moreover, ordain women, although the share of women priests is much higher in Sweden than in Norway and Finland. The Church of Sweden has also taken the most radical position with relation to family issues and sexuality – for example, adopting an official liturgy for same-sex couples. Nonetheless, the attitude toward homosexual church members is a hot issue in all three countries. In the Swedish case this became apparent when two priests in the Gävle parishes declared in a local newspaper that they were in favour of same-sex weddings taking place in church.

The Nordic case studies also demonstrate how majority churches have, step by step, integrated changing attitudes to gender and family into their theological self-understanding. This is acknowledged by many interviewees representing the populations in Gävle, Drammen and Lahti. Participants in a focus group in Drammen, for example, say that while the position of the church in society is now weaker, it has become more liberal in its orientation, less judgemental, and more tolerant, which they see as positive (Angell and Wyller 2006: 127). Similarly, an elected representative of the church in Gävle comments in positive terms that the role of the church in public debate has changed in recent decades: while the church previously attracted publicity because it took a negative stance against abortions,

---

[5]   Parishes who are strongly opposed to women's ordination may ask to be put under the authority of one of the 'flying bishops' instead of the local diocesan bishop, who is no longer considered appropriate in that he has ordained women to the priesthood.

today it publicly advocates gender equality and gender-neutral marriages (Edgardh Beckman et al. 2006: 78).

Other voices are more critical. These do not, as in Italy or France, represent organized groups of active Christians, but rather a more secular public – groups of people who continue to hold the folk-churches in high regard. Their expectations, however, are turned at times into deep disappointment, and often because of conflicts relating to gender. For example, several Swedish interviewees comment spontaneously on the internal resistance to women's ordination as being a problematic issue for the church. One says pessimistically, 'It is something which is deeply rooted, it is difficult to change, just as in the military' (Edgardh Beckman et al. 2006: 51). Rather more positive is the voice of a Finnish interviewee who expresses high expectations about the power of women to effect changes in the church, through their deeper involvement in social issues:

> Men could go on arguing about power, they could keep the theology. Women could take over the diaconate and social work entirely. We could even have a separate national-level bishop for the diaconate! The voice of the whole of Finland! I bet the voice and teachings of Jesus would be more visible in this way, through the diaconate. (Yeung 2006: 194)

Less optimistic, however, are the representatives of the local population (and, to some extent, the public authorities) who maintain that the public discussion on women priests and the rights of homosexuals erode credibility and trust in the church as a promoter of gender equality. The debate on women priests continues in Lahti, as in other Finnish parishes, and is perceived negatively by the interviewees. A young man says, 'All these discussions on women priests and gays and stuff, it really is quite depressing to listen – it is like gosh, we have already moved on from the days when grandpa bought his first watch – don't they get it?' (Yeung 2006: 194).

Critical Potentials of a Gendered Perspective

The previous section has summarized the results from the case studies gathered under four headings, drawing together the similarities across national and denominational boundaries, but also exploring the knowledge to be derived from the variations between the cases. We observed that social care is a highly gendered area in the churches, with strictly divided roles for women and men; women are primarily located in relational caring work and men in more technical and organizational roles, as well as in the higher levels of decision-making. We found social care to be paradoxically regarded: highly valued on the one hand (in terms of theology and rhetoric), but less so on the other hand (in terms of money and access to influence). Furthermore, we found the gendered structure of church-related social work to be understood as 'natural' and obvious, sometimes even willed by God, and very seldom questioned. Somewhat contrary tendencies were found in a range of internal church conflicts related to social changes with regard to family, gender and sexuality.

It is now time to draw the threads of the chapter together, by returning to the basic question asked by WREP: that is the present and possible future roles of the majority churches in the organization of welfare in Europe. In gender terms, the question could be narrowed to the churches' potential role in relation to a damaging *deficit* in care. This deficit is linked in turn to a construction of caring as a solely female task, devalued in terms of money, power and status.

There are – as described in all three of the thematic chapters in this book – a range of reasons in favour of giving churches an increasing role as agents of welfare, the most significant of which will be recalled here:

- The churches have a long tradition of defending values of solidarity and care, but these are under threat in the market-oriented climate of twenty-first-century Europe. Caring for the poor and the sick has a strong theological basis both in the Bible and in tradition. Starting from this grounding the churches have the potential to act as counter-cultural forces, raising prophetic voices as well as providing services.

- The churches have impressive institutions at their disposal, with human, financial and logistic resources available for the provision of services to those excluded from other benefits. The financial position of the churches varies, but in many parts of Europe it remains a relatively wealthy institution.

- The share of the population belonging to the majority churches involved in WREP varies from about 50 per cent in England up to 95 per cent in Greece, but across the board there are still no other institutions, apart from the state itself, that can compete with the churches in terms of popular, if not always active, support.

- The expectation that the churches should act in favour of weak groups is generally high among the European populations. Surveys in the Nordic countries, for instance, show that 90 per cent of adults consider it important that 'the church invests resources in helping the elderly and the sick' (Bäckström et al. 2004: 98). As argued by a representative of the local authorities in the Finnish case, the voice of the church is welcome in a 'society controlled by the successful, a society of the apostles of efficiency and of productivity – and it is this side of the church that Jesus would choose if He lived today' (Yeung 2006: 169). In a similar vein our researcher in Germany reports that welfare activities and diaconal work are perceived as relevant reasons to remain a church member, even among people who are not religiously active (Leis-Peters 2006: 83).

The arguments in favour of a more active role in welfare for the majority churches of Europe are therefore strong.

In an increasingly secular Europe, there are additional reasons for the churches to embrace requests for increased social involvement. Such involvement, for instance, may strengthen their popular support, which to varying degrees is threatened in late-modern society. That said, there are also risks in extending the churches' role in this field. This is especially the case in light of the close relationship between ongoing changes in gender roles and the crisis in the welfare state. For example:

- Several of the major church traditions take conservative stances in relation to gender, sexuality and family. An increased role for the churches may therefore counteract actions taken in society as a whole to increase gender equality – actions which are, in turn, closely related to improvements in welfare for families in Europe. We must also remember that gender equality is a value formally adhered to in European directives (however much it is yet to be realized in practice). This means that the credibility of the churches as actors in the social field cannot be isolated from their positions with regard to these issues.

- The resources available to the churches – both financially and with regard to the voluntary contributions of women – are clearly finite, due to a combination of decreasing membership and increasing demands on women in the labour market. The WREP data tell us that women's voluntary labour is a valuable resource for churches and society; however, a continued reliance on female voluntary and low-paid work renders the churches dependent on models of gender and family that are increasingly out of date. It is risky, therefore, to rely on them as more than a temporary solution.

- There is a potential conflict between the increasing demands on the churches as welfare providers and the prophetic role of the churches. This is especially important from a gender perspective. To the extent that the contributions of women seem not to give them full access to decision-making and public roles, the prophetic role of the churches will necessarily be limited. But the stakes are higher than this: the churches may contribute to their own downfall by devaluing the work of women. A representative of the church in Gävle expresses this very explicitly: 'Some say that now that there are more female priests, it will turn … from a so to speak respected job, to a lower paid caring profession with the arrival of all these women on the scene' (Edgardh Beckman et al. 2006: 60). This statement both constructs the church as a passive object of the 'invasion' of women priests and – at the same time – devalues femininity and caring. The church, however, is faced with a choice: to contribute to this devaluing of women, or to work conscientiously against it.

A Gendered Typology

In short, the gendered aspects of the role of European majority churches are contradictory and difficult to interpret in a clear-cut manner. The churches are still patriarchal in many respects; but at the same time they are full of women who voluntarily take on a range of serving functions and find meaning in so doing. The churches take a conservative position on many issues; but they can be surprisingly radical in other ways. What, then, are we to make of these contradictions? What do they really say? To facilitate the discussion, a typology will be used, illustrating two types of church which seem to emerge from the material. As ideal types, they do not exemplify any specific church or case study, but are constructions built on particular traits found in the empirical material. The aim of the typology is to suggest an interpretation of the results – one of several possible – that may contribute to a deepened understanding of the role of the majority churches in the future organization of welfare in Europe.

The first church type we will call the 'church with a male face', as it is primarily represented by men and associated with male leadership. This type fits well with the stereotypes that have been described and criticized by feminist theologians in recent decades – stereotypes that are frequently found in media and secular rhetoric. It has a male-dominated leadership, with the authority to interpret and represent the tradition. It is hierarchically structured and manifested in strong church institutions, locally represented by the parishes. Women and lay people in general have a subordinate role, the content of which has been wittily summarized as 'pay, pray and obey'. This subordinate role is legitimated by theologies ascribing a mainly caring role for women, but refusing space for the ordination of women to formal ministries. Finally, this church type is primarily realized in liturgy: dogmatic belief is crucial to its self-understanding, and on ethical issues it takes a conservative stance.

Evidence of the 'church with a male face' is relatively easily identified in the material from the case studies. Sometimes it arises in data on power structures and representation, but just as often it appears in expectations levelled against the churches – both from inner circles of church members and from public authorities, a wide variety of organizations and groups within the population. These expectations are sometimes of a positive kind (wanting the church to represent traditional ideals), but very often they are negative (seeing the church as lagging behind or wishing to go back to 'the days when grandpa bought his first watch').

The second type will be called the 'church with a female face', as it is primarily represented by women, who play a crucial and idealized role as providers of care. To the extent that women are leaders in this structure, their leadership is restricted to certain levels and/or specific areas. It may be combined with ordination, but may also be expressed in voluntary work, in associations, lay movements or religious orders, as well as in informal groups at the parish level. This church is primarily realized not in liturgy and dogma, but in social practice, emphasizing a commitment for others at home or abroad. The 'church with a female face' is anchored in the Bible and tradition, but has a hybrid character: it is realized both in a traditional institutional form, and in alternative ecclesial structures. In ethical issues it is attuned to the needs and tendencies of the surrounding society. The church with a female face moves quite freely between private and public spheres, seeking support and strength wherever it can be found. It is not dependent on public attention; rather it tends to shy away from too much publicity, giving priority to 'doing what has to be done'.

The two types of church are related to each other in a way that can be likened to the famous psychological image constructed by Edgar Rubin, apparently showing a vase, but with the contours of the vase revealing two faces turned towards each other. What Rubin wanted to demonstrate was that our perception leads us to see either the vase, or the faces, but not the two images simultaneously. In a similar way, we are seldom able to recognize the church with a female face at the same time as the church with a male face. Rubin's concern was the psychology of perception, but in our case it is likely that the reasons behind our restricted understanding have to do with the authority and self-understanding of the church with a male face, in that it claims exclusive access to the truth. Just as the two faces in Rubin's image are formed by the contours of the vase, so has the church with a female face been shaped by the contours of the church with a male face. In fact the church with a female face is both the consequence and the prerequisite of the church with a male face, in the sense that much of the popular support for the church with a male face has its roots in the activities of the church with a female face. A rather drastic formulation comes to mind, uttered by a church president interviewed by a team from the World Council of Churches in relation to the Decade of Churches in Solidarity with Women (1988–1998). Inspired by the decade, he said, he had discovered that women kept his church alive: 'They do everything that we men decide without them … if they were to leave, we would have only decision-makers and no doers' (World Council of Churches 1997: 34).

The church with a female face and the church with a male face, then, are dependent on each other, but not in a symmetrical way. The church with a female face has had less influence than the church with a male face in drawing the contours between the two, and according to scholars of other religions, this is not a uniquely Christian trait. Using a somewhat different terminology, borrowed from the anthropologist Robert Redfield, Kajsa Ahlstrand has argued that each world religion has this type of male-dominated leading tradition – in Redfield's terminology its 'great tradition' (Ahlstrand 2001). The great Christian tradition has, according to Ahlstrand, been characterized by its transmission through male religious specialists, confessing its faith in the Triune God, who has taken flesh in Jesus, called Christ. It has special places for its cult, ruled by the religious specialists, and has an otherworldly aim. By contrast, the 'little tradition' is primarily transmitted by women. It sees God in Jesus and angels, but also in nature, and in grandma. Its cult takes place in the home, in graveyards and in nature. Its aims belong to this world and relate to fertility, health and well-being, and a hope of reunion with beloved ones after death. The 'great' and 'little' traditions are not self-contained entities, but continuously influence each other. However, women have regularly been excluded from interpretative and transmitting authority in the 'great traditions' of the world religions.

Ahlstrand's discussion is used, but also criticized, by Helene Egnell in her doctoral thesis on Christian feminist approaches to religious plurality (Egnell 2006). Building on the work of other anthropologists, Egnell avoids the value-laden labels 'great' and 'little', and chooses the term 'religion as practised' in contrast to 'religion as prescribed' to characterize her material. In line with Ahlstrand, however, Egnell's dissertation points to the fact that a major change is taking place today, with women questioning the limitations set by authoritative interpreters from the 'great' or 'prescribed' traditions, and claiming authority for themselves both as transmitters and interpreters of their traditions. In this way they bring with them experiences and practices from the 'little' or 'practised' traditions.

This argument has much in common with the contested areas of authority we have found in our results. As we have seen, a lack of priests and financial resources brings about change in the roles of clergy and laity in several of the WREP cases. In some traditions, ordained ministries undergo a change through the opening-up of ordination for women. At the same time, the roles of women evolve due to the fact that women increasingly take part in the labour market. Traditional structures of authority are shaken, by the decrease in the institutional authority of the churches overall, and a corresponding normalization of democratic structures even in church settings. This, together with the individualization of society at large, leads people to claim personal authority in ethical issues related to gender, family and sexuality.

Returning to the double image of Rubin's vase and the two faces, it could be argued that the changes described by Ahlstrand and Egnell (and exemplified in our case studies) have to do with the fact that the contours of religious traditions today are influenced both by structural social change and by the conscious efforts of women and men within these traditions. An example of the latter, mentioned in the Italian case study, is the movement We Are Church[6] which attempts to renew the Catholic Church from the grassroots. The effects of these attempts are cumulative, such that when we look at the picture expecting to see a vase, it may have taken another shape; and when we look for the faces in the contours of the vase, they may no longer fit our expectations.

What, then, are the implications of this restructuring for the role of the churches in the future organization of welfare in Europe? Will the two church types be forever locked into the gendered spaces assigned to them? Can the image be redrawn into one whole picture, where the two aspects can communicate and thereby critique and correct each other? Is there, perhaps, a third way? Can the contours that have separated the two church types from each other be redrawn in a way that makes the envisaging of new types of church possible: churches

---

[6]   See note 4.

with renewed and potentially more egalitarian gender relations, and innovative theological visions for the role of the churches in welfare?

One obvious source for new visions concerning gender relations in the churches is feminist theology. And ecclesiology, as the field dealing specifically with how churches understand themselves and their role, might be the most fruitful place to start. As a field of academic research, however, feminist ecclesiology is not yet fully developed. Nonetheless, some basic traits may be identified, all of which are characterized by visions of a new community where justice and solidarity stand at the centre. Different theologians have stressed different aspects of this vision: Rosemary Radford Ruether, among the pioneers, launched the concept 'women-church', by which she meant 'that women themselves, gathered in faith communities, were church, exemplars of the "people of God", not in the sense of excluding men, but in the sense of being empowered as women to define their own religious needs and experience and to move to organize communities to serve these needs' (Radford Ruether 1992: 194). A network called 'Women-Church' was established in the mid-1970s, starting with a convergence of Catholic women in Detroit, articulating demands for the ordination of women as well as for changes in Catholic views of ministry and church. The network still exists, as a coalition of 'Catholic-rooted organizations … committed to an ekklesia of women that is participative, egalitarian and self-governing', working for 'the recognition and empowerment of women in church and society'.[7]

The concept of an '*ekklesia* of women' (with the last word sometimes written 'wo/men') relates to a theoretical idea developed by the Catholic feminist theologian Elisabeth Schüssler Fiorenza, referring to a political category including not only women but also oppressed and marginalized men (Fiorenza 1994: 191). *Ekklesia* means assembly, and in Fiorenza's vision this is a democratic assembly of free citizens, irrespective of gender. Awaiting its realization, she argues that the idea of the *ekklesia* of wo/men can serve as 'a critical democratic space from which feminists can speak in order to change hegemonic "common-sense" theological discourses' (Fiorenza 1994: 27). In order to underline the egalitarian and justice-oriented dimension of her vision, Fiorenza also uses the expression 'discipleship of equals' (Fiorenza 1993). From a Protestant perspective, Letty Russell (1993) has formulated a related vision of a 'church in the round', a round-table church where justice is integral to the constitutive traits of the community.

Feminist ecclesiology is thus characterized by a strong commitment to justice and solidarity, and to egalitarian forms of community-building: ecumenically open, but also open towards people of different faiths, including secularized Christians seeking new forms of spiritual nourishment. As shown above, feminist ecclesiology as an academic field has developed in close relation to activist movements within different church traditions. This does not mean, however, that there is an identity or even close similarity between feminist ecclesiology and the church type which in this chapter we have called 'church with a female face'.

---

[7]   See http://www.women-churchconvergence.org/home.htm for more details.

Feminist theologians have taken a conscious stance against the patriarchal traits of the church, and claimed their space in traditional hierarchies and traditional fields of academic theology. Many of them would agree with Natalie Watson, who in the introduction to her overview of feminist ecclesiology states, 'I am entering a conversation to which I have not been invited' (Watson 2002: 5).

Conversely, many, probably a majority, of the women involved in church-related social practice are quite content with not being invited into any ecclesiological conversation at all. The church with a female face is characterized precisely by its capacity to fill the space left by the contours of the church with a male face, and to use that space in a way that creates meaning and satisfaction. The church with a female face allows women certain independence, and offers a feeling of importance for its contributors. Indeed the women involved may, as formulated in the Greek case, express a sense of pride in their work:

> Welfare activity is considered important, and their service to people in need is ... an important role that they can play within the church. In this sense, women working within church welfare services may be considered to be functioning as if they were deaconesses ... without any resentment that they are not official, ordained deaconesses. (Fokas 2006: 260)

Such a statement complicates things for feminist theologians. The very presence of ladies in sewing circles collecting money for the poor, of priest's wives helping their husbands in the parish without pay, of deaconesses helping the sick and poor, or of female volunteers assisting the elderly is problematic. It is particularly difficult to handle from a feminist justice-based perspective, where serving has been criticized as a gendered relationship of power – one that presupposes that women will serve men and women of higher social status. The fact that some women voluntarily want to serve, with neither payment nor substantial influence on decision-making, could mean that the women involved do not want to be liberated from these structures of power and gender. Rather than engaging with the reality of church social work and idealizing the church with a female face, most feminist theologians have therefore penetrated the discourse of the church with a male face, claiming access to interpretative authority over liturgy, biblical exegesis and dogmatics – that is, to the centres of power.

In relation to the two church types, then, feminist theology may be criticized for being more occupied with the reality of the church with a male face than with the agency of women within the church with a female face. An interesting question arises from this line of thought: whether, from a feminist perspective, the existence of the church with a female face could be reformulated as an *ekklesia* of wo/men in embryonic form, in which some women have fought their way to a certain amount of influence within the limits set by the contours of the church with a male face. But if these contours were blurred or shaken, new possibilities might open up for women if they could only imagine these to be achievable. The church with a female face could, in this way, provide building blocks for realizing an alternative vision – one characterized by the values of care and solidarity. As we saw in the introductory section of this chapter, these are values that are under increasing pressure in Europe today.

A dialogue between the church with a female face and feminist theology might seem even more utopian than a dialogue between feminists and the present church hierarchies; nevertheless, both sides might have something to gain from this encounter. On the one hand, the church with a female face might offer a dimension of care to feminist theology; on the other, the church with a female face could be enriched and inspired by the conscious claims for justice raised by the feminist movement. The dialogue envisioned here has been formulated in the work of feminist ethicists such as Virginia Held, who argue that a perspective of care and a perspective of justice should not be allowed to rule each other out. Rather, they should encourage us to 'begin to think about how society should be reorganized to be hospitable to care, rather than continuing to marginalize it' (Held 2006: 18). This could be seen as the deepest challenge discovered in the forms of religion documented in the WREP case studies.

A Queer Role for the Church?

As shown in the foregoing discussion, the problem of stereotypical gender roles related to structures of power and influence is a hindrance for the churches in responding to such a challenge. Most researchers on welfare and gender agree that if welfare provision is to flourish in accordance with more equal opportunities for women and men, the role of men in society has to undergo radical change. Feminist researchers have argued for a re-conceptualization of citizenship to include not only the right (and obligation) to paid work for both men and women, but also the right to receive and to have time to give care to others (Abrahamsson et al. 2005: 91). One of the proponents of such a vision is Nancy Fraser (see above). Fraser's alternative vision (1997) for the organization of welfare, intended to balance elements of similarity and difference in the lives of women and men, is called the universal care-giver model, and is designed to deconstruct the opposition between bread-winning and care-giving. It renders the current life-pattern of many Scandinavian women (that is, part-time professional work coupled with part-time unpaid responsibility for caring and housework) the norm for everyone, including men. Fraser imagines a social world in which every citizen integrates wage-earning, care-giving and political engagement, as well as involvement in the associational life of civil society. Her proposal has been received positively, not least because it addresses the shortage of caring resources that currently burdens Western societies. But researchers have also underlined that the proposal is visionary and requires radical changes in present gender roles if it is to succeed (Borchorst and Siim 2002).

Based on our case studies, it does not seem likely that the European churches will have much to contribute in response to such a challenge. Stereotypical female and male roles flourish in the churches to the same extent as in the rest of society, if not more so. An increased role for the churches in welfare might even have a negative effect on strivings towards gender equality. On the other hand, at least theoretically, the churches have resources in their theological traditions for challenging these gender stereotypes. There are contradictory elements in the material if it is scrutinized not only for its maintenance of the status quo, but also for its deviations from the norm. These deviations, moreover, could be used as resources in the search for a third way beyond a gendered devaluing of care. Specifically, and making use of queer theory, it could be argued that these resources are found in the queer aspects of both church types (Edgardh 2009). After all, the church with a male face is sometimes represented by celibate men dressed in robes, giving their lives in defence of values that are at odds with modern ideas of personal success. Similarly, the church with a female face may show traits other than female self-sacrifice and obedience, when we look more closely at female leaders raising their voices with considerable confidence both in their churches and in society. Behind these 'queer traits', if we may so call them, we find the authority of worldly powers being destabilized by the experience of the greater power of God, not least as revealed in the biblical stories of Jesus that so often turn stereotypes upside down, even when they involve gender. One example might be the story in John 13, where Jesus encourages his male disciples to follow his example and wash one another's feet, in order to be one another's servants. This story is frequently read in many church traditions, but the gendered implications of the story are seldom alluded to except in feminist interpretations.

Downplayed as these resources may be in the ordinary church life of the case studies, they have the potential to offer men and women alternative platforms both for caring for one another and for raising their voices in public debate. If this potential is fulfilled, the churches may well find a prophetic ministry deeply anchored in the gospel *and* very much needed in a secular post-industrial Europe, where values associated with serving, mutuality, solidarity, patience and vulnerability are out of fashion. But if the churches choose simply to respond passively to requests from outside, relying on women to maintain their voluntary work along traditional lines irrespective of ongoing changes in gender roles and family structures, their contributions are likely to be temporary, and will be perceived as expressions of inferiority rather than prophetic strength. From a gender perspective, therefore, it is crucial that the churches distinguish between the traditions of social engagement that express their theological identity, and the ballast of conservative values about gender and family to which these traditions are so closely connected. In short, a third way is necessary, to break the deadlock of the gendered dichotomy between the church with a male face and the church with a female face – be it a queer church, a church with a *human* face, or whatever label we choose to put on it.

A Challenge for Research

Researchers may formulate challenges for churches and societies, but even modest self-reflection forces us to admit that the academic study of religion is itself part and parcel of the reality discussed in this chapter. Redrawing old images of gender will therefore necessitate a redrawing of certain aspects of this field. Such rethinking is, of course, already in train, amongst other things in questioning the assumptions of older versions of secularization theory. A driving force in this respect can be found in comparative studies, which show that religion has developed differently in societies that are experiencing modernization: America, for example, is different from Europe, and both are different from Latin America, Africa and Asia (Davie 2002; Berger et al. 2008). The argument in this chapter, however, underlines the need to include a gender dimension in this discussion. Our results disclose a form of religion, in our typology called the church with a female face, which is insufficiently acknowledged in the research so far.

The British sociologist Linda Woodhead argues that sociology of religion has lagged behind many other disciplines in taking gender seriously (Woodhead 2005; 2007; 2008a). This has to do with the male bias inherent in the assumptions of the classical narratives of secularization, as developed by Max Weber and Karl Marx, but also by scholars such as Peter Berger. These narratives have supposedly been gender-inclusive, but have failed in reality to take account of the different positions of women and men during the period of industrialization. According to Woodhead, there are many detectable differences in patterns of secularization between women and men. She also suggests that, while modernization has meant a decrease in the public role of religion, the realms of family and church life have been drawn closer to each other in a way that has affected them both. This was particularly true of the nineteenth century, which in fact became the most – not the least – Christian century of all time, but with the difference that Christianity became increasingly feminized (Woodhead 2007). This feminization has continued into the twentieth and twenty-first centuries, religion being increasingly carried by women. While traditional religious forms such as liturgy have lost ground, other aspects, like community work, voluntary and lay work, and social contributions both nationally and internationally, have evolved. In our own terminology, the church with a female face has become more important, while the church with a male face has lost some of its former influence.

These changes have not, however, been adequately treated in the study of religion. Social work related to the churches has seldom been included in church statistics. Nor has it been included in quantitative studies used to measure degrees of secularization through enquiries into religious belonging, adherence to certain beliefs or attendance at church services. It seems therefore that even scholars of religion have overlooked the importance of social work in the religious life of the churches. In other words the continuing religious presence highlighted in our case studies has sustained itself, despite the fact that neither the official churches nor the great majority of scholars have paid more than distracted attention to it. Social scientists have looked at the picture of the vase, without noticing its alternative features.

As Linda Woodhead points out, a move from gender-blindness to a more conscious attention to gender is likely to lead to serious re-examination of some foundational concepts within the field, including the concept of 'religion' itself. This is important, she argues, given that the most androcentric aspects of Christianity have shaped sociological understandings of religion, just as they have shaped the self-understanding of the churches (Woodhead 2007). It is likely that more attention given to the social role of the churches would lead us to question some very basic assumptions about what religion is – assumptions which have been shaped by the church with a male face. Approaches to religion focusing on the church with a female face would, therefore, give a very different picture of the religious situation in Europe – one that is able to envisage new, and as yet undiscovered, images of the church.

Chapter 4

Thinking Theologically about Welfare and Religion

Thomas Ekstrand

'The church and its members represent the basic message that people have to take care of one another.' This was the response that a Swedish local government official gave when she was asked about the role of the Church of Sweden in the welfare system. She did not consider herself a believer – although she belonged to the Church of Sweden. Nor, however, did she doubt that the church was a witness to the values of caring and love (Edgardh Beckman et al. 2006: 48).

Why do churches engage with social welfare issues? How do they understand their roles within European societies? What kind of values do they argue for, and why? And how do the statements of the official leaders on social policy issues relate to the standpoints taken by the churches at a local level? These are theological questions with both simple and complex answers, depending on how one approaches them. The simple answer would be to say that love of your neighbour is a central aspect of the Christian faith, and that Christian love is not just benevolence in general, but requires action in some form. Furthermore, the churches see themselves as instruments of God's salvation in the world. This self-understanding would be supported by referring to divine revelation in some form.

But even if there is some truth in this shorthand interpretation, things are not that simple. Already several ambiguities can be found. What, for example, is meant by 'church' in the first place? Is it the ecclesial apparatus with bishops, ministers and legally recognized organizations? Or does 'church' refer to the communion of all believers? And what should we understand by 'salvation'? Does it mainly concern the afterlife in heaven, or is salvation also – and perhaps even primarily – to be understood as the development of right relations in *this* world? If the questions are posed in this way, it is obvious that the arguments put forward for the theological standpoints mentioned above become much more complicated.

It is also necessary to qualify the concept 'theology'. As a basic definition 'theology' means reflection on the content of faith, or an interpretation of the meaning of religious practice. Defined in this way, theology can occur on very different levels. It can be a distanced academic reflection, or the reflection of those actively involved in a certain practice. It can be more or less elaborated, and more or less spelled out. In some sense, it might even be said that a given religious practice implies a certain theology, even if this is never developed theoretically.

Purpose and Aims

The aim of this chapter is to offer a theological interpretation of the European majority churches' involvement in, and views on, welfare provision. This will be divided into the following sections.

First, I will give an overview of the church traditions covered in the study, with respect to their social doctrines. 'Social doctrine' refers to a vision of what constitutes a good society from a Christian perspective, and what the church's place in such a society might be. By implication, 'social doctrine' also covers the churches' critique of present social evils and ideas about how these should be remedied. The overview will focus on official and traditional doctrine, as it can be found in documents issued by church authorities, confessional statements and other similar texts. In the terminology of the previous chapter, it could be said that I focus mainly on the social doctrine of the 'church with a male face'. Since 'social doctrine' according to my definition also includes the churches' understandings of their own role in society, I will also touch upon questions of ecclesiology.

Next, I will offer an analysis of the empirical material collected in the WREP project, with regard to the explicit and implicit theology and social doctrine of the churches in the various case studies. The analysis of the empirical material will then be related to what has been identified as the official or traditional doctrine. The focus will be on possible tensions between local levels and the official versions. By identifying such tensions, questions about the multifaceted character of ecclesial identity will be brought to the fore.

Finally, the analysis will identify some specific theological problems facing majority churches involved in welfare provision and opinion-forming activities. It will be argued that these problems can be summarized under the concept *identity*. Several questions will be considered, including the following: are the churches putting their religious identity at risk by becoming large welfare providers in the European welfare states, or conversely do they *express* their 'true' identities by accepting this role which, at least in some sense, is recognized as a partner by the state? I will not try to offer any outright answers to these questions, but will rather point to ways in which such questions can be approached theologically.

My analysis will not include questions about the causal relations between theological ideas and societal developments. Questions such as those raised by Max Weber in his classic study on the Protestant ethic, about the relation between Reformed belief in the doctrine of predestination and the development of capitalism (Weber 1922; Ekstrand 2000), are more accurately described as sociological or historical rather than theological. That said, and as Manow has shown, the impact of theological and religious traditions has been somewhat neglected in research on the development of European welfare states (Manow 2004; van Kersbergen and Manow 2009a).

Some Methodological Considerations

In 2006, the *International Journal for the Study of the Christian Church* devoted a special issue to the concept 'operative ecclesiology'. The guest editor, Sven-Erik Brodd, following the French theologian Yves Congar, explained operative ecclesiology by stating that '[T]he idea is that the piety and liturgy found in various traditions actually say something about the self-understanding of these traditions' (Brodd 2006a). Operative ecclesiology is thus an analytical concept referring to understandings of what the church is or ought to be, which are 'hidden' in ecclesial practice. Operative ecclesiologies are implicit and reflected in different church activities, such as liturgy (Edgardh Beckman 2006), music (Brodd 2006b) and preaching (Fahlgren 2006). By reflecting on a specific activity of the church it is possible to infer an implicit idea of what the church is and ought to be. This might or might not be consistent with official doctrine or with the operative ecclesiologies of other church activities.

In my analysis of the empirical material, I will pay attention to operative ecclesiologies and to other implicit theological ideas,[1] as they might be understood from the case study reports. For example, in the Greek case study, an informant says, '[T]he church is love. People offer themselves in the name of love' (Fokas 2006: 243). In claiming that 'the church is love', the informant implicitly prescribes what the church *ought* to be; and, from this, it is possible to infer at least some tentative traits of an operative ecclesiology and social doctrine.

In order for such inductive interpretations not to be arbitrary, it is necessary to have an adequate hermeneutical model on which the interpretations can be based. I have found the Swedish historian of philosophy Anders Wedberg's idea of theory extension and Cristina Grenholm's concept of reconstructive interpretation useful in this regard (Wedberg 1968; Grenholm 1990). Interpretations of church practice and informants' statements about this practice are not systematically developed theologies, but they can be seen as *fragments* of theology. A theological analysis of operative ecclesiologies and implicit social doctrine is about filling in the gaps between these statements, thereby reconstructing a theological position out of the fragments. Of course, it is important to remember that such a reconstruction cannot claim to state what the informant or the practitioners *really* think theologically; but it can offer a reasonable interpretation of the implicit and operative theologies underlying practice. Furthermore, a reconstructive interpretation is not a causal explanation of a specific church practice. It is rather an argued proposal for what a more explicit theological basis of a specific practice *could* look like.

---

[1]   Jonas Ideström's important book *Lokal kyrklig identitet – en studie av implicit ecklesiologi med exemplet Svenska kyrkan i Flemingsberg* (Ideström 2009) was published after this chapter was drafted, but is recommended to those interested in the study of implicit theologies. That said, Ideström's method is more informed than my own by theories of organizational identity.

My reconstructive interpretations in this chapter have been guided by the following principles: the principle of logical coherence; the principle of discursive context; the principle of local context; and the principle of generosity (Edgardh Beckman et al. 2006). A reconstructive interpretation has to be logically coherent with the material on which it is based. If, for example, a reconstructive interpretation of a local church's social doctrine is based on interview material, the interpretation must be consistent with what is said by the interviewees. Furthermore, it assumes that there are no *intended* incoherencies in the material interpreted. When, in spite of this, the material is unclear, a reconstructive interpretation tries to reduce unintended incoherencies in the material in order to present a coherent interpretation of implicit and operative theology.

A reconstructive interpretation also has to pay attention to both the discursive and local contexts of the material interpreted. A text or a statement made by an informant is part of a specific discourse. This means that the same expression can have different meanings in different ecclesial discourses. A trivial example could be the term 'bishop'. The functions of a bishop are very different in the Greek Orthodox Church, the Catholic Church in France and the Lutheran Church of Norway.[2] This also means that it is reasonable to assume that theologically-laden expressions in the material are used in a way that is common within the specific tradition to which they belong, unless it is explicitly said to be otherwise. A reconstructive interpretation has to take into account the specific local context of a document or an interview.

Lastly, it is necessary for the interpretation to be generous. This means that it should try to do the material interpreted as much justice as possible. Contradictions or irrationalities have to be analysed in ways favourable to the text or interviewee, and should not be presented as arising from a lack of theological capacity. This is especially significant since the author of the present chapter is himself an ordained deacon in the Church of Sweden, and is thus deeply influenced by one of the traditions studied. I have tried to be as generous as possible in my analysis of Catholic, Orthodox and Anglican perspectives, but the reader should be aware that the section on Lutheran social doctrine is written by an insider, while all the other traditions are in some respect at least approached 'from the outside'.

Something should also be said about what I have called the official or traditional social doctrine of the church traditions included in the project. It must be stressed from the beginning that documents produced by church authorities on social doctrine have a very different status in each of the traditions analysed. For

---

[2]   I will use the term 'Catholic' instead of 'Roman Catholic' since this is the term preferred by Catholics themselves. It should be noted, however, that theologically, Lutheran, Anglican and Orthodox churches also claim to be 'catholic'. In the present chapter, 'Catholic' is used to mean Christian individuals and institutions in full ecclesial communion with the Pope.

the Catholic Church, the *magisterium* – the teaching office of the Church – has a claim to be *the* authoritative interpreter of Catholic doctrine. In the Orthodox, Anglican and Lutheran Churches, the status of bishops and other church leaders is different. As a consequence, the official documents published by these churches do not claim a similar authority to their Catholic equivalents (Curran 2002). It is necessary therefore to widen the scope of analysis to a brief sketch of the social doctrines of these traditions in general. For example, in the Lutheran case, the doctrine of the 'two kingdoms' will be presented, even if this is not a salient feature of the teaching of the Church of Sweden today.

The Churches' Social Doctrines

Catholic Social Doctrine

In 2004, the Pontifical Council for Justice and Peace at the Vatican published a *Compendium of the Social Doctrine of the Church* with the explicit intention – in the words of its president Cardinal Martino – to 'give a concise but complete overview of the Church's social teaching' (Pontifical Council 2004: xvii).[3] It is argued that the social teachings of the church are based on a view of humanity's place in God's creation, and, following from that, 'man's place in nature and in human society' (*Compendium* § 14).[4] The *Compendium* identifies four basic principles of Catholic social doctrine, namely the principle of the 'dignity of the human person'; the principle of the common good; the principle of subsidiarity; and the principle of solidarity (*Compendium* § 160; compare Hornsby-Smith 2006).

Human dignity   The theological foundation for the principle of human dignity lies in the understanding of every human being as created in the image of God. This means, that God has bestowed 'an incomparable and inalienable dignity' on every human being (*Compendium* § 105). The understanding of every human person as made in the image of God also implies that human beings are social and

---

[3]   In referring to church documents, I will follow conventional usage and reference the relevant paragraph of the text, rather than page numbers. This is helpful in that paragraphs are normally numbered in the same way in different editions and translations. In the bibliography all such documents are listed under the institution responsible for them or under the relevant Pope. Official documents issued by the Catholic Church can be found on the Vatican website. O'Brien and Shannon (1992) gather a number of texts on Catholic social thought into a single volume.

[4]   The language of the *Compendium* is not always gender inclusive, and often uses 'man' for 'humanity' and 'human being'. I have used the inclusive concepts as far as possible, but in quotations and when for some other reason it seems necessary, I have retained the *Compendium*'s usage.

relational in their essence, since they are created to live in relationship with God. The social character of human existence is expressed in the fact that God created humanity as men and women. There is a 'dynamic reciprocity' between men and women, manifesting the relationality which is a fundamental component in human nature (*Compendium* § 108–12). Men and women have, as human beings, equal dignity, according to Catholic social teaching.

Being created in God's image and likeness, human beings are free and conscious persons. This, in the view of the *Compendium*, makes human beings unique. Freedom is a prerequisite for human beings to achieve the highest goal of their existence: to live in relation with God. A good society, therefore, has to foster human freedom and respect the dignity and uniqueness of every person. No human being may be treated as a means 'for ends that are foreign to his own development'; and, *vice versa*, it is not possible to build good societies unless individual persons live morally (*Compendium* § 131–4).

Also connected with the idea of human dignity is the understanding of humanity's sinful nature. Humanity after the fall is understood to be affected by sin in such a way that human nature is defective: there is an inclination towards evil in every human person. This 'tragedy', as the *Compendium* expresses it, is at the root of all social evils. Sin causes alienation from one's true self, from God and from fellow human beings. In the most profound sense, sin is a violation of human dignity. Furthermore, sin is always at its roots individual and personal. Social evils are the product of the evil moral actions of individuals. In a sense it is possible and legitimate to speak of social or structural sin, connoting unjust social conditions. But this must not be done in such a way that sin's fundamental personal and individual character is played down or denied (*Compendium* § 115–19). Following Pope John Paul II in the encyclical *Sollicitudo Rei Socialis* (1987), the *Compendium* states that today, social sins can be divided in two main groups, namely the 'all-consuming desire for profit' and the striving after power (*Compendium* § 119).

From this view of humanity follows the strong affirmation of human rights in Catholic social doctrine. Human rights are based in the dignity of the human person, and are not a result of political decisions or individual choices (*Compendium* § 152–4). Ultimately, they are bestowed upon human nature in God's act of creation. In the encyclical *Centesimus Annus*, John Paul II lists those rights which he thinks are the most important – the right to life, the right to live in a united family, the right to develop one's intelligence and freedom, the right to work and to support oneself by working, and the right to establish a family and to have children (John Paul II 1991: § 47). Other popes have presented other lists of human rights, including the right to a decent standard of living, and the right to emigrate and immigrate (John XXIII 1963).

The common good   The common good is the second principle presented by the *Compendium*. For a definition the *Compendium* refers to the pastoral constitution of the Second Vatican Council (1965), *Gaudium et Spes*: 'The common good indicates "the sum total of social conditions which allow people, either as groups or as individuals, to reach their fulfilment more fully and more easily"' (*Compendium* § 164; *Gaudium et Spes* § 26). All human people have therefore the right to the goods necessary for their flourishing as persons. One of the main purposes of the social order is, accordingly, to guarantee a just distribution of goods. In Thomistic philosophy, the basic definition of justice was the principle of *suum cuique* (to everyone her or his due). This was further specified as three types of justice: commutative, distributive and legal. According to Curran (2002) this Thomistic understanding is still the basis of the understanding of justice in the social doctrine of the Catholic Church.

While commutative justice is concerned with private goods, as for example contractual agreements between individuals or institutions, and legal justice concerns the right and duty of everyone to participate in government, distributive justice is a concept used for reflection about how the resources – but also the burdens (e.g. taxation) – of the common good in society should be distributed among its members. Even if there is little discussion of the vast modern philosophical debate on distributive justice in the official documents, it is quite clear that Catholic social doctrine holds that a just distribution of the common good should be based on the *needs* of members of society. Similarly, the burdens should be distributed according to the capabilities of those carrying them (Curran 2002).

The 'preferential option for the poor' expressed in Catholic teaching is based on this understanding of distributive justice. In *Sollicitudo Rei Socialis* (§ 42), for example, John Paul II (1987) stated that Christians cannot ignore the needs of the poor and those 'without hope of a better future'. To do this would be a grave offence to God, and would put one's own salvation at risk (*Catechism of the Catholic Church* § 1033). Social organization, including the distribution of property, should therefore make a preferential option for the poor. But the Catholic Church does not prescribe how this should be done in each particular case. On the contrary, the *Compendium* states that the concrete organization of the polity falls outside the church's legitimate competence, since the state and the church are autonomous from each other. This does not exclude the right to mutual criticism or the possibility of co-operation. The latter is preferable when it can be done without danger to the identity of the church, since both church and state exist in order to promote the temporal and eternal good of every human person (*Compendium* § 424–7).

Subsidiarity   The principle of subsidiarity is often presented as the hallmark of Catholic social doctrine, spelled out in several official church documents, and not least in Pope Pius XI's encyclical *Quadragesimo Anno* (1931), commemorating the fortieth anniversary of the encyclical *Rerum Novarum* (Leo XIII 1891). In *Quadragesimo Anno*, the pope stated:

> It is an injustice and at the same time a grave evil and a disturbance of right
> order to transfer to the larger and higher collectivity functions which can be
> performed and provided for by lesser and subordinate bodies. Inasmuch as
> every social activity should, by its very nature, prove a help to members of the
> body social, it should never destroy or absorb them. (Pius XI 1931: § 79)

The principle of subsidiarity is based on the idea that society is organized on different levels, and that the higher levels are obliged to offer help (*subsidium*) to lower levels so that these can fulfil the functions proper to them. At the same time, the higher levels should not interfere with the operations of the lower levels. All social action and responsibility should therefore be taken at the lowest organizational level possible. For example, the principle of subsidiarity means that the state should not take over functions which belong to the family, a point heavily stressed by John Paul II (1981) in his Apostolic Exhortation *Familiaris Consortio* (§ 45–6).

Of special interest in this context is the importance of the principle of subsidiarity for the understanding of the welfare state in Catholic social doctrine. In the encyclical *Centesimus Annus*, John Paul II (1991) criticized what he conceived as an over-ambitious welfare state, which he named the 'social assistance state'. The social assistance state is, according to *Centesimus Annus*, characterized by far-reaching bureaucracy and large public spending, both of which cause civil society gradually to lose its sense of responsibility. According to the encyclical, the situation of the needy is better understood by those who are close to them than by an extensive bureaucracy (John Paul II 1991: § 48). The principle of subsidiarity requires that the state respects and supports the smaller entities of society, such as the family and non-governmental organizations. By promoting a number of social organizations, the state also safeguards pluralism and democracy (*Compendium* § 187).

One of the core values in the principle of subsidiarity is the value of participation (*Compendium* § 189). All human beings have the right and the obligation to participate in those social processes which affect their lives. This means a right and a duty to participate in government, but also in community-building more generally. The principle of subsidiarity thus aims at securing the likelihood of participation by locating responsibilities as close to the persons concerned as possible.

Solidarity The fourth principle of Catholic social doctrine is the principle of solidarity. As a moral virtue, solidarity is defined as 'a firm and persevering determination to commit oneself to the common good; that is to say to the good of all and of each individual, because we are all really responsible for all' (John Paul II 1987: § 38). As a social principle, solidarity means therefore recognizing the responsibility for the common good. This is shared by both rich and poor. The rich should acknowledge their responsibility for those who are less fortunate, and the poor should do what they can to promote the common good in their striving for better conditions (John Paul II 1987: § 38–9).

Finally, it should be noted that Catholic social doctrine is not only diverse but is continually developing. The modern reflection of the *magisterium* on social issues started effectively with Leo XII's encyclical *Rerum Novarum* in 1891; among the latest major papal documents on social issues can be found *Novo Millennio Ineunte* (covering such areas as international debt, poverty and ecology) (John Paul II 2001; Hornsby-Smith 2006), the encyclicals *Deus Caritas Est* (Benedict XVI 2006) and *Caritas in Veritate* (Benedict XVI 2009). The *Compendium* itself, published at the request of Pope John Paul II by the Pontifical Council of Justice and Peace, marks the ambition of the Catholic Church to offer its social doctrine to all peoples. At the same time, however, concrete Catholic social action is not a mere reflection of Vatican teachings. There is often a critical tension between local churches on the one hand and the authorities in Rome on the other. In France, for example, this can be illustrated by the reaction to the removal of Bishop Jacques Gaillot from the Diocese of Evreux. Although Pope John Paul II's dismissal of Gaillot was caused by conflicts over a wide range of issues, it was also perceived by many French Catholics as a reaction against rather too radical social activism (Valasik 2006).

Orthodox Social Doctrine

For historical as well as theological reasons there is no unified and official Orthodox social doctrine comparable to that set out in the Catholic *Compendium of the Social Doctrine of the Church*. The most authoritative texts are the writings of the church fathers, decrees by the ecumenical councils and various local synods, and statements made by the hierarchy. Depending on the local context, the contents of these statements and decrees may vary and at times even be contradictory.[5]

Basically, the Orthodox Church looks to the first Christian centuries and regards the teaching of the church fathers and ecumenical councils as the authoritative exposition of doctrine. Much of the later theological reflection takes the form of comments on the patristic texts. This also gives the social teachings of the Orthodox Church their special character: Orthodox theology is not predominantly an academic activity – although this might also be important – but is deeply embedded in the liturgy and spirituality of the church. Any reflection on Orthodox social doctrine has to take this into account. As will be discussed below, the social teaching of Orthodoxy is closely connected to the understanding of salvation as transformation, which in its turn is based on how Orthodox theology understands the whole of the Christological drama, and especially the resurrection of Christ.

In line with this, Michael Plekon, in his article on 'Eastern Orthodox Thought' in the *Blackwell Companion to Political Theology* (2007), concludes that there is 'no single Orthodox social and political theology'. According to Plekon, this does not mean that the theology of the Orthodox Church is uninterested in the affairs of

---

[5]   I am indebted to Effie Fokas, the researcher for the Greek case study, for advice in writing the section on Orthodox social doctrine.

the world. On the contrary, it believes that since God was incarnated into creation, the world is 'the only place where the drama of salvation occurs' (Plekon 2007: 104).

Even if Orthodox social doctrine is intrinsically multi-faceted, Plekon identifies five theological themes which, he claims, permeate Orthodox political and social thought. The first is an 'authentic concern for the material realities of this world'. With reference to St. John Chrysostom, Plekon argues that the Orthodox faith sees Christ in the suffering neighbour, and therefore metaphorically celebrates 'the sacrament of the brother and sister' in him or her. The second theme is a radical personalism. This, according to Plekon, means that Orthodox social doctrine focuses on the individual who suffers, but without neglecting the structural causes of suffering – attention to which is the third theme. The fourth theme is the 'constant eschatological reference' of Orthodox theology: it is central that the kingdom of God is already present in the world. The kingdom of God is, of course, seen as a future state of righteousness when Christ has returned in glory, but it is also present in the Divine Liturgy, in which the love of the Trinity is celebrated. The fifth and last theme is the belief in transformation. Salvation is understood as a means to the ultimate goal of creation: the deification of humanity, 'and by them, of the whole universe' (Lossky 1978: 110). This belief in transformation, according to Plekon, applies to humans as individuals, but also to social relations, in order for them to be in tune with the life of the Trinity.

These themes are closely interconnected, and in the following analysis I shall propose that the themes of eschatological reference, personalism and belief in transformation can be seen as three focal points of Orthodox social doctrine, while the two other themes identified by Plekon are consequences of these overarching foci. However, it must be stressed again that in identifying these key terms, I am offering an *interpretation* of Orthodox social doctrine, and not presenting a statement by a church authority comparable to the Catholic way of organizing the *magisterium*.

Eschatology: the kingdom of God   Apart from the patristic period, the era of the Byzantine Empire is the second most formative period of Orthodox theology, and is often regarded as a model for the church, as is evident from the statements of Archbishop Christodoulos of Athens (see below).[6] This being so, Byzantine views on the relationship between church and state still play a role in Orthodox theological reflection on these issues – though they should not, of course, be seen as the only factor underpinning the understanding of church–state relations. Indeed the nationalism of the nineteenth century and the subsequent establishment

---

[6]   Christodoulos's statements should not, however, be seen as representative of the Orthodox clergy or indeed the hierarchy in general. See Chapter 2 of this volume. I have used English language translations of Christodoulos's texts throughout. During the time that Christodoulos was Archbishop of Athens, these texts were available on the official website of the Church of Greece. This is no longer the case.

of national churches independent from the patriarchate of Constantinople in the Balkans and in Greece have considerably weakened the universal perspectives of the old Byzantine church (Runciman 1968), a development which has also had some effects on social doctrine.

That said, according to the modern Orthodox scholar John Meyendorff, Byzantine understandings of the relationship between church and society are eschatological in character. The key idea lies in the fact that the Kingdom of God was manifested in the Byzantine Empire, and that it would be possible to create a good society and a good world order if the whole world were to be subdued to 'the power of the one emperor and to the spiritual authority of the one Orthodox priesthood' (Meyendorff 1983: 214).

For Meyendorff, this was essentially an expression of a holistic anthropology; it did not accept distinctions between 'the spiritual and the material, the sacred and the secular, the individual and the social' (1983: 215). The Byzantine ideal was a 'symphony' between the divine and human in a Christian society, where the church and the state co-operated (Papadakis 1988). Of course, it was only possible to uphold this symphony in a state that understood itself as Christian *and* Orthodox; the fall of the Byzantine Empire, as well as the establishment of Communist rule in eastern Europe, was therefore a severe blow to the self-understanding of the Orthodox Churches. Under such circumstances, the church either worked out a kind of *modus vivendi* with the state, or chose the path of martyrdom and persecution. Due to the fundamentally different ecclesiology of Orthodoxy, an organized resistance like the Catholic opposition in Poland was difficult to imagine (the notable exception being the role of many clerics in the Greek war of liberation from Ottoman rule at the beginning of the nineteenth century).[7] Still, the church developed a wide range of social provision under Ottoman rule, since the Orthodox Greek population within the Ottoman Empire was organized as the *rum millet* – the Roman nation – and was allowed a certain amount of self-governance under the Ecumenical Patriarch (as *ethnarch* – governor of the people) (Constantelos 2003).[8]

In contemporary Orthodox thinking, the view of the relation between church and state is, of course, conceptualized rather differently. The Orthodox Church supports democracy and promotes the respect for human rights, even if there is also some Orthodox critique of the United Nations' 'Declaration on Human Rights'. This criticism focuses not so much on the actual *content* of the declaration, as on the basic premises on which it is built. Human dignity and human rights are, from

---

[7] It should be noted that much of the church hierarchy, including the Ecumenical Patriarch, did not support the independence movement, influenced as it was by secular ideology. This did not save the Patriarch from martyrdom, however, since as the responsible ethnarch of the *rum millet* (Roman nation) he was executed by Ottoman authorities for his failure to guarantee the loyalty of the Greek population (Clogg 2002).

[8] In imperial Russia, the church had rich opportunities to develop welfare activities. For a discussion of this point, see Belopopsky (2004).

an Orthodox perspective, ultimately based in the belief that humanity is God's creation. In so far as human rights discourse is related to liberal individualism, Orthodox theology is critical of this perspective. Being created by God, humanity ought to constitute a fellowship bound together by love.

This has been acutely formulated by Archbishop Anastasios Yannoulatos of Tirana in his book *Facing the World*:

> Here lies the decisive importance of the Christian understanding of *agape*, Christian love. It is this alone that can transform society from a heap of individual grains of sand, each isolated from and indifferent to the next, into an organic whole composed of cells, each contributing to the growth of all the others. Every person has a 'right' to be loved by the other people in society; God himself, in his love, has given us this right. In order to be truly free, every person must love, for it is in love that freedom is fulfilled. In the Orthodox doctrine of the Holy Trinity, personhood and society become harmoniously linked: the person is fully incorporated into society, yet the integrity of personhood is fully preserved. (Yannoulatos 2003: 71)

Based on this idea of love, the state is understood as having the task of promoting social cohesion and the material and spiritual well-being of all its citizens. For example, in a letter to the President of the European Commission, Archbishop Christodoulos (the Primate of the Greek Orthodox Church at the time of the WREP enquiry), stresses the vision of an active welfare state as an 'integral part of the Christian perception of society'. A good society, according to this vision, is characterized by a balance between striving for economic growth and social responsibility. The Archbishop also points out that technological development must 'be connected with sociality and spirituality' (Christodoulos 2005).

In two interesting speeches published in English, Archbishop Christodoulos reflects further on the role of Christianity, and especially Orthodoxy, within the European Union. The Archbishop argues that European civilization is intrinsically Christian. Striving for a united Europe is connected to the ideals of the Byzantine Empire, which, according to the Archbishop, was an expression of the idea of a 'Christian commonwealth'. In a controversial argument based on this premise, the Archbishop concludes that peoples whose civilizations are not shaped by Christianity do not belong in the European Union. Consequently, he also argues for the inclusion in the proposed constitution of a reference to the Christian heritage of Europe (Christodoulos 1999a; 2003).

There is a somewhat ambiguous attitude towards the question of church–state relations in Orthodox social doctrine. On the one hand, modern Orthodox theology accepts that the state is not intrinsically Orthodox. But on the other, there is still an expectation that the state will promote the Orthodox identity of the nation and will support the majority church. This is evidenced by the *Bases of the Social Concepts of the Russian Orthodox Church*, published by the Jubilee Bishops' Council of the Russian Orthodox Church, which among other things argues that the church 'has the right to expect that [the] state, in building its relations with religious bodies, will take into account the number of their followers and the place they occupy in forming the historical, cultural and spiritual image of the people' (Jubilee Bishops' Council 2000: III, 6). In Greece, too, representatives of the hierarchy express the view that there should be a close co-operation between church and state in order to preserve the close connection between national identity and Orthodox faith (see, for example, Christodoulos 1999a).

Personalism The second theme to be discussed here is the personalism of Orthodox social doctrine. Personalism is a somewhat elusive philosophical and theological concept, associated with French philosophers such as Jacques Maritain and Gabriel Marcel and the so-called Boston School of Personalism in the United States. The Swedish theologian and ethicist Elena Namli offers a definition of personalism by saying that 'a personalist chooses to put person and personal relations in focus for her/his theories'. She concludes the definition by saying that in this approach, the personal always has priority and cannot be reduced to or explained by non-personal factors (Namli 2000: 76).

Personalism understood in this way is commonplace in Orthodox theology. For example, Archbishop Yannoulatos states that any work for social and political change has to start with a transformation of the individual's heart: 'The secret of substantive change, the guarantee of change, and the dynamic through which change occurs all lie hidden within the process of restoring and purifying the human person' (Yannoulatos 2003: 167). This stress on personal change as a basis for social change has given Orthodox ethics an ascetic character: in order to live a moral life, it is necessary to liberate oneself from desire. This ascetic and personalist position can lead to an ethics of action – or, in the words of Yannoulatos: 'The Christian believer stands before every one of God's creations with respect and love in his heart, not thievery' (Yannoulatos 2003: 172). But it can also lead to a passive quietism, which glorifies suffering as a moral quality in itself.[9]

Two other basic concepts in Orthodox social doctrine, closely connected to the theme of personalism, are *diakonia* and *philanthropia*, meaning 'social service' and 'love of human beings'. *Diakonia* can be understood as the church's work to liberate humanity from everything which stands as a hindrance to salvation (Molokotos-Liederman and Fokas 2004). *Philanthropia* is a central concept in Orthodox theology, implying a constant, undefined state of giving which could correspond to any type of need or want, and which stems from nothing more and nothing less than love of one's fellow human being. This should be distinguished from the related concept of *philoftoxos*, meaning 'friend of the poor'. *Philoftoxos* could be seen as one instance of the broader concept of *philanthropia*, connoting giving directed specifically to economically deprived people (Fokas 2006: 258; Constantelos 2004).

---

[9] For a critique of this trait in modern Orthodox ethics, see Namli (2003).

The Orthodox theologian Thomas Hopko, in his article 'On Stewardship and Philanthropy' (2003), discusses the theological understanding of *philanthropia*. Philanthropy, he concludes, is ultimately based in God's nature, which is characterized by giving. The Trinity itself is, by essence, giving: the Father must, by nature, share his divinity, which is the *ultima ratio* for him to beget the Son and to breathe forth the Spirit. Creation and incarnation are a consequence of God's giving nature. God can therefore also be named *philanthropos* – the Lover of Humanity – as is repeatedly done in the Divine Liturgy, and philanthropy can be seen as related to the life of the Trinity.

Living in relation to God therefore means to give oneself and one's possessions for the benefit of others. This is not merely a question of giving material assistance. The virtue of *philanthropia* is also to be exercised by those who do not possess anything (or who, due to illness, cannot offer help in other ways), by offering 'spiritual acts of mercy'. Hopko remarks: 'Not all can work and assist. But all can pray, all can weep, and all can express co-suffering love with mercy for all, without discrimination or condition' (Hopko 2003: 143). Furthermore, philanthropy of all kinds is not restricted only to other Christians, but should extend to the whole of humanity. It is also interesting to note Hopko's argument that Christians in politically powerful positions should use their position in order to exercise *philanthropia*, even if they cannot openly do so 'in Christ's name'. As exemplars from Orthodox history, he mentions the Roman/Byzantine imperial figures of Constantine and Helen, Justinian and Theodora, as well as Russian rulers such as Vladimir and Olga (Hopko 2003: 147).

Within the sphere of *philanthropia* also comes love of one's family. With reference to the First Epistle to Timothy (1 Timothy 5:8), Hopko concludes that God despises those who do not care for their own family. The same stress on the spiritual importance of love and care for the family is expressed in various public statements by Orthodox hierarchy. For example, Archbishop Christodoulos, in a message to the Hellenic Gerontological and Geriatric Association, states that the family is the 'healthy nucleus of society'. It is therefore regrettable that those who are elderly 'waste away alone and distressed, far from the warmth and comfort of a family and with the bitter complaint of abandonment on their lips' (Christodoulos 1999b). This stress on traditional 'family values' is by no means exceptional, and can be found in various statements of Orthodox hierarchy. As has been discussed in the previous chapter, however, this is likely to reinforce the subordinate role of women both in society and in the church.

Transformation   Belief in the possibility of transformation is the third and last theme of Orthodox social doctrine to be discussed here. As will be shown, it is closely connected to the theme of personalism, and is based in the Orthodox view of human nature and salvation. Orthodox anthropology and soteriology view human beings as free and responsible agents, as images of God. As such, human beings are called by God to become like God. The process of becoming like God – theosis or deification – is, in fact, the ultimate purpose of human existence (Meyendorff 1983: 163). Salvation, in Orthodox understanding, is the healing of the rupture in divine–human relations caused by human evil and death, through the incarnation, death and resurrection of Jesus Christ. However, unlike its counterparts in much traditional Catholic and Protestant theology, this salvation is not primarily understood in legal terms, but as a transformation – assisted by divine grace – into the likeness of God.

Orthodox theological anthropology is thus more optimistic about the capabilities of sinful humans to transform their lives. This does not mean that the reality of sin is denied, but it means that human beings are still free to choose good instead of evil. Archbishop Yannoulatos argues that through the incarnation of the Son, God offered humanity 'a new way for the human person to advance toward "communion" with the trinitarian God, and also with other human beings, who are images of God' (Yannoulatos 2003: 60). Since, according to this anthropology, human beings are still free to choose life instead of death, there is also a conviction in Orthodox social doctrine that it is possible to transform society into a community characterized as '*koinonia agapes*' – a communion of love (Yannoulatos 2003: 58).

As we have seen, however, the personalist aspect of Orthodox social doctrine implies that any real transformation for the better of human societies must start in the transformation of persons. No real and lasting change in social conditions can be achieved if it is not based on a spiritual transformation of the persons who together make up society. Social justice which is not based on 'individual honesty and genuineness' is therefore 'a mere chimera' (Yannoulatos 2003: 167). This combination of personalism and belief in transformation is also present in public statements by Archbishop Christodoulos. In his message of 1 May 1999, for example, the Archbishop stated that various 'socio-political systems', however well-intended, have not been able to solve the social problems which first gave rise to the celebration of Labour Day on the first day of May. The church, however, 'heals the person and his problems in a social place where it lives, works and creates' (Christodoulos 1999c).

Orthodox theology and spirituality is sometimes – even by intra-Orthodox observers – described as other-worldly (Meyendorff 1983). There is some truth in this description. Stressing the personal, and developing a spirituality of *theosis*, the Orthodox Church in many ways fosters an ascetic ethic, which might (at least by modern secular standards) seem quite uninterested in the affairs of this world. On the other hand, the ascetic ethos – perhaps most clearly expressed in Orthodox monastic life – is also a pointer to an ideal of what just relations in the world ought to look like, offering thereby resources for a critique of social evils. As is obvious from Orthodox Church practice, this does not in any way exclude organized social work, but it does give Orthodox social doctrine a different character from its Protestant and Catholic counterparts.

Lutheran Social Doctrine

As in the Orthodox case, and unlike the Catholic situation, Lutheran social doctrine cannot be based on the authority of a universal *magisterium*. There is no church authority even remotely similar to the pope or the Vatican. The confessional documents from the sixteenth century are still held in high esteem, but they were written in a totally different social, political and religious context, and their real importance for contemporary Lutheran theology is debatable. They are still commented on by theologians, and referred to in church documents, but their authority is indirect and limited.

That said, Lutheran churches publish documents on social issues. For example, in 1993 the bishops' conference of the Church of Sweden published *Rich and Poor – A Letter from the Bishops of the Church of Sweden about Justice and Morality in the Global Economy*. In the first pages of this document, the Swedish bishops claim that 'the pattern of this world is best perceived from the perspective of the poor' (Church of Sweden 1993). Another example can be found in *Towards the Common Good – Statement on the Future of the Welfare Society by the Bishops of the Evangelical Lutheran Church of Finland* (Evangelical Lutheran Church of Finland 1999). Here the Finnish bishops argue that a commitment to the welfare state has deep roots in the Lutheran tradition, in which public authorities are seen as God's instruments for setting a limit to selfishness and promoting the common good. The state and civil society, as God's instruments, should therefore take responsibility for a just distribution of the common good.

The Evangelical Churches in Germany (EKD), a union of the different Protestant Churches (Landeskirchen) of Germany, have also published a number of reports on social-ethical issues, as have the different Landeskirchen.[10] The EKD, for example, has published statements on the health care system in Germany (EKD 2002a) and on the legislation on immigration in Germany (EKD 2002b). The Lutheran Church of Norway has done likewise, as for example its 2005 document on issues of immigration in Norway, arguing for a more generous policy (Church of Norway 2005).

There is therefore no lack of documents from the Lutheran Churches on social doctrine, which in various degrees refer to the Lutheran tradition and to the confessional documents from the sixteenth century. However, their formal status as authoritative statements is not clear, and they are often highly debated within their respective church traditions (see, for example, Grenholm 1994 for a critique of the Swedish bishops' document *Rich and Poor*).[11] Thus it is almost impossible

---

[10]   The member churches of the EKD are not only Lutheran, but also Reformed and Uniate. The bi-confessional character of church life in Germany makes the German case slightly unusual. That said, the Catholic Bishops' Conference and the Protestant churches frequently work together in the area of social policy.

[11]   This is also true of Catholic documents, but the formal status of these is laid down in church law, at least when it comes to documents published by the Vatican or various bishops' conferences.

to define what official Lutheran social doctrine really is. However, in order to create a point of reference for the theological analysis of the case studies, I will give a short overview of what could be considered traditional Lutheran social doctrine. In this context, 'traditional' means Lutheran doctrine as formed in the Reformation period. It should not be assumed that this corresponds directly to the contemporary teachings of Lutheran Churches in general, though it is of course part of their legacy.

In an article on themes and challenges in Lutheran ethics, the American Lutheran theologian Robert Benne has identified four central aspects of a Lutheran view on the public role of the church (Benne 1998). These aspects are: salvation versus human effort; the purpose of the church; the 'twofold rule of God' (the 'two kingdoms' doctrine); and the paradox of human nature and history. In what follows, I use Benne's four themes to frame my overview.

Salvation Traditional Lutheran theology is characterized by a sharp distinction between salvation, which is solely God's work, and the moral efforts and achievements of human beings. Salvation is something brought about by God's activity, and is based on the salvific work of Christ in his death on the cross and in his resurrection. This also means that salvation, in traditional Lutheran terms, is primarily about the forgiveness of sins. That is, salvation is about humanity's relationship to God, rather than the relationships between human beings. Of course, this does not exclude a social dimension to salvation in Lutheran theology, but a morally perfect order is something which belongs to the eschatological future, when God creates a new heaven and a new earth. All social realities in this world will therefore be permeated by sin. Accordingly, there is in traditional Lutheran theology a decisive ban on any confusion between salvation and human effort, both when it comes to personal salvation and to the remedying of social evils. However, this does not mean that questions of social ethics are of no concern to Lutheran theology. On the contrary, since moral efforts are not in any way a prerequisite for salvation, Christians are free to pursue moral goals as valuable in themselves (Benne 1998: 18–19)

The church This view of salvation is closely related to the second aspect, the purpose of the church. The church is the herald of the gospel in the world (on the concept 'herald', see Dulles 2002). In Benne's terminology, the gospel of salvation in Christ is the 'core vision' of the church, the central aspect of its identity. Fundamental moral convictions – in Lutheran theological vocabulary, 'the law' – are closely connected to this core. But, in Benne's view, there are also 'concentric circles' around this inner core. These are of a more speculative and less authoritative character. They consist of the 'theological reflections of the church, including its social teachings'. Since these do not belong to what is essential to the church's identity, there is room for a variety of standpoints, not least when it comes to opinion on public policy (Benne 1998: 20–21)

According to the traditional Lutheran view, the church's identity rests in its witness to the gospel. The church, as an organization, cannot claim any privileged insights in political matters, even if God's law, as proclaimed by the church, has consequences for politics. The traditional Lutheran position on the relation between gospel, law and politics is often summarized under the heading 'God's twofold rule' or the 'two kingdoms' doctrine.

The two kingdoms   As Benne says, the notion of God's 'two kingdoms' is perhaps one of the most misunderstood Lutheran theological doctrines (Benne 1998: 22). Max Weber and Ernst Troeltsch both claimed that the social doctrine of Lutheranism fosters quietism and passivity, compared to the Calvinist view on the Christian's calling in the world (Troeltsch 1992; Weber 1990; Manow 2004). The reason for this alleged quietism is often declared to be the Lutheran idea of God's twofold rule of the world. However, the doctrine can also be used as a theological basis for holding the state responsible for its shortcomings, as is done in the document *Towards the Common Good – Statement on the Future of the Welfare Society*, presented by the Finnish bishops.

The basis for the doctrine of God's two kingdoms is the Lutheran conception of an essentially sinful humanity. Since human nature is characterized by a radical evil, often named original sin, God has to deal with humanity in two ways. On the one hand, God's love requires that God puts things right between God and creation. This is achieved by the salvific work of Christ, and the good news of salvation through faith in Christ is proclaimed by the church as the herald of the gospel. At the same time, however, God also has to deal with the consequences of human evil in the world, by putting a limit on it. This is the realm of the law, which is God's instrument for regulating the affairs of sinful humanity. The law in this sense could roughly be defined as the moral order laid down by God in creation. The law, furthermore, has two functions. The first is to set a limit to sin. This function is often called the political or civil use of the law. This use of the law exists for the sake of order, and aims at creating a good and ordered society. The second function is the theological use of the law. In this sense, the law exists to convince humanity of its sin and therefore of its need of salvation (Lohse 1999: 267–76).

The two kingdoms of God are therefore related to the law and the gospel respectively. In the spiritual kingdom God relates to humanity in all things necessary for salvation. In this respect, God governs through the gospel, without any coercion. In the worldly kingdom, which is also called the kingdom of the sword, things are very different. Here, God governs through the political authorities, and ultimately by coercion – 'by the sword'. For Luther, it is impossible to think that sinful humanity could be governed by the gospel alone. It is necessary to put a limit on sin, in order to preserve justice and peace (Lohse 1999: 314–24; Luther 1900). The worldly kingdom is therefore also God's kingdom, and Christians can be said to be citizens of both kingdoms. As believers in Christ, they are members of the spiritual kingdom, but as those who live in a social context, they are members of the worldly kingdom, living under the law. This means that human beings, as citizens of the latter, are called to serve God through their vocations in civil life, and thereby to contribute to the flourishing of creation.

The church is primarily called to proclaim the gospel. Since the law is God's law, however, the church cannot refrain from proclaiming the law as well. But what does this mean in practice? In the history of Lutheranism, this question has been answered in two ideal-typical ways (Benne 1998: 22). In what might be called the quietist-passive model, the two kingdoms doctrine has been interpreted as saying that the church should not speak out on public issues, since the church's business is to care for individual salvation. It is not the church's task to criticize those who 'carry the sword', since they do this on God's behalf. Even if the political authority is tyrannical or evil, therefore, a Christian should not resist it in any active way. When the church preaches the law, it should do so solely for the salvation of individual souls, and leave the care of politics to the worldly kingdom. Unsurprisingly, this quietist-passive model fell into disrepute after the Second World War, since it was used as a way to legitimize Lutheran passivity or even collaboration with Nazi authorities (see Forrester 1997: 210; Normann 1998; Lazareth 2001).

The second ideal-typical model of the two kingdoms doctrine I will call the political model. The political model also recognizes that God rules the world in two ways of radically different natures, but it does not accept that the church should only preach the gospel and the law in its theological sense. It is, rather, the task of the church to bear witness to the fullness of revelation, to both gospel and law, while respecting their different characters. The church does not, and should not, strive for the 'sword', in the sense that the church should not seek political power for itself. But since the political authorities have a God-given task, they also have a responsibility towards God to promote justice, peace and good order. It is this way of applying the doctrine of God's two kingdoms that can be seen in the Finnish Lutheran bishops' *Statement on the Future of the Welfare Society*. The public authorities and civil society have a God-given task to promote the common good. Human communities are created by God and should distribute the goods of creation according to the principle of love:

> The principles of the social thought of the church, i.e. those of communio and
> of public authority, are based on the belief in the Creator, the source of all good,
> who has placed the law of love into every human heart. The very core of this
> teaching is the Golden Rule. (Evangelical Church of Finland 1999)[12]

In a statement following a consultation held by the Lutheran World Federation (LWF), entitled *Reclaiming the Vocation of Government*, the church's responsibility to criticize governments if they fail to live up to God's vocation to 'promote

---

[12]   Here, as elsewhere, where reference is made to a document available electronically, no page number is given.

justice and peace, and to keep life human' is firmly underlined (Lutheran World Federation 2004: 3). The document clearly states that the church does not possess any privileged political insights. It is thus not the church's business to participate in day-to-day policy making. Nonetheless, it *is* the task of the church, on the basis of its faith, to remind governments of their God-given purpose to 'exercise public stewardship of the common good' (2004: 3). As part of civil society, the church is also called to contribute to the common good by its diaconal work (2004: 4).

Human nature   The fourth aspect identified by Benne is the paradox of human nature and history (Benne 1998: 26). In Lutheran theology, human nature is affected by the radical evil of sin, but at the same time is created in God's image. As God's image, every human being has the capacity to act morally. Furthermore, from a Lutheran perspective it is also necessary to affirm an infinite human dignity. Since God has both created and redeemed humanity, human beings are infinitely valuable. It is this tension between humans as sinful, and at the same time of infinite worth, that is paradoxical. On the one hand, humans are capable of doing good, but on the other, everything they do is affected by sin. This means that it is impossible for a perfect social order to be created by human efforts. The best humanity can do, in Benne's interpretation of Lutheran thinking, is to 'strive for relative gains' (Benne 1998: 27). A perfect community can only be brought about by God, and this should make Lutheran thinking utterly sceptical about any idea of realizing any political or social utopia this side of the *eschaton*.

Anglican Social Doctrine

As is the case with the Lutheran and Orthodox Churches, the Church of England and the Anglican Communion do not have any central authority which can define social doctrine in a way that can claim to be binding for all Anglicans. Any discussion of official Anglican social doctrine has therefore to be based on a reconstructive interpretation of various sources. A second point concerns the distinction between the worldwide Anglican Communion and the Church of England. The Church of England is the mother church of the Anglican Communion, and the Archbishop of Canterbury is both Primate of the Church of England and 'central focus of both unity and mission' in the Anglican Communion (Lambeth Commission on Communion 2004, *Windsor Report* § 109), but this does not mean that the Archbishop of Canterbury or any other part of the Anglican Communion can define doctrine in a way that is binding on all Anglicans. It can be said, however, that the Archbishop of Canterbury is in a broad sense expected to express the views of the Anglican Communion, in that it 'looks to the office of the Archbishop to articulate the mind of the Communion especially in areas of controversy' (*Windsor Report* § 109).

William Temple (1881–1944) is probably the best known and most influential Archbishop of Canterbury in the field of social doctrine. He is claimed to have coined the term 'welfare state', as opposed to what he perceived to be the nature of the German nation – a *warfare* state.[13] Temple's position on social doctrine has been described as a 'third way' standpoint, understanding state and church as 'two elements of God's plan, with specific tasks to perform' (Middlemiss 2002: 45). At the Malvern Conference in 1941, Temple formulated his position as follows: 'It is the duty of Lambeth to remind Westminster that Westminster is responsible to God; but this does not mean that Westminster is responsible to Lambeth' (quoted in Middlemiss 2004: 177).[14] In many ways, the Church of England still fulfils this function of being a 'critical partner' of the state (Middlemiss Lé Mon 2009: 269).

One of Temple's successors, Rowan Williams (the current Archbishop of Canterbury), has expressed a similar view when saying that Christianity can be seen as a 'critical friend to the state and its laws'. Christianity, says Williams, asks about 'the foundations of what the state takes for granted and often challenges the shallowness of a prevailing social morality; it pushes for change to make the state a little more like the community that it is itself representing, the Kingdom of God' (Williams 2007).

Middlemiss (2002) constructs an ideal type of Anglican social thought in the twentieth century, based on an analysis of the theologies of William Temple, David Jenkins and the *Faith in the City* report (Archbishop of Canterbury's Commission on Urban Priority Areas 1985). The basic features of her ideal type can be summarized under three headings, which will structure the following analysis. These are: that the church has an obligation and a right to interact with the state in social issues; that the church relates theological principles to social policy by the method of middle axioms; and that the social teachings of the Church of England are largely developed in the due processes of committees, but the influence of individual theologians, and especially the bishops, is also important.

Interaction with state and society on social issues The interaction between church and state in social policy formation is in many ways facilitated by the fact that the Church of England is an established church and its senior bishops remain for the time being members of the House of Lords. This fact in itself gives the episcopacy of the church both the right and the obligation publicly to comment on and to influence social policy. It also provides an opportunity to make the church's activities within the welfare sector more visible. One relatively recent example is the initiative of the Archbishop of Canterbury to hold a debate in the House of

---

[13] On this and Temple's social theory, see Middlemiss (2002) and Middlemiss (2004). See also Temple (1942).

[14] 'Westminster' refers to the British Parliament, and 'Lambeth' to the Anglican Church and especially to the Archbishop of Canterbury, whose residence in London is Lambeth Palace.

Lords on 'the contribution of the role of the churches in the civic life of towns and cities' (*Hansard* 19 May 2006: 501–70).

In his opening remarks in this debate (Williams 2006), the Archbishop pointed to the role of religious organizations in the regeneration of deprived urban areas. Religious organizations have a continuous presence in these areas and will not go away simply because a government-funded project ends. Partly because of this, religious organizations are seen by many as trustworthy partners in the sense that they 'provide a pool of volunteer enthusiasm' needed for successful community development. In the conclusion to his speech, the Archbishop pointed to the special role of the Church of England, which by its presence in all areas of the country 'embodies a sort of popular awareness of where this particular kind of social capital may be found'. In connection with this, he referred to the then imminent publication of the report *Faithful Cities*, produced by the Archbishop's Council's Commission on Urban Life and Faith (2006). Through this initiative in the House of Lords, the Archbishop was able to highlight the publication of this report, the content of which will be discussed below.

Theological reflection and social policy   The second heading in Middlemiss's ideal type concerns the efforts of the Church to relate theological reflection to questions of social policy. William Temple did this by a method of 'middle axioms'. The basic principles of this method were laid out by Joseph H. Oldham in *The Church and its Function in Society* (Visser't Hooft and Oldham 1937: 210), and were then taken up by Temple. The latter's use of middle-axiom thinking has exercised a strong influence on the way that the Church of England operates when reflecting theologically about social issues.

The method of middle axioms presumes that the Christian faith contains general beliefs and ethical norms which have to be related to social policy by some sort of intermediary principles. For example, a general belief or ethical imperative in Christian faith is that one should love one's neighbour as oneself. This does not say much about the precise political position a believer should take. From the general principle, however, it can be argued that we ought to provide for the material well-being of all. Accordingly, the middle axiom that we should have a public social security system can be inferred. This still leaves room for serious disputes – about how much tax should be paid and what kind of social assistance should be offered. The use of middle axioms is thus a way to formulate relevant Christian standpoints in a specific context, while still leaving it open to policy-makers and specialists to discover the proper means to achieve the desired ends (Chapman 2004).[15]

---

[15]   The question of whether middle axioms can logically be deduced from basic principles such as the belief that human beings are 'children of God' is beyond the scope of this analysis. For a discussion of this and related matters see McCann (1981); Preston (1983); Kamergrauzis (2001); Storrar (2004); and Dackson (2006). See also Middlemiss (2002) for a detailed analysis of Temple's thought.

In other words, there can be basic Christian agreement on middle axioms, alongside substantive disagreement about how these axioms should be implemented in practice. A method of middle axioms can also facilitate co-operation between different denominations and faith traditions, since they can provide a basis for co-operation on specific issues, whilst accommodating the fact that the faith basis for each partner may be quite different (see Atherton 2003: 129). As Middlemiss (2002) points out, Temple's own use of the middle-axiom method was noticeably cautious in offering concrete policy directions, leaving this to individual Christians in their role as citizens. Later Anglican social thought has been less wary about offering statements regarding national policy. However, the primary principles as formulated by Temple are still quite visible in the social doctrine of the Church of England.

For example, in 1986 the Social Policy Committee of the General Synod Board for Social Responsibility published *Not Just for the Poor – Christian Perspectives on the Welfare State* (General Synod Board for Social Responsibility 1986). The report is one of the most important Church of England documents on the welfare state published in the last 25 years (Middlemiss 2004: 178), and can be understood as an instance of middle-axiom method. Following a brief introduction, the report sets out an analysis of 'Welfare in the Light of Christian Belief'. In this primarily theological discussion, the committee underlines the unique value of every human being, which places an obligation on us all not to treat 'some as of more value than others' (§ 2.8). The report also stresses what is called the 'interdependence in human life', thereby pointing to a conviction that human life is dependent for its flourishing on a mutual giving and receiving between human beings. Thirdly, the report highlights the 'biblical concern for justice and for the poor' (§ 2.23), and the church's calling to bear witness to the coming of the Kingdom of God. In its witness, the church must pay heed to the paradoxical character of the Kingdom, as something which is both already present and at the same time yet to come. This means that the church has to transcend the provision of individual charity, and work for radical social and political change, but at the same time not fall prey to utopianism. In order to be effective, the church in its political action has to be realistic and base its actions on detailed economic and political analysis.

The following chapters are mainly devoted to such an analysis. At the end of the report, the committee returns to policy questions, and formulates five possible models for how welfare services might be provided. Only two of these models are seen as compatible with the primary principles advocated in the theological analysis. The structure of the *Not Just for the Poor* report is thus an example of an argument 'from the general to the specific' (Chapman 2004), where primary principles are applied via detailed argument and analysis in order to formulate more specific guidelines for action.

In the more recent *Faithful Cities* report, a similar approach is applied.[16] The report presents three 'key convictions' which form the basis of its work. These are worth citing at length:

> First, we understand God to be the source of all life from whom all creation draws its purpose and character. Secondly, we understand that to be human means that we are made 'in the image and likeness of God', and that therefore each person possesses an innate and irreducible dignity. Thirdly, our traditions speak of humanity being called into relationship with God and that human purpose and destiny is fulfilled in relationships of mutuality, love and justice. (Archbishops' Council, Commission on Urban Life and Faith 2006: § 1.10)

In the following chapters, the report explores the 'faithful capital' which is represented by various religious communities in British society. Both by their sheer presence in deprived areas, and by their specific activities, they represent resources for urban regeneration. With reference to the term 'social capital', these resources are labelled 'faithful capital'. The commission concludes its report by offering a set of recommendations to faith communities and government in order to further a just society.

The method of formulating basic principles of Christian faith from which a more detailed standpoint on social policy can be developed seems to be the 'standard' method in the reports analysed so far. My third example refers to a speech given by the Archbishop of Canterbury in Singapore in May 2007 (Williams 2007). The Archbishop spoke on the theme 'Christianity: Public Religion and the Common Good'. In his speech, the Archbishop presented two principles which the Christian faith offers as a basis for a just society. The first is the conviction that human dignity is based in God's creation. The purpose of human existence is ultimately defined by God, who calls human beings and 'continues to call them and to offer them what they need to fulfil their calling'. The second principle is what the Archbishop calls 'the pattern of the Body of Christ', referring to 1 Corinthians 12:12–31. Christians are called to live in interdependence with each other, as parts of the same body. The church is called to live out this vision, and to influence society by bearing witness to its ideals. But the church should not seek political power:

> [T]he Christian is not seeking to make the state into a church, but is proposing to the state and to the culture in general a style and direction of common life – the life of the Body of Christ – that represents humanity at its fullest. (Williams 2007)

---

[16]   This report was written by an ecumenical and inter-faith commission, with representatives from major Christian denominations, and one member from the Muslim community. The initiative for the commission, however, was taken by the Church of England, which also held the majority in the commission.

Common features It is already clear that committee processes (the third feature of Middlemiss's ideal-typical construction of Anglican social thought) are an important way in which the Church of England develops its social doctrine. One further point is, however, important. This concerns the common features of Anglican social doctrine, where I will take as my starting point Alan M. Suggate's 1987 study of the significance of William Temple's thinking for Christian social ethics. In this Suggate identifies three basic principles, which can function – slightly revised – as a summary of Anglican social doctrine in the present analysis. There are: the principle of the freedom and dignity of every human person; the principle of the sociality of persons and of interdependence; and the need to serve the community or the common good.

Anglican social doctrine stresses that every human person has an infinite worth as a creature of God, and must never be treated as a means toward other ends. Respect for human dignity implies the fostering of freedom, in the sense that all persons should have the possibility to realize their full potential. This implies a concept of freedom that stresses not only formal autonomy, but also a material freedom to realize one's preferences together with others. The second common feature is the stress on human interdependence (and, ultimately, dependence on God). This point is made in all the documents analysed here and could be understood as a critique of any policy which gives priority to the individual person to the extent that the communal character of human existence is downplayed. One frequently repeated example is the critique of neo-liberal solutions to the problem of welfare in *Not Just for the Poor* (§ 7.33, 7.47). A system of welfare that relies on private charity and the family for support of the needy does not, according to this report, take seriously that 'there are responsibilities which must properly be assumed by society as a whole', since we are dependent on a larger societal context for the conditions of our social situation.

The third common feature is the strong emphasis on the church's obligation to community service. Reports such as *Faith in the City* and *Faithful Cities*, statements made by the hierarchy of the church, and the concrete actions of the church on both national and local levels, all bear witness to this fact. It should also be noted that the sense of obligation to serve the community – whether local, national or indeed international – is connected to the ecumenical spirit of the Church of England. At the local level the church co-operates with other churches and denominations on a wide range of issues, and at both national and international levels, it is an active partner in more formal ecumenical co-operation (Middlemiss 2004).

Themes in Local Theologies

As we saw in Chapter 3, ecclesiology is a theological subdiscipline which explores the self-understanding of Christian churches. It can be thought of as the study of the Christian churches' view of their own identity. In his pioneering book *Ecclesiology in Context*, the Dutch practical theologian Johannes A. van der Ven discusses identity as a fundamental concept in ecclesiology; in this he makes a distinction between the *basis* and the *identity* of a local church (van der Ven 1996).[17] The basis of a local church is the specific Christian and church tradition to which it belongs. For example, the Catholic parishes in Vicenza have the Catholic Church, its traditions, history and structure as their basis. It is a major thing for a local church to change its basis, and is seldom done. To change basis means to dissociate oneself from a tradition. Even if a local church or its representatives criticize the church leadership or traditional theology, they seldom contemplate a change of this nature.

They might, however, want to transform the *identity* of the local church. Van der Ven identifies four dimensions of a local church's identity: context, convictions, vision and mission. The *context* refers to the geographical, cultural, political, legal and social setting of the local church, which determines the presuppositions for the church's reflections on its own place in that society. For example, the French idea of *laïcité* – implying a strict separation of church and state – makes the situation of the French Catholic Church radically different from that in Germany or Italy, even if the basis of the local church in each of these cases is the Catholic tradition. In a similar fashion, the state–church character of the Lutheran Church of Norway gives it a different outlook from the Church of Württemberg. Questions about the organization of the church can also be subsumed under this dimension.

The *convictions* of a local church are the answer that the church would give to the question: 'What do we believe?' These convictions make up the doctrine of the church, covering a wide range of questions about God, salvation, human nature, morality and so forth. According to van der Ven, convictions of this sort also underpin the answer the local church would give to a further question: 'Who are we?' – thereby expressing its *vision* for the church community. This vision could be expressed in some sort of ecclesiological model, as for example 'the people of God', or 'folk church', or it could be a more vaguely formulated idea of the church as an instrument of God's love (van der Ven 1996: 152). Closely connected to the vision of the church is its view of its own *mission*. In expressing its mission, the church answers the question: 'What are we striving after', or 'What is our perceived *task*'? Asking about mission in this context means posing questions about the church's specific focus: should this be exclusively on spiritual matters, or should the church also engage in struggles for social justice (van der Ven 1996: 152)?

In analysing the implicit and explicit theologies of the local churches that have been studied in the WREP project, I will make use of van der Ven's dimensions of identity. However, I have simplified the model in order to make it more useful in the context of this study. Specifically, vision and mission will be discussed under the same heading. Structuring the theological interpretation of the case studies

---

[17]   The term 'basis' might seem somewhat awkward in English. However, since it is the term used in the English translation of van der Ven's book *Ecclesiology in Context*, I have kept it. An alternative concept could perhaps be *fundamental identity*. For a critical perspective on van der Ven, see Ideström (2009: 49–50).

according to this model has several advantages. First, it will make it easier to identify tensions between the local and national/international church structures. For instance, by making a distinction between the basis and the identity of a church it will be easier to interpret the fact that some Catholic interviewees want their church to change in a direction which, from a more conservative and 'official' Catholic point of view, could be seen as a move towards the 'Protestantization' of the Catholic Church. But even the interviewees who wish for major changes in their church do not, it seems, want to convert to Protestantism, presumably because this would imply a shift of ecclesial *basis*.

Secondly, using van der Ven's dimensions of identity will make it easier to identify theologically relevant themes and draw fruitful comparisons between the cases. By differentiating between questions belonging to context and questions pertaining to vision or mission it will be easier to point to similarities (perhaps unexpected ones) between cases belonging to different ecclesial bases, and to discuss the relation between social context and theological outlook.

Dimensions of Identity I: Contexts

One of the most theologically complicated questions emerging from the case studies concerns what kinds of organizations and activities count as belonging to the church. This might seem a strange question, but it is in fact one of the most important theological aspects of the study. From a sociological point of view, it might be possible to stipulate a relevant definition of 'church', thereby demarcating what kinds of activities and organizational structures should be included. But when it comes to theology, there is a normative aspect already present in the material which makes this much more complicated.

In almost all the cases studied, the majority church is clearly present in different organizational structures, and it is not self-evident what should or should not be counted as 'church'. The most obvious problem is the ecclesial character of more or less independent Christian organizations operating within the welfare sector. Do they belong to the church or not? What would a 'yes' or 'no' to this question imply theologically? In the Swedish case this problem is illustrated by the Holy Trinity Association for Diaconal Work (Heliga Trefaldighets Diakoniförening), or the Diaconal Council, as it is called in everyday speech. The Council is an independent foundation which offers financial assistance, but also tries to provide long-term solutions to the social problems of people in need. It is chaired by a senior priest from the parish of Heliga Trefaldighet in Gävle. Apart from the requirement that the chair of the foundation should be a priest in this parish, there are few formal ties between the Diaconal Council and the Church of Sweden in Gävle. However, it might very reasonably be assumed in the eyes of the public and indeed of most church employees that the work done by the Council is a part of the activity of the Church of Sweden (Edgardh Beckman et al. 2006).

A similar case is that of the Church City Mission in Drammen, Norway. As in Gävle, there are two different types of church-related agents operating in the field of welfare in Drammen: the Church of Norway parishes, and church-based associations like the Church City Mission and the ecumenical Blue Cross, which mainly work with people addicted to drugs. The Church City Mission's activities are relatively limited, but – as we have seen already – it is held in high esteem both by church representatives and by the population at large. As Angell and Wyller show (2006; Angell 2010), the Church City Mission presents a challenge both to the municipality and the local church. The leader is the only church representative who stands out as a significant critical voice, often writing articles or being interviewed in the media on social and ethical issues.

Among the Lutheran churches included in the study, the German case is of special interest with regard to the relationship between church structures in a narrow sense and church-affiliated organizations. This is significant not least because of the size of the latter. In Reutlingen, the impressively large diaconal institution Bruderhaus Diakonie is one of the major church-related actors within the area of social welfare. At the same time, as pointed out by Leis-Peters (2006; 2010), there is an ongoing debate in Germany about how the different church-related welfare organizations relate to theological understandings of the church. The large diaconal institutions operate much like companies, and receive direct funding from the state. Within the church, therefore, their Christian identity is sometimes questioned. At the same time, however, the work of the diaconal organizations is often seen as contributing to the good reputation of the church; as a result church leaders underline the importance of keeping the church and the diaconal institutions together (July 2005).

The nature of the relationship between the church structure and church-related associations is also an issue in the Catholic and Orthodox cases. In the Catholic case, Caritas is perhaps the best known organization, working in social and development issues all over the world. Caritas Internationalis is an umbrella organization for the various national Caritas associations, such as Secours Catholique France and Caritas Italiana. Caritas is formally recognized by the authorities of the Catholic Church, and often headed up by members of the hierarchy on both international and national levels. Associations such as Caritas have a long history within Catholicism, and are recognized in official church statements as a way of organizing lay participation in the church's ministry. In the Apostolic Exhortation *Christifideles Laici*, Pope John Paul II (1988) stated that the organization of the laity in church-related associations is an outflow of the mission given to all Christians in baptism. They do not need any specific authorization from the hierarchy, as long as they conform to certain criteria of ecclesiality, such as giving priority to 'the call of every Christian to holiness', and expressing communion with the pope and church authorities (*Christifideles Laici* § 30). This freedom to form lay associations is also recognized in Canon Law.

There is therefore a formal recognition of these associations as expressions of the church's mission in the world; at the same time they are recognized by Canon Law and the church authorities as being authentic actions of the church. The data from our case studies tell us, however, that their relationship to the church structure is not always perceived in this way. As one of the church representatives in the French case study puts it:

> If all of a sudden there were no more Catholic welfare associations, the state couldn't manage! But people have problems seeing the link between the church as an institution and the fact that the Secours Catholique helps thousands of people. (Valasik 2006: 149)

In the Orthodox case of Thiva and Livadeia, there are various private institutions with no formal or administrative links to the Church of Greece, but which still claim to be a part of the church and guided by Orthodox faith. In Darlington also, there are independent welfare organizations with imprecise relationships to the Church of England. At the same time, there is a relatively high degree of ecumenical co-operation on welfare issues, a particular characteristic of the English case. Together with other denominations, the Anglican parishes co-operate in the Town Centre Churches' Group. There is also a Town City Mission, founded in 1838, which works on an ecumenical basis, alongside several other organizations which present themselves as working within a Christian perspective (Middlemiss 2006).

Another issue raised by the contextual dimension is that of structural tensions within the church. A good example can be found in the tensions between local parishes and the diocese of Vicenza. The parishes in the urban area of Vicenza are relatively wealthy and active as welfare providers. Not only do they constitute 'small welfare centre[s]' (Frisina 2006: 186) in their local setting, but they also support overseas activities, such as missionary schools and hospitals. The bishop, according to Frisina, has tried to create a coherent structure of the diocese's welfare activities, but this has been difficult due to the parishes' desire to act independently.

At a much more serious level, the tensions between the former Bishop of Evreux, Jacques Gaillot, and the Pope, offer a further illustration of structural tension. Monsignor Gaillot was dismissed as Bishop of Evreux by Pope John Paul II in 1995, after long-standing conflicts with the church authorities on a wide range of issues. The removal of Gaillot, although within the limits of the canonical authority of the Pope, caused great unease within the Diocese of Evreux, and indeed among many Catholics in France (Valasik 2006). One interviewee expresses her feelings as follows:

> I felt it was really unjust, let's say there was my first reaction and then another later. When it happened, my reaction was, well, if that's what the church is, as Rome knows better than we do, I give up. Completely discouraged. My second reaction was: we let everyone against him act as they wanted to and did we, ourselves, speak strongly enough to Rome, saying we were happy as we were? So there's a sort of guilty feeling somewhere, we didn't do our job. We let others act for us. (Valasik 2006: 150)

This quotation, as well as the example from Vicenza, shows that at times there can be a distinct lack of confidence between the different organizational levels of a church. These two examples are both taken from a Catholic context, but similar tensions can be found in other case studies – as in the Greek case, where (as we have seen already) there is considerable evidence of distrust regarding the national church in general and Archbishop Christodoulos in particular (Fokas 2006; Fokas and Molokotos-Liederman 2010). Using van der Ven's terminology, one of the theologically interesting questions to which these observations gives rise is how far distrust between the local levels and national/international levels in a church can go, before this affects not only the identity but also the basis of a local church.

In my view, both the relationship of the more or less independent church-related organizations to the church, and the issue of tensions between different organizational levels, could be interpreted theologically as questions about the connection between *autonomy* and *communion*. Werner Jeanrond (2001) has offered a theological interpretation of the link between the church and the autonomous human being in the contemporary European situation. According to his analysis, the church is often confronted with conflicting expectations from its members. On the one hand, the church is expected to respect members' autonomy, but on the other it is also expected to provide a community where people can find comfort and security. From the perspective of the church authorities, this can be problematic, since it is difficult to develop a stable community of people who have autonomy as their top priority. Jeanrond asks whether the Christian congregation is simply a 'function of the individual Christian's interest for developing full autonomy and personal identity' (2001: 136), or, conversely, whether the individual is merely a function of the church. He argues for a 'mutual critical relation' (2001: 144) between the autonomous person and the church as a community. For Jeanrond, autonomy is related to the Christian understanding of love: without autonomy, there can be no true love. The community and the individual should therefore relate to each other in love.

Jeanrond's argument is theologically controversial. I will not dwell further on its shortcomings here, but will rather point to the fact that the relationship between individual autonomy, the autonomy of the local church or church-related organizations, and the church as a national or international organization, is theologically complex and needs reflection on multiple levels. Tensions caused by a striving for autonomy on the one hand, and respecting the identity and basis of the church organization and tradition on the other, can moreover be found in several of the case studies (Valasik 2006; 2010; Fokas 2006; Fokas and Molokotos-Liederman 2010; Frisina 2006; 2010). However, such tensions are not only found in the church. Rather, as Pettersson has pointed out in Chapter 2, they are examples of the wider process of individualization and the growing suspicion of large organizations that are commonplace in late modern European societies. Nonetheless, they pose a particular challenge to the Christian churches. All denominational traditions analysed here confess, in the Nicene Creed, their belief in the fundamental unity of the church. What this means in practice, and how important it is in relation to other aspects of the tradition, continues to be debated.

One solution might be that the church at all levels ceases to worry about institutional unity, affirming instead an autonomous search for meaning, independent of the ecclesiastical structures. This seems to be the conclusion of a priest in our English case study, whose answer to the question about his wishes for changes in the church is worth quoting at length:

> I think that whereas perhaps ten years ago ... one would have wanted to argue with people about how the institutional church was still really important, that it was worth fighting for, that even though they had been hurt by it and felt that it wasn't meeting their needs they needed to stick by it instead of looking for anything else. I don't think we would bother arguing now. You know if the church is stopping them doing whatever it is that gives life meaning, their dance or their music or whatever, well maybe they need to pursue that and maybe what the church, what they imagine the church is saying to them doesn't matter so very much. There is a kind of a more real, more ... that there is an invisible church. I think that we were always told that that was just some kind of heresy really, but I think that maybe that is the case, that maybe there is a church there that is people meeting together, where they happen to encounter one another as Christians that is the church and I think what one perhaps wants to say to people, well if you are meeting with your fellow Christians and if you love God and Jesus then that is fine, do that, that is the church and don't worry about the Church of England and all its trimmings. (Middlemiss 2006: 37)

Dimensions of Identity II: Convictions

There are, of course, many theological differences between the denominational traditions studied here – both in general, and with regard to social doctrine. To mention one example, traditional Lutheran and Orthodox interpretations of human nature and salvation are very different; Lutheran theology stresses that salvation is primarily about the forgiveness of sins, whereas Orthodox theology understands salvation primarily as *theosis*. And just as the doctrine of the two kingdoms is connected to a Lutheran understanding of salvation, so too are Orthodox personalism and the understanding of salvation as *theosis* related to each other. Differences such as these should not be downplayed, even if the social doctrines espoused by the traditions and the church leadership are not much reflected on at the local level – and even if local church representatives sometimes explicitly distance themselves from such teaching (Edgardh Beckman et al. 2006: 70).

One striking observation from our case studies is, however, that representatives of all the local churches represented in WREP often – but by no means always – express *similar* convictions and theological arguments with regard to social doctrine, ecclesiology and social work. When the Bible is referred to, for example, it seems as if the same verses function over and over again as scriptural references in arguments about church and welfare. Most such references are indirect and quite short. Generally it can be said that representatives of the public authorities and the population as a whole refer to New Testament texts, almost always the gospels. Representatives of the church do likewise, but they also include reference to the prophetic literature in the Old Testament (Middlemiss 2006). Among the New Testament texts, Jesus' saying in Matthew 25 that what we have done to those in need, we have done to him, is referred to by a number of the interviewees (see Edgardh Beckman et al. 2006 and Fokas 2006). The commandment in Matthew 22:39 to love one's neighbour as oneself is also referenced by representatives of the local churches, as well as by public authorities and the population as a whole, as one of the core values of the Christian ethos (as in Fokas 2006 and Yeung 2006). Unsurprisingly, the parable of the Good Samaritan is frequently cited as a reference point (Leis-Peters 2006).

Two central concepts in Christian social ethics are *love* and *justice*. Being biblical concepts, they have been considered essential characteristics of God in Christian theology through the centuries. Their exact meanings and implications for Christian practice have, of course, been fiercely debated, as has the question of their mutual relationship (Forrester 1997). In what follows, I shall use love and justice as analytical tools in order to structure the basic theological and ethical convictions of the local churches in the case studies. The character of the empirical material does not allow for any detailed analysis of the meaning given to these concepts. As analytical tools, therefore, I define justice and love in the widest possible sense. Love indicates the will to do good to our fellow human beings or, indeed, to the whole of creation (Forell 1989). The implication of this meaning of love is that it is not motivated by self-interest. It is our neighbours who are in focus, and they are seen as ends in themselves, not as instruments for realizing our own hopes and desires.[18] Justice indicates ideals of how goods, burdens and power should be distributed in a morally acceptable way.

The relationship between love and justice in Christian ethics has been understood in different ways. Kamergrauzis (2001) identifies three models for how this connection could be interpreted. The first model is called the 'independent ethics of love' (Kamergrauzis 2001: 99). According to this model, love and justice are conflicting values. Love is understood as personal and self-sacrificial giving. As such, it is mainly an ideal for personal relationships, and cannot be a foundation for social ethics, which instead should be governed by justice (understood as something quite different, giving to each person a fair share of goods). The second model is the 'identical ethics of love', and does not recognize any distinction between justice and love (Kamergrauzis 2001: 100). Either love is reduced to justice, or justice is declared irrelevant as a principle in Christian ethics. The third model is the 'relational ethics of

---

[18]   By this I do not claim that love cannot also include love of oneself. I cannot discuss this question at length, but the ideal of self-sacrificing love is also problematic in that it tends to reinforce the subordination of women within welfare, since women constitute the vast majority of welfare providers. See Chapter 3.

love', according to which love and justice are different but related principles (2001: 102). According to this model, justice is seen as an approximation of love. Love, in this sense, is the moral principle of the Kingdom of God. But in an imperfect world with scarce resources, justice is needed. However, the principle of love is also a part of the principle of justice, implying that all persons should be treated as ends in themselves.[19]

In the Greek case, love is seen as the basic moral principle of the church. This could be understood as an expression of Orthodox personalism, stressing the self-sacrificing love of Christ as a model for Christians. A representative of a welfare institution of the church says,

> Our church is based on offering [*prosfora*], sacrifice, self-denial – at least, this is what Christ taught us: love others as yourself. Not that we all Orthodox people or societies, or anyone, do this. But these are the prototypes of our church, [to do this] without expecting something in return. (Fokas 2006: 245)

Another interviewee (Fokas 2006: 252) in a privately-run welfare institution argues that 'welfare is not something for me to pull out my wallet and give in the form of money'. Rather, she argues, 'what needs to exist is the power of love'. Welfare should be an outflow of love. If social work, like visiting the lonely or helping the sick, should 'happen for some personal interest [gain] or in an offensive way, better that it doesn't happen'. According to this interviewee, it seems to be the quality of the intention that determines the moral value of the action. She is by no means unique in the Greek case study, where love is seen as the core value of the church, formulated in meta-ecclesiological terms in the statement 'the church is love'.

From statements such as these it is, of course, difficult to say anything about how love is related to justice. The sentiments are compatible both with the model of an independent ethics of love and with the model of an identity between love and justice. The understanding of justice as an approximation of love is, however, more difficult to reconcile with the importance of sacrificial love as a motive for true welfare, since the latter standpoint puts more weight on the intentions guiding actions than on the outcomes. But since justice is not alluded to as a central concept in the theological reflection of the Orthodox Church in Thiva and Livadeia, it seems reasonable to conclude that an identity model accounts best for the obvious emphasis on love as the guiding principle of the church's welfare activities. It could also explain the rather hesitant attitude towards the church's participation in public debate, remembering that most church representatives emphasize the need for humility in the church's approach.

The Italian case gives a very different picture. If the Orthodox Church in Thiva and Livadeia stresses the value of self-sacrificing love, representatives of the

---

[19]   The third model is perhaps one of the most influential models in Christian ethics in the twentieth century, with advocates such as Reinhold Niebuhr and Ronald H. Preston.

Catholic Church in Vicenza understand welfare as being connected to 'citizenship rights', the 'fight against poverty' and a 'redistribution of wealth' (Frisina 2006: 191). Moreover, the Ursuline nuns in Vicenza stress the importance of the church's prophetic role, and the necessity to work for the rights of deprived people. They also stress the gendered aspect of social injustice, pointing to the fact that poverty 'afflicts above all women: foreign women, divorced or separated Italian women, single mothers' (Frisina 2006: 194). There is an evident conflict in the Italian case study, in which some of the participants in the focus-group interviews feel that the church is not radical enough, and that there is a tension between the 'official/institutional church' and the 'church from below' or the community of believing citizens (Frisina 2006: 202; 2010).

The Church City Mission in Drammen, Norway, explicitly stresses the relationship between love and social justice, prioritizing the needs of the weakest members of society. A statement on the value-basis of the Church City Missions in Norway says,

> Our goal is to meet people with love and respect. We are present in town on behalf of Jesus Christ. In all our activities where other people are involved our view of man is the most decisive factor influencing how we behave [...] Our view of the person provides us with a view of society which commits us always to talk and act on behalf of the lowest ranked people in society. (Angell and Wyller 2006: 105)

Similarly, the parish union in Lahti, Finland, stated in 2004 that the social work of the church aims to promote 'Christian faith-based justice, participation and neighbourly love in the lives of individuals and the society, as well as globally' (Yeung 2006: 159). In the Finnish case, as elsewhere, there are, of course, different opinions among church representatives regarding how much emphasis the church should put on social justice in general and welfare activities in particular. Some argue that the church's main role is spiritual and has to do with the care of the religious rather than material needs of people. Even so, it is clear that the concept of justice is more important in both the implicit and explicit theologies of the 'Western' cases in WREP than in the 'Eastern', Orthodox case.

If, in the case of Thiva and Livadeia, the understanding of the connection between justice and love in Christian ethics lies somewhere between an independence model and an identity model, it seems reasonable to interpret the other cases – generally speaking – as instances of the relational model. The core value in these cases seems to be the love of Christ, which Christians ought to imitate. In practice, however, this is often seen as a commitment to social justice and advocacy of the welfare state, including sharp, sometimes very sharp, criticism of the present social order.

In sum, there seem to be significant differences between the Orthodox case on the one hand, and the 'Western' cases on the other hand, when it comes to the basic convictions of the local churches. Orthodox personalism must not be confused with individualism: it is deeply communitarian in character. The differences, however, should not be exaggerated. It is more a question of where one starts. Orthodox social doctrine is combined with a more optimistic anthropology than many of its Protestant and Catholic counterparts. It assumes (see above) that any real transformation of society must start with the transformation of persons. If people are transformed, justice will be the result. In a more pessimistic anthropology, as is the case in traditional Lutheranism, it is considered unrealistic to hope for real moral transformation of persons this side of the second coming. This in turn implies that 'love' has to be approximated in justice, a principle that can guide social policy and action.

This analysis of justice and love as basic convictions of the local churches can, then, be concluded as follows: despite the fact that many of the local representatives are critical of the hierarchy of their churches, they seem to be more or less in tune with the main characteristics of the social doctrines of their respective traditions. The reasons for such consonance are worth pondering.

Dimensions of Identity III: Visions and Missions

It is obvious from the case studies that there are many operative ecclesiologies at work in the respective local churches. In some cases the respondents feel that there is a distinct conflict between their ecclesiological ideal and the teachings of the church hierarchy and/or other ecclesiological ideals at the local level. In other cases, the level of tension is much lower. With this in mind, the operative ecclesiologies present in the different localities will be organized with the help of the following model, consisting of two ideal-typical theological visions for the church, and two ideal-typical understandings of the church's mission within the field of welfare (see Figure 4.1).

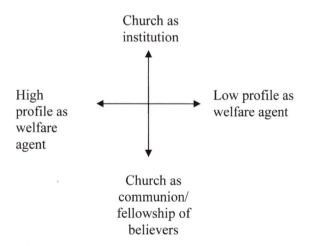

Figure 4.1   The vision and mission of the churches as welfare agents

The first axis in the model is marked by the ideal-typical visions of the church as *institution* and the church as *communion* or *fellowship of believers*. An ecclesiology that lays a lot of weight on the institutional character of the church emphasizes the organization as theologically the most central aspect of the church. This understanding of the church as primarily an institution can be conjoined with different denominational traditions: in the Lutheran tradition, for example, some of the Nordic conceptions of the folk church come close to this type. In Swedish folk-church ecclesiology it has been common to understand the Church of Sweden as an 'institution of grace'.[20] According to this kind of thinking, the church as an institution is a creation of God placed in the world as a means of salvation through its celebration of the sacraments and its proclamation in words and deeds (Ekstrand 2002). In Catholic theology, an institutional understanding of the church was commonplace until the Second Vatican Council (Dulles 2002). It based its ecclesiology on the understanding of the church as a perfect society (*societas perfecta*), organized hierarchically with the ministers of the church as governors and teachers, and the laity as receivers of the grace administered by the church.

At the other end of the axis is an understanding of the church as a communion or as a fellowship of believers. 'Communion' and 'fellowship of believers' are two variants within this ideal type. Both stress the social character of the church, but the church is not seen primarily as an institution, even if the need for organization is acknowledged. 'Communion' in the present analysis refers to ecclesiological positions that stress the organic and mystical character of the church, as well as interpretations of the church as the people of God (Dulles 2002). 'Fellowship of believers' refers to understandings of the church that tend to be more individualistic in their approach and interpret the church as an association of the followers of Christ (Kärkkäinen 2002; Dulles 2002).

The second axis has at its poles two ideal-typical understandings of the mission of the church as a welfare agent. I have chosen to label these as 'high profile' and 'low profile' respectively. Each of these profiles has two dimensions, which can be described as 'emphasis on social work' and 'emphasis on prophetic voice'.[21] As we have seen in Chapter 2, these dimensions do not necessarily go together: a church can have a low profile on one of the dimensions, and a high profile on the other. Basically, however, the two ideal-typical poles of the axis reflect different understandings of the church's primary tasks. A low profile as welfare agent (in one or both dimensions) tends to go together with the view that it is not the church's business to engage in the everyday affairs of this world, but rather to prioritize the eternal well-being of its faithful. In this account, if the church should act within the welfare field, care must be taken that this does not distract it from its primary

---

[20]   The term 'institution of grace' corresponds to the Swedish 'nådemedelsanstalt' and the German 'Gnadesanstalt'.

[21]   I am indebted to Anne Birgitta Pessi, the researcher for the Finnish case, for Figure 4.1 and for the concepts outlined in this section (Pessi 2010).

task. A high profile as welfare agent implies that the church's active engagement is seen as an important way of fulfilling its calling in the world.

Visions In the Swedish case, there is a tendency towards an institutional understanding of the church, even if more communion-centred perspectives can also be found. A priest in Gävle asserts that the Church of Sweden is not centred on its members. The Church is not trying to convert people, but to be a part of society's everyday life. One point often made by the representatives of the church in the Swedish case is that the church is open for everyone, irrespective of their religious qualifications (Edgardh Beckman et al. 2006: 72). Interestingly, the most outspoken critique of the ideal of the open and welcoming folk church is offered by a local official who has left the church: 'If you are going to be a member of the church, you should have faith. I am sceptical about the idea of the folk church, because it encompasses everything' (Edgardh Beckman et al. 2006: 73).

In Darlington, representatives of the Church of England who were asked about their wishes for changes in the church gave one very clear answer: for the most part they did not wish the church to be disestablished. According to Middlemiss (2006; 2010), they argued that the present parish system, where the church is present in every part of the country, is an important aspect of the church's character. Stressing the parish system as a theologically important aspect of the church could reasonably be interpreted as leaning towards the institutional ideal-type – but the picture is not so clear-cut. The priest in Darlington already quoted (Middlemiss 2006: 37) seems – somewhat hesitantly – to question an institutional understanding of the church. According to him, 'maybe there is a church there that is people meeting together, where they happen to encounter one another as Christians that is the church'. Such a view is a clear example of the 'fellowship' type of ecclesiology.

Leis-Peters (2006; 2010) observes that when the churches run social services with public funding, the services have to be open for all, irrespective of their affiliation to the church. It also requires a high level of formal organization. As Leis-Peters points out, this is not ecclesiologically neutral. The Evangelical Lutheran Church of Württemberg is considered to be a stronghold of Lutheran pietism, which is associated with a congregational ecclesiology. In such a pietistic notion of the church, the social work of the congregation should direct itself primarily towards its own members. It might therefore be expected that the church representatives in Reutlingen would score close to the communion/fellowship of believer type of ecclesiology. However, this does not seem to be the case; an overwhelming majority of the respondents advocate a more open folk-church approach, which would score closer to the institutional ideal-type in my model. Leis-Peters proposes three possible explanations for this unexpected outcome. First, an obvious reason is a reluctance to put public funding at risk by arguing for a less open approach to social service. The second explanation argues as follows: if you are working within the social service organizations of the church, you are already likely to have a more open ecclesiology, of a folk-church nature. Thirdly, it might be the case that people's theological approaches change when they begin to work in the area of welfare provision (Leis-Peters 2006: 114)

What is especially striking in the French and Italian cases is that many respondents speak about tensions between the hierarchical church on the one hand and more radical laypeople, priests and members of religious orders on the other. This perception seems to be shared both by representatives of the church and by the population at large. It should be noted, however, that the case study reports do not give a total picture of the Catholic Church in Evreux and Vicenza. It is not possible to say therefore if this tension represents a more general view, or is merely the position of a minority.

As already noted, one participant in a focus group in Evreux strongly criticizes the Catholic Church, seeing Jacques Gaillot as a notable and positive exception: 'The Roman Catholic Church is against everything: condoms, sexual relationships … It's not concerned by the fact that AIDS is rampant in Africa! And when there's a good one, he gets fired!' (Valasik 2006: 153). Indeed the Gaillot affair seems to have caused a long-lasting trauma for the Catholic Church in Evreux, and brought ecclesiological problems to the fore in many different ways. Some church representatives feel 'completely discouraged' (Valasik 2006: 150) by the actions taken by Rome, while others point to the universal character of the church and the role of the Pope as its leader. For example, a priest expresses a certain irritation regarding a question on this matter by saying that the church is not a democracy, and that he could not therefore be expected to have an opinion (Valasik 2006: 151). Another church representative, commenting on those who left the church in the wake of the affair, says:

> They were seeing the church differently, with a different face, incarnated by Jacques Gaillot. But one has to be rational, was it the man or was it the message? The universal church has a leader, the Pope, so either you are in the church or you are not, it's complicated. (Valasik 2006: 151)

In the Italian case, representatives from private social organizations, at least, wish the institutional side of the church to be played down. One respondent says that he 'who loves his life is ready to lose it, the church has always told this to others … But the institution refuses to die, it goes on … ignoring the suffering of those who try to tread on new paths' (Frisina 2006: 206). The same respondent also makes a clear distinction between the official church and the ideas he has found in mystical literature. According to him, this means a refusal to acknowledge institutional boundaries in religion. Questioning the need for the church as a mediator between God and humanity, he continues: 'We worker-priests suggest a lighter kind of mediation, a democratization of the church … But the church as an institution is still enormously heavy' (2006: 210).

The more or less radical critics of the Catholic Church in Evreux or Vicenza, then, whether they consider themselves members of the church or not, seem to make a distinction between two ways of being church, roughly corresponding to the ideal-types of the church as institution and the church as a fellowship of believers or communion. In their opinion, the church organization is hierarchical and undemocratic, with a leadership that shows little acceptance of more radical perspectives about the church and its engagement with society. Perhaps another way of typologizing these tensions is to use the distinction between the 'church with a male face' and the 'church with a female face', as in Ninna Edgardh's contribution to this volume. The 'church with a male face' would, roughly, correspond with the understanding of the church as an institution, while the understanding of the church as a fellowship of believers has close connections with the 'church with a female face' as described in the previous chapter.

It is interesting to note that the official teaching of the Catholic Church – at least since the promulgation of *Lumen Gentium* (the dogmatic constitution on the church) by the Second Vatican Council (1964) – has avoided overemphasizing the institutional understanding of the church. Instead, it has interpreted the church as the body of Christ and the people of God. These meta-ecclesiological metaphors would score closer to the communion type of ecclesiology as described in my model. But *Lumen Gentium* also stresses the hierarchical nature of the church; and, at least in the eyes of the critics in Evreux and Vicenza, it seems to be this dimension that comes to mind first. Whether or not this should be seen as a real conflict between official teachings on the church and the operative ecclesiologies at work at the local level is not possible to say on the basis of the evidence from the cases – but it can, at least, be said that such tensions exist.

In the case of Thiva and Livadeia, the ecclesiological pattern is different. This is not unexpected, since Orthodox theology differs in many ways from Catholic and Protestant thinking. The church is not so much described as an institution, but nor is it a fellowship of believers in the pietistic sense. Rather, the church is understood as a mystical communion. There is considerable critique of the church on the national level raised by the respondents, not least of Archbishop Christodoulos. One respondent says: 'Sometimes we feel that the Archbishop, Christodoulos, speaks for the Church of Greece. This is wrong. He expresses the voice of the church, and this he should do when he is invested the authority by the Holy Synod' (Fokas 2006: 246). The national leadership is seen as communal in character, and the Archbishop is criticized for adopting a more individualistic leadership role.

Conversely, several respondents in the Greek case stress that the church is love. On the one hand, this describes their view that the motives of church representatives in the sphere of social welfare are more altruistic than those of civil servants. It can also, however, be interpreted as a sign of the communion perspective of Orthodox ecclesiology. As Archbishop Anastasios (Yannoulatos) writes, the church is seen as Christ's 'mystical body' (2003: 202). Of course, it still has institutional traits – but it is, essentially, a divine communion of love.

In conclusion, it must be stressed that there is always a danger in constructing ideal types of ecclesiology. No ideal type can lay claim to cover reality in all its complexities. Moreover, reducing the ideal types to two, as I have done in analysing the visions of the local churches in the case studies, might seem an illicit over-simplification. However, as long as it is remembered that ideal types are constructed *for analytical purposes only*, I think it is legitimate. All the local churches studied in the WREP project are majority churches, and are closely connected historically with the culture of their respective countries. They are also relatively large organizations, and in the Catholic case international. This makes the ecclesiological aspect of the institution especially interesting. Whatever the theological ideal might be, the local churches in these cases cannot avoid being parts of a large organizational structure as long as they retain their ecclesial basis. It is for this reason that we need to identify how different ecclesiological ideals – explicit or implicit – relate to the given character of the institution.

From this point of view, one of the most interesting results of the analysis is that the institutional character of the church seems to be most radically questioned in the Catholic cases of Evreux and Vicenza. In the Scandinavian cases, this is not perceived as a major issue in the same sense, even if there is criticism of the church. In the English case, disestablishment is not seen as an attractive option by most representatives of the Church of England. That said, being an established church also implies being a relatively well-defined organization. Indeed there is a very Anglican tension between being both in favour of establishment and at the same time advocating a more radical interpretation of the church as a fellowship of believers.

A less unexpected finding is that the Orthodox case differs from its Protestant and Catholic counterparts. The institutional side of the Orthodox Church is not regarded in the same way – as a result, the need for a structured organization is not really questioned. Conversely, it is possible to be quite critical of the organized church without this leading to a questioning of one's Orthodox identity, which seems to indicate an understanding of the church as communion rather than primarily as an institution.

Missions   It is obvious from the case studies that the church representatives do not reject church involvement in welfare provision as such (see also Chapter 2). But there is a wide range of opinions about whether it should have a high or low profile, and whether priority should be given to the dimension of social work or the dimension of prophetic critique. There is, moreover, no *logical* connection between how a specific ecclesiological position scores on the institution–communion axis and how it scores on the welfare–profile axis. It is, in principle, possible to combine either an institutionally-oriented or a communion/fellowship-oriented ecclesiology with any position on the profile scale. In practice, however, it might be more difficult, especially if an emphasis on the prophetic voice is combined with a *de facto* institutional ecclesiology. Large ecclesial organizations, especially if they have public funding for welfare schemes and/or have a very pronounced folk-church character, may find it difficult to be a critical voice in society. This may, therefore, lead to tension between a theologically argued will to be prophetic, and an implicit theology in which social work is prioritized.

A representative of the Church of Sweden expresses very clearly how difficult it might be to combine the role of being a folk church – with a vast majority of the population as members – with having a high profile in prophetic critique:

> But a voice, which puts the pressure on the authorities to prioritize this or that
> – I do not think that the church can be that … The role of the lobbyist does not
> suit the church. But I believe in pointing out difficulties and drawing attention to
> minorities with problems, and such things. (Edgardh Beckman et al. 2006: 54)

In both the Swedish and the Norwegian cases, it is also clear that the church has not been very active in trying to influence local politics on a broad scale. Analyses of local newspaper debates show that in Gävle church representatives seldom take the opportunity to debate controversial issues in the media. And in Drammen, it is almost exclusively the leader of the Church City Mission who acts in this way, at least as evidenced during our period of research. In the Finnish case as well, church representatives seem reluctant to be too critical in local policy debates.

This relatively low profile with respect to the dimension of prophetic critique does not always correspond to what many respondents think should be the case. Many of them, for example, make comments like the Norwegian interviewee who stated, 'Yes, in principle the church should engage itself [in the public debate]. It should be active, speak up, be critical and creative' (Angell and Wyller 2006: 120). One way to interpret this tension could be to say that there are differences between the explicit and implicit theologies of the church when it comes to the importance of prophetic critique. Another angle of interpretation is that 'individuals matter' – to use a phrase from Per Pettersson's contribution to this volume. If and when a church employee or volunteer feels strongly about the prophetic role of the church, he or she will personally engage in the public debate as a church representative.

In all the Scandinavian cases, church respondents are generally positive about the church's engagement in practical social work. But this is often combined with advocacy of a strong welfare state, which in practice means a more limited, complementary role for the church. Indeed some respondents are quite critical towards the church's role in social work, like the Finnish priest who says, 'We should not have the present form of welfare at church at all in Finland! They should simply focus on spiritual work or on aiding third-world countries' (Yeung 2006: 176).

If one were to assess the Scandinavian cases in terms of how the mission of the church as welfare agent is understood in the operative ecclesiology of the local churches, it is difficult to avoid the conclusion that a low profile is preferred. With few exceptions, the local churches are not very active in public debates and policy formation – even if they express a wish to be more dynamic. When it comes to social work, they quite consciously take on a complementary role to that of the public authorities. This could be seen as the Lutheran two-kingdoms doctrine put into practice, even if it is not explicitly perceived as such by the church representatives themselves. But the Lutheran doctrine also contains resources for criticism of the state. These critical resources seem to be applied more on a national level than the local, as in the Finnish bishops' document *Towards the Common Good*.

It is obvious that the church has a high profile as an active welfare agent in the German case. This is due to the structure of the German welfare system in general, and is unsurprising. But there is also much agreement on the importance of prophetic critique among church representatives, who have often reflected both theologically and practically on what this dimension might mean in practice, despite the difficulties of discerning exactly how the churches should act in this respect. Of course, as one of the interviewees argues, complexity is not in itself an argument against participating: 'Anyway, I think it is important that the church says: "This is wrong!" Even without having an alternative solution. Because it is important to continue to think about alternatives' (Leis-Peters 2006: 93).

In the Greek case, church representatives are somewhat hesitant about the dimension of prophetic critique. On the one hand, they suggest that the church should take part in public debate – but, on the other, it should do so very carefully, and act in a humble way. As one priest argues: 'I don't think the church should have a public voice on every issue ... this is not the nature of the church. It is not the job of the church to solve social problems. That's the job of the state' (Fokas 2006: 246).

The Church of England has a unique opportunity to voice criticism at a national political level, since its senior bishops still have seats in the House of Lords. This aspect of its establishment is considered an opportunity by respondents in Darlington. Being a part of the established political structures, the church can influence policy-making in the 'kind of traditional Church of England way of doing it, behind the scenes' (Middlemiss 2006: 35). Many local church representatives argue that expressing a prophetic voice is a specific task for the national church and the bishops. This kind of reasoning articulates the advantages of being an established, or at least legally privileged, church. Establishment means influence, and influence can be used in many ways: in order to legitimate, but also to question the social and political order. Nowhere else in the project has this been as clearly stated as in the case of Darlington. On the other hand, nowhere else in Europe does the church have similar representation in parliament.

In the French case, the principle of *laïcité* functions as an overarching principle in the church's reflection on its role as a welfare agent. Interestingly there is no clear evidence of church representatives radically questioning the principle as such. This also frames the understanding of the mission of the church as a welfare agent. *Laïcité* is, as Valasik (2006; 2010) argues, internalized in the thinking of the Catholic Church in France. This means that the church does not really have the option to be a strong prophetic voice, pressing for changes of policy in the public sphere. This does not, of course, prevent active lay people, priests or members of religious orders from having strong opinions on welfare policy and its provision by both the state and the church, but the framework of *laïcité* makes it difficult to conceive of a politically active church. A comparison with the Catholic Church in Vicenza makes this point clear. In Vicenza, Caritas plays an important role in welfare provision, and at least some of the church representatives argue for a politically active role. One respondent, for example, declares that the church has to 'exert pressure for the introduction of a minimum wage, for a change in immigration laws (people must have the right to move freely!), for a change in tax policies so that they are more progressive and the wealthy actually pay more than the poor' (Frisina 2006: 193).

As with the analysis of the visions of the local churches, constructing ideal types of different understandings of the church's mission as a welfare agent is complicated and runs the risk of over-simplification. But it also makes it quite clear that there is no obvious connection between the official social doctrine of the different church traditions and the implicit and explicit theologies at the local level (with the possible exception of the Orthodox case). For example, the fact that the Lutheran Church in Reutlingen is a major welfare actor while the Church of Sweden in Gävle is not cannot be explained by reference to Lutheran social doctrine. Rather, traditional doctrine should be seen as a resource for theological reflection as the local churches continuously interpret their mission as welfare agents. Similarly, standpoints about whether the church should have a high or low profile as a welfare agent, and whether it should prioritize the dimension of social work or prophetic critique, cannot be deduced from any of the social doctrines presented in this chapter. Rather, the local churches must relate their tradition to the circumstances in which they understand themselves to be called by God to be witnesses of salvation – and the case studies give ample evidence that they are doing precisely this.

Concluding Remarks

A very clear and important finding of our analysis is that, within the area of welfare provision, there are relatively few *theological* conflicts between official doctrine and local theology. Local theologies on welfare can usually be interpreted as falling within at least some of the possible interpretations of the official doctrines. This does not prevent individuals from having serious misgivings about official doctrine, but in general the local churches seem to fit quite well into the frameworks of central teaching. When the representatives of the local churches do criticize the leadership of the church, this is more likely to be related to ecclesiological questions such as the role of democracy in the governance of the church, or the relationship between clergy and laity, than to social doctrine proper.

However, this does not mean that there are *no* theological problems to be solved. In these concluding remarks, I do not aim to present solutions, but rather to point to three theological observations that can be made on the basis of the empirical material in relation to the official social doctrines of the churches. By posing these observations, I want to highlight some of the theological problems facing majority churches as welfare agents in contemporary Europe.

The first and most basic observation relates to the question of identity. Especially within the contextual dimension, this becomes very clear. The individualizing processes of modernity quite clearly affect the identity of the local churches, prompting a number of searching questions. Should the churches, as one priest in

Darlington seems to argue, accept that Christians do not have to worry about 'the Church of England and all its trimmings', or, similarly, *any* institutional church? It is easy to see that such a standpoint has consequences for the local church's ability to be an active welfare agent. Collective action, whether in welfare provision or as a prophetic voice, demands some sort of organization with which the members feel solidarity. One of the main theological challenges to the majority churches posed by the individualizing tendencies in modernity is, therefore, how to develop an ecclesiology that can foster solidarity in church members. Such an ecclesiology has to accommodate the fact that it is unrealistic to expect submission to a single view on any theological question, but that it is still important to be related to the basis (in van der Ven's understanding of the term) and tradition of the church.

Secondly, the case studies point to the social doctrines of the churches as resources for prophetic critique. Several of the respondents feel that it is one of the most important tasks of the church at the national/international level to be a prophetic voice in the area of welfare. And in order to be taken seriously in the debate, the churches need to have a considered position on social doctrine. All the traditions analysed in this study have rich resources to build on in this regard, but within the field of gender equality in particular these are often a two-edged sword. As Edgardh has shown, the credibility of the churches when it comes to gender equality is questioned by many Europeans. Specifically, the traditional church teachings on the family are problematic as resources for promoting full equality between men and women. Questions about gender equality, same-sex relations and conceptions of the family are therefore sources of conflicts within several of the majority churches in Europe, and between the official teachings of the churches and the norms prevalent in European societies at a whole. By tackling these questions, church leaders risk alienating either the conservative members of the church, or those striving for reform. As has been shown in this study, questions about family and gender are closely connected to the churches' role in welfare provision. Theological reflection must therefore be an integral part of this work.

Thirdly, it must be noted that although the churches in WREP belong to different denominations and local contexts, they confront very similar challenges. For example, the cultural and social processes of late modernity give rise to similar questions of identity for local churches all over Europe, all of which respond by adapting their traditions to the present situation. At the same time, the churches share many convictions within the welfare area. Specifically, they all stress the need for churches – and society at large – to imitate the love of Christ. They all point to the moral imperative to see social policy and welfare provision from the perspective of the least advantaged in society. They all are witnesses to hope for a radical change in relationships through the coming of the Kingdom of God. And as such, they make a vital contribution to the capacities of Europe to consider viable alternatives to the present situation.

Chapter 5

Welfare and Religion in Europe: Themes, Theories and Tensions

Anders Bäckström and Grace Davie

The concluding chapter to this volume is divided into two unequal parts. The first is relatively short and draws the threads of the previous chapters together. Despite the fact that each chapter is written from the viewpoint of a different discipline, and relates the material in WREP to very different bodies of literature, a number of common themes emerge which merit attention simply by the fact that they are constantly being drawn to our attention.

Four of these are particularly striking: the role of volunteers and volunteering in the welfare systems of Europe; the taken for grantedness of key ideas and key institutions (notably the presence of the historic churches, and the gendered nature of care); the effects of engaging in welfare on the identity of modern churches; and the continuing tension between the prophetic (or political) role of the churches and the hands-on delivery of care.

The last of these acts as a bridge to the main body of the chapter which is organized around a series of *theoretical* rather than policy tensions, all of which relate very closely to the WREP data, but invite further exploration. In pursuing this agenda the following format is adopted. In each section, the relationship between religion and welfare provides the starting point for the discussion, which is then enlarged to encompass both different empirical examples and broader theoretical issues. The aim is to address new fields of research – those that are opening up for scholars of all disciplines who are struggling to keep up with the growing visibility of religion in late modern societies. These fields are closely interconnected – there are several places where they intersect and overlap. The following pages should be read with this in mind.

Recurring Themes

This section examines four recurring themes. Both Per Pettersson and Ninna Edgardh, for example, write at length about volunteers and volunteering; both of them notice the dominance of women in this category, and both recognize the 'taken-for-grantedness' of this situation. Edgardh herself, this time with the support of Thomas Ekstrand, examines the ways in which this state of affairs is legitimized (an important aspect of the 'taken-for-grantedness'), recognizing that certain kinds of theology can be deployed to this effect. Similarly, Pettersson and Ekstrand are both intrigued by questions of identity and role. What effect does the engagement of churches and church-related organizations have on the identity of these institutions, what precisely should they be doing, and who should be doing it (returning us once again to gender)? What role, finally, does theology play in determining these choices?

Volunteers and volunteering are essential to the work of the European churches – and even more so in terms of their welfare activities. Clearly this is more apparent in some cases than in others and relates, very directly, to the financial situation of the institutions in question. The more paid employees that the church can afford, the less there is for the volunteer to do. At one end of the spectrum lie the well-funded Lutheran churches of northern Europe; at the other can be found the Church of England, which like many other British institutions, relies to an extraordinary extent on unpaid labour. That said, a black and white distinction between paid employees and unpaid volunteers is not helpful. What emerges, in fact, is a continuum, which includes ordained personnel (of various kinds), full-time lay professionals with considerable responsibility, assorted part-time workers, and an equally wide range of volunteers. It would be a mistake moreover to assume that only the full-timers are professionally trained. Both part-timers and volunteers bring with them a wide range of skills and training acquired elsewhere, and in many parts of Europe volunteering as such is becoming increasingly professionalized.

It is clear, however, that distinctive patterns emerge, in which gender is a dominant and totally accepted feature – our case studies are full of evidence to this effect. For how long this will be the case is a different matter, bearing in mind the following paradox. The more that churches rely on unpaid labour – or indeed on lay people of all kinds – the greater the opportunities for women, not least in positions of leadership. The logic is inescapable. The irony is even more obvious in situations where the priesthood as such is denied to women, a situation exacerbated by the rapid decline in ordinations in the Catholic Church. In France for example, women are undertaking hitherto unimaginable and very responsible roles.

An additional question cannot be avoided: is this dependence on volunteers as asset or a liability? Precisely this point was raised in Chapter 2 and in the conclusion to Volume 1 – it relates to the relative merits of state- and church-based welfare.[1] On the one hand are the neutral, well-trained and salaried professionals employed by the state; on the other are a wide variety of personnel, paid and unpaid, who between them offer a more personal, but at times haphazard, system of care. Volunteers are an essential, but necessarily 'fragile' element of the latter. They represent excellent value for money, but are limited in what they can do.

---

[1]   Bäckström and Davie (2010: 186–7). It is important to remember that these are ideal types. Reality almost always falls between the two extremes.

Given appropriate tasks and training, volunteers excel; overburdened and taken-for-granted, they and the system they sustain collapse together.

The taken-for-grantedness of the majority churches as a whole is an important finding in WREP, a situation that mirrors very clearly their counterparts in the welfare state – most of all the health services. Both are seen as public utilities: there at the point of need for those who need them, but very largely taken for granted in the meantime. Once again, the point was raised in Volume 1 and linked to the discussion of vicarious religion (Bäckström and Davie 2010: 191–2). Here a rather different aspect requires attention: it concerns the methodological implications of this situation. Time and time again, our respondents omitted important aspects of the churches' work in their accounts, simply because they took these for granted. In a very real sense, the work was 'invisible' until it was needed – very often at the turning points in life when the need was acute. In a rather similar way women were 'invisible' in a wide range of caring roles. Over and over again our respondents express surprise that the researcher should even ask the question about the different roles of men and women in the provision of care. But here – once again – there is evidence of change. Indeed in this case the irony is complete: women have become 'visible' because they are no longer there. As increasing numbers of women find outlets for their talents in the labour market, their domestic and voluntary roles necessarily diminish leaving behind a 'deficit in care'. Solutions to this problem vary – from institutional care (staffed very largely by women) in the north, to 'replacement' in the form of immigrant women employed in the household further south.

What then should the churches – these taken-for-granted institutions – be doing? Here Pettersson and Ekstrand pose a similar and penetrating question. If churches engage in welfare (however defined) does this affirm their primary identity or challenge this? What in other words is the underlying task of the church? Is this to preach the gospel in a strict and rather narrow understanding of this term; or is it to 'embody' the gospel in the sense of acting out, and thus defending, the values of care in secular society. Ekstrand approaches the question theologically, demonstrating the rich and very diverse resources available to the dominant European churches and the different ways in which these have been deployed to justify a range of responses to these issues. For this reason, identity becomes a dominant theme in his chapter. Pettersson considers the question sociologically, seeking to locate (or more accurately re-locate) the welfare activities of the churches, paying attention not only to the identity of the churches themselves, but to their evolution as one organization among many in late modern societies. A second question cannot be avoided: what is it that distinguishes the churches from their secular equivalents and how best can this be expressed? Much of Pettersson's analysis is concerned with this issue.

By different routes, both authors reveal a persistent and perplexing dilemma, the essence of which can be expressed as follows. Is it possible for the churches to sustain effective partnerships with the state in the delivery of service without compromising their essential ministry? Pettersson offers the following example.

Churches are increasingly obliged to compete with other providers for the delivery of care. The consequences are worrying (at least for the churches) in that contractual arrangements with local authorities almost always imply, either explicitly or implicitly, a reduced religious profile. In other words the church is obliged to restrict its scope to social issues only and, in that sense at least, to change its identity (returning to Ekstrand's dominant theme). Interestingly, exactly the same point has been raised in more recent discussions in Britain. There are times when the challenges of collaborating with the state outweigh the (financial) advantages of contractual engagement. Church-related organizations should think carefully before embracing this option.[2]

A fourth theme – mentioned in all three of the preceding chapters – concerns the tension between the provision of services as such and role of the churches as a critical or prophetic voice. As Ekstrand demonstrates, there are strong theological justifications for both roles, but it is not always easy to combine them. Interestingly, the leader of the City Mission in Drammen achieves precisely this. Indeed his credibility as a 'prophet' is to a large extent underpinned by his work with substance abusers – each reinforces the other. Here, however, is an individual with considerable room to manoeuvre, able to act independently if needed. That is not the case for many organizations and their leaders who are dependent on the state for finance and are not, therefore, in a position to criticize still less to prophesy; it is unwise to bite the hand that feeds you. That said, it is clear that European citizens welcome the prophetic role of the churches: this is the voice that they want to hear. It is, however, almost always a male voice – a point emphasized by Edgardh, though she too notes a welcome exception. The Ursuline nun from Vicenza most certainly speaks prophetically, articulating with some force a feminist critique of the economic and social situation in north Italy.

The examples above are indicative rather than exhaustive. Quite clearly, much more could be said. It is time, however, to place these reflections in a broader context – that of the changing nature of religion and religious activity in modern Europe.

Religion in Modern Europe: More or Less?

The first question is in many ways very simple: is there more or less religion in Europe in the early decades of the twenty-first century than there used to be? The following discussion will take the mid post-war decades as a benchmark, bearing

---

[2]   Note for example Beckford (2009), Dinham et al. (2009), and the contribution of Margaret Harris to 'Faith and Policy – Where Next for Religion in the Public Sphere?', an event sponsored by the AHRC/ESRC Religion and Society Programme together with the Faiths and Civil Society Unit, Goldsmith's College, and held at the British Library Conference Centre, London in July 2010. For more information and downloads, see http://www.religionandsociety.org.uk/events/featured_event.

in mind that any date selected for this type of comparison is to a considerable extent arbitrary. Interestingly, the WREP material – though in itself ambiguous – is relatively precise on this issue and offers an excellent point of departure. In almost every one of our case studies, the role of the churches in the delivery of welfare is expanding rather than contracting. The reasons for this are complex, and – for the most part – lie outside (a long way outside) the influence of the churches themselves. They have been discussed in both this volume and in the one that preceded it and reflect both internal and external factors.

The key points are easily summarized. No longer is it possible to assume that there will be sufficient people in employment in any given country to sustain an increasingly dependent population – be they elderly, newly-arrived and in search of a job, victims of political unrest in a relatively distant country, or simply young people pursuing an extended education in order to survive in a rapidly changing economy. Such challenges are exacerbated by continuing shifts in gender roles, as fewer and fewer women consider themselves full-time, home-based carers (of the young, the old, the sick or whoever). At the same time, the pressures of the global economy increase with corresponding effects on public expenditure in the national context. Such pressures were already visible at the time of WREP fieldwork and were becoming more so almost by the day: since then, in many parts of Europe, they have reached crisis point. One effect, most surely, will be drastic reductions in state-provided welfare and a profound questioning of the post-war assumptions on which the system was built. A second question is inevitable: how will the system evolve? Or to put the point even more directly, who or what will replace the elements that the state can no longer afford?

It is clear that these changes take place differently in different parts of Europe and depend considerably both on the stability of the economy in question and the degree to which an independent welfare system had been established in the first place. As ever the north and the south of Europe reveal contrasting profiles. But in every case – to a greater or lesser extent – the demands on the churches as welfare providers (both formal and informal) have increased. In the north, relatively well-funded churches fill small, but increasingly visible gaps in equally well-funded welfare systems. In the south, notably in Italy and Greece, the churches have never really ceded their place to a secular welfare system which remains rudimentary. Here even incipient welfare is under strain leaving more rather than less for the churches to do. In between there are many different variations on this theme, which was explored in detail in the case studies found in Volume 1.

Such a situation places the churches in a difficult position – the more so in that the increase in the demand for welfare has come at a time when the churches themselves are contracting. How then should they respond? In terms of policy, answers to these questions vary considerably. Both questions and answers need, however, to be placed in a wider perspective.

The first point is very clear: in most (if not quite all) parts of Europe, the conventional indicators of secularization are rising rather than falling, a trend unlikely to reverse even if it slows down. This is particularly the case in relation to active rather than passive membership, a trend with important (and often very direct) consequences for financial resources. That said, it is important neither to generalize, nor to oversimplify: northern Europe is more secular on all the conventional indicators (belief, practice, the importance of God in people's lives etc.) than the south, but membership per se remains high in the Nordic churches, bringing with it appreciable sums of money in the form of church tax.[3] The English church is very different and is depleted in almost every sense (i.e. in terms of both members and money). So also is the French, but for rather different reasons – here the Catholic Church still suffers from its 'defeat' by a hegemonic and morally authoritative state. In Germany, traditionally wealthy churches are losing both people and money on a hitherto unimaginable scale – exacerbated in the case of the Catholic Church by the recent revelations of child abuse (itself historic but with huge implications for the current situation). In Italy and Greece, the indicators of attachment stay high, but – very often – mask widespread internal changes, not least the loss of authority on the part of traditional hierarchies. Lay voices become increasingly important.

It is the combination of these factors which is important: on the one hand is the demonstrable increase in welfare provision on the part of the churches and in the demand for this; on the other is the overall decline in the number of people actively involved in these institutions and in the resources available to them. Unsurprisingly, managing this situation generates tensions. Among these is the increasingly noticeable 'gap' between active and passive membership in the constituencies of European churches – a continuing theme in social scientific analyses of religion in Europe (see below). Most interesting from the point of view of WREP is the fact that these very different constituencies reveal rather different attitudes towards the provision of welfare. Specifically, those on the fringes of the churches tend to appreciate the contributions to welfare undertaken by the churches and want these to increase (Bäckström et al. 2004); not all of them, however, recognize the financial demands that these initiatives make on contracting institutions. The more active members, conversely, are all too conscious of such constraints and are correspondingly cautious in their planning – a contrast clearly reflected in the WREP data (especially the German case), and discussed in detail in Pettersson's contribution to this book.

In terms of the question set out at the head of this section, a rather different point must now be introduced – one that will be developed in more detail as the chapter progresses. It concerns the growing visibility of religious issues in the *public* debates of both the European Union itself and of its constituent nations.[4] Two rather different examples come to mind: the first concerns a wide range of

---

[3]   As indicated in the introduction, the membership rates of the Nordic countries are now beginning to fall.

[4]   As will be made clear in this chapter, the growing 'visibility' of religion can be interpreted in different ways. It can indicate a substantive change in the religious field; it can also imply a shift in perception rather than reality.

bio-ethical issues which relate very often to the beginning and ending of life, and – consequently – to delicate issues of quality of life or well-being (i.e. welfare in its broadest sense). Necessarily these debates provoke religious as well as moral reflections – the churches, moreover, are very much present in the discussion, sometimes controversially, sometimes less so. A second set of issues reflects the continuing struggles to accommodate diverse religious minorities in a part of the world dominated by Christianity for nearly two millennia. The implications of such minorities for welfare as such formed the basis of Welfare and Values in Europe (WaVE), the successor to WREP. Their presence, however, raises a huge variety of issues concerning the public as well as private dimensions of religion in modern European societies.

At this stage, it is important to stress the juxtaposition of the two trends described in this section. On the one hand is the increasing secularization of the European populations as a whole; on the other is the re-emergence of religious issues in public debate. The *combination* is necessarily difficult. In many respects the process of secularization is remorseless: large numbers of Europeans have lost not only the narrative of their own religion, but the vocabulary and sensitivities that are necessary to talk about religion per se. At precisely the same moment, the salience of religion grows in the public sphere. The consequence very often is a public debate of poor quality, at times detrimental to all parties (see for example Davie, quoted in Woodhead with Catto 2009: 38).

From Obligation to Consumption: The Growth of the Market

A second tension must now be addressed: the shift right across Europe from a culture of religious obligation in which citizens are under some sort of pressure to belong to the majority church in their country to one in which such people are entirely free to make their own decisions with respect to their religious, and indeed their secular lives (Bäckström et al. 2004; Bäckström 2010; Davie 2002; 2006; 2007a). There can be no doubt that this entirely positive transformation has been taking place right across Europe for decades, if not centuries. It is also gathering pace. It remains, however, varied, complex, long-term and for the time being incomplete. One way of grasping what is happening is to regard this as a shift from 'opting-out' to 'opting-in'. In the opting-out model, an individual is a member of the historic church unless he or she decides otherwise. Historically, moreover, such decisions normally implied joining another church or religious organization rather than simply ceasing to be a member – both forms of 'dissent', moreover, required not only initiative, but (at times) considerable courage. In the opting-in model the same individual is only a member of the historic church – or indeed of any other – if he or she makes a conscious decision to become so. Membership, in other words, is chosen rather than imposed and cannot simply be assumed. The default positions change accordingly.

One very clear illustration of this process can be found in the changing nature of baptism in the Church of England. Historically, this has been as much a mark of Englishness as of Christian conviction, indeed for many people rather more so. There have, moreover, been several phases in this history. Initially baptism was associated with coercion with serious penalties for those who refused the rite. Bit by bit this evolved into a rather softer notion of requirement or duty (which was more or less rigorously enforced), and which mutated in turn into encouragement (reflecting a policy of welcome to all those living in a designated area – the parish). Currently this essentially 'open' policy is giving way to a much more selective process in which only the children of the faithful are allowed the sacrament (at least in some parishes). The very rapid decline in the proportion of infants baptized in England in recent decades should be seen as both cause and consequence of this situation,[5] and for this reason it is not, taken in isolation, a reliable indicator of secularization as such. It is much more accurate to say that baptism, in this particular case, is changing in nature: it is becoming increasingly a sign of membership in a voluntary organization rather than an indication of membership in a national church. In short it is something chosen rather than ascribed. Theologies adapt accordingly (Croft 2006).

In terms of the case studies represented in WREP, however, England is something of a special case – the decline in rates of baptism is much less marked in most of the other case studies. Nor is this simply a clear-cut theological issue in which Protestant and Catholic countries move in different directions. As already indicated, the Lutheran countries of northern Europe retain a strong sense of membership (illustrated by high levels of baptism, and indeed confirmation – especially in Finland). In the Protestant churches in Germany, however, membership is beginning to fall fast, a situation exacerbated by two generations of communism in the East – in this part of Germany the indices of secularization (including baptism) are some of the highest in the world. The Catholic experience is similarly uneven: it ranges from a church which has largely lost its authority over the population as a whole (in France), to one where the national impact is still strong if increasingly controversial (in Italy). In between can be found the Catholic Church in Germany which has, on the whole, retained members more effectively that its Protestant counterpart, but is currently under considerable strain. It is important, finally, to signal the Greek case in this discussion, where the elision of national and religious identity remains very largely intact. Greeks most certainly are members of the Orthodox Church unless they opt out – and even if they do 'leave the church' they retain very largely the culture of Orthodoxy if not its belief system.

All that said, almost no adult is *obliged* in late modern Europe to go to church for whatever reason, and any attempt to insist otherwise is quite rightly opposed. The outcomes of this situation are, however, complex – not least in terms of the

---

[5]   Up to date statistics for the Church of England can be found on the following website: http://www.cofe.anglican.org/info/statistics/.

growth and decline of religion. If it is clear, for example, that the actively religious in Europe are considerably less numerous than their equivalents in previous decades, they are almost certainly more 'religious', in the sense that their motives for attending church are less mixed than was the case historically – a fact that bedevils questions about the strength (or otherwise) of religiousness in this part of the world. In a very real sense, less can mean more.

At the same time, there is a marked growth all over the continent of religious alternatives (both Christian and other) as the market in religion grows. This, in itself, encourages people to choose the kind(s) of religion that suit them best. An important point follows from this: this is not necessarily a somewhat casual pick and mix situation often associated with the word 'consumption', though this may occur in some cases. On the contrary, these can be very serious choices with considerable implications for both private and public life. It is also important to remember that such choices cross-cut denominational boundaries (Pettersson 2000). There is a significant group of people, for example, who *choose* to remain, indeed to become, active and loyal members of the historic churches. This is very different from the larger and rather more passive constituency, who continue to be members of the majority churches in a technical sense but have made no decision at all. As ever the situation is ambiguous, but can, perhaps, be summarized as follows. On the one hand, the majority churches remain influential institutions in late modern European societies and can claim the allegiance of significant numbers of people, keeping in mind that the nature of this allegiance varies considerably. On the other, these churches have lost almost entirely the capacity to control the beliefs or the behaviour of the great majority of European citizens – an entirely positive shift.

A primary reason for this development lies in the core of the secularization process as it is articulated by both Martin (1978) and Casanova (1994) – that is in the growing autonomy of education, health and welfare, indeed of the state itself, as each of these sectors detaches itself from the authority of the churches. No longer, therefore, can the latter influence what goes on outside its own increasingly circumscribed sphere. Indeed attempts to do this are met with instant disapproval. The gradual – and seemingly inexorable – growth in the structures of secular society constitutes the other side of the coin as each of the institutions listed above works out not only its organizational forms but the professional codes that underpin these. In terms of welfare, this was the process discussed at some length in Volume 1, both in general and in particular, recognizing that this was essentially a national project – it took place differently in different places. An effective welfare state remains none the less a common aspiration of all Europeans and indeed of the European Union itself.

It is abundantly clear, however, that the welfare systems of modern Europe reviewed in detail in this project are *less* inclusive and *less* monolithic than they used to be, a trend that is likely to continue and in more ways than one. Firstly, for the reasons already stated, all such systems are less and less able to offer a comprehensive service from the cradle to the grave. At the same time, increasingly difficult questions arise about who is and who is not included in the system (i.e. who is and who is not entitled to welfare) – a central issue of the WaVE enquiry that followed WREP.[6] Thirdly, such services that do continue in existence are changing in nature. In theory at least, modern welfare systems are increasingly designed to 'serve' customers or clients who are free to make choices about how to access the things that they require from this sector. The same, of course, is true in health and in education: in every case the language of service is increasingly giving way to a discourse of purchasers and providers. Shifts in discourse, moreover, reflect deeper realities as the rules of the market begin bit by bit to assert themselves. New actors enter the scene and include for-profit as well as non-profit organizations – a change described in detail in Chapter 2.[7]

In short, instead of one comprehensive system replacing another, both the institutions in question (the religious and the secular) are subject to similar pressures as the public are encouraged to decide for themselves the particular packages that they are willing to purchase. It is, moreover, extremely clear from the WREP data that the 'markets' that are emerging overlap as the churches join other service providers in the social economies of Europe's towns and cities. This is especially true where the churches remain significant providers of welfare. Exactly who does what varies from place to place – as both Esping-Andersen and Martin predicted. A number of tendencies can, however, be discerned across very different cases. It is clear, for example, that majority churches are able to remain important players at local level and can contribute significantly to the social economy even when their voices are diminished on the larger stage. At one end of the spectrum can be found the Greek case, where our respondents not only expected the contributions of the Orthodox churches at local level, but were evidently respectful of the associated personnel. This, it seems, was entirely compatible with a developed critique of the national leadership. Very different are the almost invisible, but still effective contributions of the French church, especially to those who fall outside the formal system. Here a number of Catholic organizations, if not the Catholic Church as such, are better placed than the 'official' institutions of welfare to minister to the *sans-papiers*. If not strictly speaking a black market, this is most certainly a grey area. A third example can be found in Sweden, where a church that is no longer

---

[6]   The focus of the Welfare and Values project is captured in the following sentences. 'The project aims to generate new insights into religious, minority and gender related values which impact on social change in European society. WaVE starts from the assumption that concepts such as "cultural identities" and "values" can best be understood by looking at the ways in which they are expressed and developed in practice. The project therefore studies the interactions between diverse value systems as seen from the perspective of welfare. Who offers what to whom and for what reasons are understood in the project as critical markers of values in a given context.' See http://www.crs.uu.se/Research/Concluded+projects/WaVE/ for more details.

[7]   The notion of a 'market' in the delivery of service is, of course, controversial. Not everyone who is in need of welfare is in a position to choose between different options.

formally attached to the state is freer than it used to be to make a contribution to the voluntary sector, both as a provider in its own right and by raising its voice in public debate (Bäckström 2008).

The importance of the social economy or civil society as the sector of society in which these interactions and overlaps take place is paramount – a factor that vindicates very strongly the methodology of WREP and the decision to find a focus for the empirical work in a series of medium-sized towns across Europe rather than the national level. A second point follows from this: namely that in many respects there is more similarity between the WREP cases at the local level than one might expect – the same *patterns* repeated themselves in the different case studies even though the actors and organizations varied considerably. Such commonalities are all the more striking given that the development of both the majority churches and the various welfare regimes identified by Esping-Andersen are essentially national projects.

The Secular and the Religious: Mutually Constituted or Diametrically Opposed

The discussion so far necessarily merges into the next question: the extent to which the secular and the religious are mutually constituted. Empirically this is clearly the case: in each of the places considered in the WREP enquiry, the secular and the religious fit together in the sense that there is a local market in welfare to which many different actors or agents (both secular and religious) contribute. At best each fills the gaps left by the other, whether formally or informally. In practice, however, it is hard to avoid at least some duplication of roles, not to say overt competition. As the Italian case study revealed, it is not always easy for the organizers of welfare to keep track of what is happening, never mind the recipients. In some places, moreover, the competition is more formalized than in others – where the system requires that the various agents bid for contracts and deliver their services accordingly.

This interlinking of the religious and the secular in a situation which is beginning to resemble a market invites a number of more general observations. The first concerns the complexities of religious pluralism in modern Europe, a discussion complicated by the fact that a single phrase is used in many different ways (Beckford 2003). The notion of *secular* pluralism must also be introduced. As an idea this is less common than its religious equivalent, but is none the less important. Not only does it highlight once again the mutually constitutive nature of the religious and the secular, it also reveals the significance of secular elites for a full understanding of religion in Europe – recognizing their influence both for public debate and for social scientific discussion. The evident variety among such elites will be scrutinized in this section; their influence on public debate – specifically on their approaches to the secular – will be developed in the two that follow.

Religious pluralism describes two very different processes, both of which are relevant to the present discussion. The first is the growing presence of different religious communities in Europe, some Christian and some not. There is nothing particularly new about such diversity; nor has it ever been easy to manage the competing claims of many different groups, be they economic, social, cultural or religious. In the mid post-war decades, however, this process accelerated markedly as new sources of labour flooded into the expanding economies of Europe (initially to Britain, France, Germany and the Netherlands and somewhat later to the Nordic countries and the Mediterranean area). The process itself need not concern us here except to note that it created distinctive and visible constituencies all over Europe, which in the course of time made new demands on the public agenda. Of much greater importance in this context was the emergence of pertinent and specifically religious questions within this agenda, a shift which came as a surprise to significant sections of the European populations, not least its secular elites.

Before turning to the latter in more detail, however, it is important to recognize that pluralism can also be used to describe a very different feature of religious life: that is the fragmentation of a whole variety of religious and indeed other worldviews. This progressive deconstruction leads inevitably to a rather different kind of market in which individuals and communities combine and recombine these elements into packages which suit themselves. The most interesting thing from the point of view of a project such as WREP lies in the fact that a number of these packages not only relate to the welfare and well-being of individuals, but include a religious (or more often spiritual) element.[8] Here, therefore, is yet another illustration of the mutually constitutive nature of the religious and the secular but in a more individualistic sense.

The preceding paragraphs *describe* two very different processes, both of which carry the label 'religious pluralism'. The same term, however, can also be used normatively, in the sense that judgments (both implicit and explicit) are implied: is increasing pluralism in either sense a good thing? Should it be welcomed or resisted? Quite clearly opinions differ. Interestingly, a number of those who are ready to welcome the second alternative (the increasing individualization of worldviews and the freedom to explore new ways of being religious or spiritual) can be more resistant to the former (the assertion of distinctive, and at times discordant, religious voices in the public sphere). Such resistance, moreover, is more rather than less likely if minority voices, from whatever faith, challenge the values of the host community – including the notion that religion, for most Europeans, is primarily a private matter. Sensitivities about gender are another obvious flashpoint.

---

[8]   The presence of a spiritual element in all kinds of holistic therapies is well-known. A good example of sociological work in this field can be found in Heelas and Woodhead (2005). The fact that this study is based in a particular locality in the North of England means that it is of particular relevance to WREP. See also Woodhead (2008b).

Any number of examples can be cited as evidence for this claim – a chain of events that includes the heated discussions surrounding the preamble to the European Constitution, the Rushdie controversy in Britain, the *affaire du foulard* in France, the murders of Pim Fortuyn and Theo van Gogh in the Netherlands (together with the subsequent defection of Hirsi Ali to the United States), the furore over the Danish cartoons of Mohammed, and the bombings in Madrid (2004), London (2005) and Stockholm (2010). The debate about representations of Mohammed has now spread to Sweden, the legality of minarets has been challenged in a Swiss referendum, and in some parts of Europe the *niqab* has been banned altogether. A burgeoning literature in this field, both academic and other, is in itself an index of growing concern.[9]

How then do *secular* elites react? The crucial point to remember is that 'secular' as an adjective is as capacious as religious and can include not only many different ideas but many different degrees of intensity. For a start it is crucial to distinguish secularity (a state of affairs) from secularism (an ideology), just as it is important to distinguish descriptive from normative ideas about religious pluralism. Both, moreover, should be distinguished from secularization, which is a process – which some, in the name of secularism, may want to encourage, whilst others resist. But even if we limit the discussion to secularism as a world view, it is clear that there are many different possibilities: scientific, rational, political (socialist and/or Marxist), feminist, expressive, hedonistic and so on. Not all of these lead in the same direction and any one of them can be placed on a scale – or rather a complex continuum – that includes the mildest of adherents at one end and the articulate and at times vehement ideologue at the other. Regarding the former, it is difficult at times to distinguish between agnostic indifference and believing indifference – the line between them is fuzzy to say the least. Convinced atheists, conversely, know a great deal about the God(s) in whom they don't believe; they also take on the characteristics of the society of which they are part.

In terms of the case studies covered in the WREP enquiry, it is interesting to look at three examples from this point of view: France, Britain and Norway. The French case is the most clear-cut and offers ample evidence of *laïcité*, the legitimating narrative of French society including its welfare system. In terms of the present discussion, *laïcité* is best understood both as a specifically French form of secularism, and historically as the alter-ego of French Catholicism (each, in other words, required the other).[10] *Laïcité* can of course vary in its intensity, but as a cultural narrative it sinks much deeper into the population than its equivalents elsewhere. Local representatives of welfare in Evreux, for example, were resistant to the WREP researcher simply because she was asking questions about religion.

A second point follows from this and concerns the nature of the debate in France regarding religion and religious issues. In this respect, *laïcité* should be thought of as a political philosophy – i.e. as an organizing principle with reference

---

9   A reasonably up to date bibliography can be found on http://www.euro-islam.info/.

10   Interestingly, the current focus of the debate is Islam rather that Catholicism.

to which policy should be made. Here the most obvious comparison is with Britain where policies concerning religious pluralism are driven more by pragmatism than principle. Finding a solution to the immediate problem is more important than establishing the principle at stake. It is for this reason that the wearing of the veil is resisted in French schools (its presence violates the principle of *laïcité*), but is more easily tolerated in the British system, where each school adapts its uniform accordingly. That said, it is clear that the situation in Britain is beginning to change as the human rights discourse gains momentum, a shift which most certainly has solved some problems but at the same time has created others. Freedom of expression (in the form of legitimate critique or satire), for example, is not always easy to distinguish from unwarranted criticism of religion, and legislation to outlaw discrimination on the grounds of sexual orientation is likely to conflict with the rights of those who espouse more traditional forms of belief.[11]

A third point is also important in terms of the comparison between France and Britain: that is to recognize that recourse to principle on the one hand and problem-solving pragmatism on the other should not be thought of as right or wrong answers to the challenges of religious pluralism. They are simply two rather different solutions – or two ways of expressing secularism – which have emerged in different places. The point to stress is that both can be used constructively, and – more regrettably – both can be used at the expense of minorities who are less able than others to protect themselves. One point is very clear, however: they lead to very different policies with regard to religious communities. France, by and large, is looking for ways to integrate minorities of all kinds into the French system – as a result, differences of all kinds are minimized. Religion, it follows, is strictly a private matter. Britain, conversely, is closer to a multicultural model which – at its best – celebrates diversity (collective as well as individual), seeing this as a way of enriching society. Some forms of diversity, however, are more acceptable than others. Interestingly whilst social, cultural, religious and linguistic pluralisms are often encouraged, any suggestion of a legal equivalent prompts a very different response. Specifically, the idea that elements of religious law might be introduced into Europe is invariably met with hostility.[12]

The final case is Norway, where proportionally speaking there is a surprisingly large number of humanists in the population. Many of these are members of the

---

[11]   An excellent overview of the thinking about religion and belief in the context of the British Equality and Human Rights Commission can be found in Woodhead with Catto (2009). This includes a summary of recent court cases. See also the website of the Commission itself: http://www.equalityhumanrights.com/.

[12]   See for example the controversy generated by a lecture given by the Archbishop of Canterbury at the Royal Courts of Justice in February 2008. The lecture was entitled 'Civil and Religious Law in England: A Religious Perspective'. A very similar discussion was prompted by a doctoral thesis presented at Uppsala University in January 2010. See Sayed, M., 'Islam and Inheritance Law in Multicultural Sweden: A Study in Private International and Comparative Law'.

Norwegian Humanist Association which campaigns for the separation of church and state and the full equality of all religions and life stances in Norway. It actively encourages secular ceremonies for rites of passage, including 'confirmation'. Particular attention is paid to schools (including the place of religious education in the curriculum) and to young people – a separate youth organization was established in 2007. The Association becomes in fact a parallel institution to the state church and is, in many ways, similar to this. It is, for example, partly financed by the equivalent of 'church' tax (there is also an annual membership fee).[13] Above all, the tone of the debate, despite some sharp differences in opinion, is distinctively Norwegian – it is very different from the French case.

Public and Private: Unexpected Reversals in the Role of Religion

It is already clear that the *inter*relationships between the secular and the religious are closely connected to the complex links between the public and private with regard to religion – a point that must now be developed more fully. Initial (once again for the sake of argument, mid-twentieth century) interpretations of this situation went more or less as follows: scholars of religion very largely agreed that religion was disappearing from the public sphere in Europe, but that it continued to endure in the private lives of many Europeans. This moreover was a normative position: most Europeans, notably the political class and a wide range of intellectuals, deemed the privatization of religion to be a good thing. The point should not be exaggerated: until very recently religion remained an important marker of identity, of political allegiance and of voting behaviour right across Europe. As an institution, however, religion should be independent of the state (de facto if not de jure), and neither entity (state nor church) has the right to impose a belief system or specified forms of liturgy on its citizens. The state, in other words, should be strictly neutral in matters of faith.

The privatization of religion can also be approached in terms of religious practice. As the twentieth century progressed, the decline in churchgoing became increasingly evident. The fact that this happened faster in some parts of Europe than others, that the patterns of detachment varied from place to place, and that certain countries in Europe bucked the trend should not detract from the overall pattern which can be illustrated in any number of empirical enquiries.[14] Religious belief, however, proved more resilient than practice at least in the short term, a situation captured by the phrase 'believing without belonging' (Davie 1994). Not everyone agreed with the thinking that lay behind this expression but it became,

---

[13]   The Norwegian Humanist Association maintains an informative website in English as well as Swedish. See http://www.human.no/templates/Page____2067.aspx.

[14]   See for example the data generated by the European Values Study (http://www. europeanvaluesstudy.eu/) and the International Social Survey Programme (http://www.issp. org/).

without doubt, a touchstone for the debate. Central to this discussion was the long-term viability of non-institutional forms of religion. Many commentators argued, quite rightly, that detached belief was unlikely to sustain itself for more than one or (at most) two generations (Bruce 2002; Voas and Crockett 2005).

Davie herself moved on to introduce the idea of 'vicarious religion' (Davie 2000; 2007b), which evoked rather better than 'believing without belonging' the residual attachments of European people to their majority churches. This aspect of vicarious religion has been developed at length in Per Pettersson's contribution to this book which argues that institutions that continue to attract significant sections of the population as (at least) passive members must to some extent at least be considered 'public'. It is hard to disagree with this position. It prompts, however, a further question about ways of working. Are the methodologies currently in use in social science sufficiently sensitive to reveal not only the existence but the full potential of passive as well as active membership in the historic churches, and the implications of this situation for a better understanding of European societies? For a recent exchange of views on this issue, see Bruce and Voas (2010) and Davie (2010). Davie argues strongly for a more imaginative approach than is currently the case.[15]

Much more radical, however, have been the very visible changes that began to appear in the final decades of the twentieth century and which are, if anything, intensifying at the present time. The series of events or episodes which brought the question of religion to the forefront of public attention in Europe have already been listed (p. 163) – they need not be repeated again. It is important to note, however, that the great majority of these complex and difficult issues relate to the existence of Islam in Europe, rather than to the mainstream churches. Clearly there is a need for a mutual learning process, as European societies find ways to accommodate forms of religion which – simply by their existence – challenge the notion of privatization. Muslim communities, meanwhile, must find ways to live in diaspora, beyond the borders of a Muslim state. Neither the host societies, nor the incoming populations will find this process easy.

In short, a somewhat unexpected combination of events has occurred. On the one hand the privatization of religion is continuing, in the sense that religious institutions are losing their authority however this is understood; on the other religious issues are, and are likely to remain, at the forefront of public discussion. Paradoxically, the process of secularization and the public discussion of religion appear to go hand in hand (Sigurdson 2009; 2010).

Post-secular Europe: Reality or Illusion

Bearing all this in mind, an underlying question must now be addressed which reflects a continuing discussion in the social-scientific analyses of religion. It is

---

[15]   Warner (2008), Woodhead (2008b) and Riis and Woodhead (2010) make a similar point.

a discussion, moreover, that allows us to gather up the threads in this chapter. We have argued so far that both religious people and religious institutions remain important for the delivery of welfare in modern European societies especially at local level where they contribute significantly to the social economy. We have noticed in addition that religion has become an increasingly salient variable in *public* debate, even as it recedes in the private lives of significant numbers of Europeans. A third factor must now be introduced: namely the growing visibility of religion in global terms, a fact which Europeans increasingly acknowledge, and which fosters a growing awareness that the religious situation in Europe may not be typical of the modern world in general. It may in fact be an 'exceptional' case (Davie 2002).[16]

For all these reasons (and indeed many more), a lively debate has emerged in the social sciences regarding, not only the nature of the secular, but of the *post-secular* as cogent ideas in intellectual analysis. Broadly speaking there are two approaches to this question. On the one hand are those who argue that since the 1970s, there has been a marked change in the nature and forms of religion in the modern world – a trend that peaked, at least in terms of its visibility, in the attack on the World Trade Center in New York in September 2001. On the other are scholars who emphasize not so much a change in religious situation as such as a shift in the attitudes of Western scholars to this. Each of these approaches will be taken in turn.

Regarding the first option, there are some difficult issues of timing. Quite when these changes 'began' is not so easy to say, but they would include a consideration (or perhaps re-consideration) of the religious factor in the Iranian Revolution of 1979 and an acknowledgement of cultural as well as economic forces in the collapse of the Soviet Union in 1989. Attention would also be paid to a range of global regions: to the distinctive development of the United States (as a highly modern but religiously active society), to the emergence of specifically religious issues in the Middle East, to the Muslim world more generally, to the troublesome divisions of the Indian sub-continent and to the evolution of many different religions along the Pacific Rim, including China. The exponential growth of charismatic Christianity in the global South and in China would be central to these discussions, omitting the fact that the social sciences had very largely ignored this phenomenon when it first emerged in the 1960s.

The short hand for this position is 'God is back'[17] – a phrase that indicates that something *substantive* has changed regarding the place of religion in the modern world, a shift that requires the attention of scholars from many different disciplines

---

[16]   A detailed discussion of the global situation lies beyond the scope of this chapter. There is a burgeoning literature in this field. An excellent source of empirical data in a wide variety of global regions is the Pew Forum on Religion in Public Life (http://pewforum.org/Regions/).

[17]   'God is Back' comes from the title of an important, though controversial book by two senior editors from *The Economist* (Micklethwait and Wooldridge 2009).

(the economic and social sciences, international relations, development studies and so on). The situation moreover has penetrated Europe in the sense that even this most secular continent can no longer isolate itself from what is happening elsewhere. For a start, representatives of the 'rest of the world' are arriving in Europe on a daily basis – the principal reason for the complex and continuing debates about religious pluralism already noted. But quite apart from the physical presence of many very different groups of people, Europeans can no longer ignore what they see on their television screens night after night and what the internet brings into their homes at the click of a mouse – the role of the media is evident.

They react accordingly, though not all in the same way. Some wish to preserve the distinctiveness of Europe as a relatively secular enclave. Others emphasize two millennia of Christian history and resent the penetrations of other faiths. (Interestingly, each of these reactions depends very largely on the other.) Yet others are more open to the modern world in the sense that they are ready to embrace change and to live in an increasingly diverse environment. The reactions of social scientists are equally varied and range from rigorous re-affirmations of the secular nature of their disciplines to new forms of thinking that make every endeavour to accommodate the religious factor. A noteworthy example of the former can be found in a highly theoretical article entitled 'Towards postsecular sociology?' In this Gregor McLennan looks at four areas or sectors in which 'the postsecular condition' is expressed in contemporary social theory and philosophy. These include poststructuralist vitalism, transcendental realism, multiculturalist thinking and the recent contributions of Habermas to the public debate about religion. McLennan describes each of these in turn, but concludes unequivocally – by underlining very firmly the necessarily secular nature of sociology given that it is 'definitively naturalistic in its mode of comprehension' (2007: 868).

The reaction to Habermas is particularly pertinent to this chapter. In a key statement, Habermas (2006) takes as his own starting point the increasing visibility of religion in the modern world. He addresses the issue in terms of John Rawls' celebrated concept, the 'public use of reason'. The challenge which emerges is provocative: Habermas invites of secular citizens, including Europeans, 'a self-reflective transcending of the secularist self-understanding of Modernity' (2006: 15) – an attitude that quite clearly goes beyond 'mere tolerance' in that it necessarily engenders feelings of respect for the worldview of the religious person. There is in fact a growing reciprocity in the argument. Historically, religious citizens had to adapt to an increasingly secular environment in order to survive at all. Secular citizens were better placed in that they avoided, almost by definition, 'cognitive dissonances' in the modern secular state. This, however, may not be the case for much longer as religion and religious issues increasingly pervade the agenda.

An additional question follows from this. Are these issues simply to be regarded as relics of a pre-modern era, or is it the duty of the more secular citizen to overcome his or her narrowly secularist consciousness in order to engage with religion in terms of '*reasonably expected disagreement*' (Habermas 2006: 15), assuming in other words a degree of rationality on both sides? The latter appears to be the case. Habermas' argument is challenging in every sense of the term and merits very careful reflection; it constitutes an interesting response to a changing *global* environment – one moreover in which the relative secularity of Europe is increasingly seen as an exceptional case.

There is, however, an alternative point of view – the second of the approaches set out above. Protagonists of this position are less ready to say that 'God is back' for the simple reason that God never went away. The real shift that has taken place in recent decades is not so much a return of religion to the modern world, and indeed to Europe in a certain sense, as a return of religion to the consciousness of Western social science. Hans Joas, for example, challenges Habermas on precisely this point, arguing that the latter's earlier approaches to the key activities of modern societies were insufficiently sensitive to the religious factor, which was none the less present (Joas 2002: Joas and Wiegandt 2009). In other words, it is the perceptions of Habermas (and indeed many others) that have changed rather than the religious situation as such. In his own contributions to the debate, Joas himself moves in a different direction. He is more inclined to scrutinize the different understandings of the 'secular' and the very varied processes of secularization, distinguishing up to seven different meanings in the latter. It is in working through these complexities that we will find the keys to a better understanding of modernity, not in an exaggerated contrast between unitary, and thus distorting, concepts of secular and post-secular. In a more theological response to this discussion, Ola Sigurdson (2009; 2010) takes a midway position. He argues that something substantive has changed, not least in Europe, where the 'Westphalian paradigm' (essentially a territorial model) is no longer viable. It follows that neither the state church, nor its alter-ego the radical privatization of religion (believing without belonging) offer an adequate frame for the understanding of religion in this part of the world which is seeking new forms of 'embodiment'. These shifting parameters need a 'name' and for better or worse, Sigurdson labels this condition 'post-secular'.

Long-term Trajectories and Recent Change

David Martin's thinking has already been referenced at length in both this volume and in the one that preceded it. It is important therefore to consider his point of view in these evidently significant debates. Those who are acquainted with Martin's work will know that as early as the 1960s he urged caution regarding the use of the term 'secularization', noting the manifest confusions surrounding this term, not to mention its ideological overtones. Interestingly, Martin advises similar prudence with respect to the 'post-secular', fearing that the same confusions might happen again. The point is very clear in his most recent collection of essays, in which he argues for the persistence rather than the resurgence of religion, including its presence in public debate – for which reason he questions the notion (the idea itself) of privatization. Is this the correct word to describe what has happened even in Europe (Martin 2011: 6)? The interactions of the religious and secular should rather be seen in the long-term. 'Religious thrusts' and 'secular recoils' have happened for centuries rather than decades and – crucially for Martin – they work themselves out differently in different places. It follows that the indicators regarding religion in the modern world need careful and contextual scrutiny; the shorthand of 'God is back' does not, indeed it cannot, do justice to this urgent and complex agenda.

A final word of warning can be found in the work of Jim Beckford, who is as diffident about the 'post-secular' as he was, a decade or so ago, about the 'post-modern' – unsurprisingly in that his work is widely known for its precision in the use of terms.[18] Beckford discerns multiple strands in the notion of the post-secular, not all of which are compatible with each other. Such variety is not in itself a cause for concern; it may in fact be a stimulus in our attempts to understand the shifting parameters of the religious and the secular in late modern society. But we need to be clear in our thinking (Beckford 2003; 2009). In the second part of the 2009 paper – and to bring home the point about precision – Beckford explores the expanding role of faith-based organizations in welfare programmes in twenty-first-century Britain, a discussion of immediate relevance to WREP. Is the term post-secular helpful in this context? Beckford is doubtful, maintaining that the markedly ambiguous cases that he describes are more accurately explained by changes in government policy – specifically by 'the distinctive and controlling notion of "partnership"' between the state and the faith sector (2009: 16).

Concluding Remarks

It is important finally to ground this discussion in the data emerging from WREP itself. The primary aim of the project was to discover exactly what happens on an everyday basis in the fields of welfare and religion in Europe in the first decade of the twenty-first century, and to ask what this can tell us about the changing nature of European societies. In terms of religion we can conclude very simply: it is clear that the majority churches of Europe, though diminished in terms of numbers, are still important players in the lives of many Europeans (an argument for persistence) and that their roles in the delivery of welfare are growing rather than declining. It is equally clear, however, that even modest expansions in this respect stretch the assets of the churches to their limit in that their resource-base in terms of both active members and money is declining. The demands on women

---

[18] It is Beckford's work on pluralism that informs the discussion in an earlier section of this chapter (Beckford 2003). The parallels between post-modern and post-secular can of course be extended to a whole series of similar terms which denote the changing nature of late modern societies and the cultural expressions associated with these shifts. This is a controversial field.

are particularly acute – a burden which is largely invisible in that their caring role is very often taken for granted.

Edgardh's chapter deals at length with the last of these questions and concludes by underlining not only the absence of gender, but the absence of social care in most (if not quite all) conceptual understandings of religion. It follows that both of these factors should be included in empirical as well as theoretical enquiries if our understanding of religion is to be complete. Bearing these things in mind, and joining the threads of this chapter together, it is striking that gender is entirely absent as a category in the various discussions of the post-secular mentioned above, just as it was until relatively recently in analyses of the secularization process itself.[19] The role of the churches in social care fares better – in the sense that it is frequently, if at times controversially, cited as evidence in itself of the post-secular.

What then of the future? All three of the preceding chapters offer us a clue. In their different ways, they call for imaginative solutions to questions of welfare in twenty-first-century Europe – solutions that see the churches and their associated organizations as a resource rather than a problem. Such an approach implies innovative, focused and interdisciplinary thinking that not only includes both women and men, but enables them to escape from the roles which, our data tell us, are deeply ingrained in European mentalities. This way of working would concur with the views of our respondents. The great majority of these people see the historic churches as an asset in the delivery of welfare, especially when the 'official' system is under strain. Not only do these institutions offer a wide range of services, they embody certain values that – used creatively – have the potential to enhance rather than diminish the lives of Europeans. Such values operate at every level of society and in very different ways. If the institutional stabilities of the churches affirm long-term and reassuring continuities (for individuals as well as for society), the theologically-driven prophetic voice disturbs the status quo. Both are necessary.

---

[19]   See, however, the contributions of two feminist scholars to this debate (Bracke 2008; Braidotti 2008). The latter, in particular, maps the intersections between feminism and the post-secular condition.

Appendix
The WREP Team

In total, WREP has included 24 researchers from eight countries. The members of the co-ordination group are listed first, noting those who also undertook the Swedish case study. In addition to the Swedish material, Ninna Edgardh was responsible for the work on gender within WREP and much day-to-day management, Per Pettersson for the sociological analysis and overall scheduling, and Thomas Ekstrand for the theological dimension. In the remaining case studies, the senior scholar is named first, followed by the 'junior' researcher.

The Co-ordination Group

Anders Bäckström, Project Director, University of Uppsala: Sociology of religion
Grace Davie, Assistant Director, University of Exeter: Sociology

Members of the Swedish Team

Ninna Edgardh, University of Uppsala: Ecclesiology; Gender studies
Thomas Ekstrand, University of Uppsala: Theology
Per Pettersson, University of Karlstad: Sociology of religion

Specialist Advisors

Eva Jeppsson Grassman, University of Stockholm: Social work
 (now University of Linköping)
Bo Edvardsson, University of Karlstad: Business studies

Case Study Teams

Norway

Trygve Wyller, University of Oslo: Ethics
Olav Helge Angell, Diakonhjemmet University College, Oslo: Sociology of religion

Finland

Eila Helander, University of Helsinki: Church and social studies
Anne Birgitta Pessi, University of Helsinki: Sociology of religion

Germany

Heinz Schmidt, University of Heidelberg: Practical theology
  and Hans-Georg Ziebertz, University of Würzburg: Practical theology
Annette Leis-Peters, University of Uppsala: Sociology of religion

England

Douglas Davies, University of Durham: Theology
Martha Middlemiss Lé Mon, University of Uppsala: Sociology of religion

France

Danièle Hervieu-Léger, EHESS, Paris: Sociology
Corinne Valasik, EHESS, Paris: Sociology of religion
  and François Mabille, Institut Catholique, Paris: Sociology of religion

Italy

Chantal Saint-Blancat, University of Padua: Sociology
Annalisa Frisina, University of Padua: Sociology

Greece

Nikos Kokosalakis, Panteion University, Athens: Sociology
Lina Molokotos-Liederman, University of Exeter: Sociology
  and Effie Fokas, University of Exeter/London School of Economics; Political
  science

Bibliography

Abrahamsson, P., T. Boje and B. Greve (2005). *Welfare and Families in Europe* (Farnham: Ashgate).

Ahlstrand, K. (2001). 'Kvinnors bidrag till religionsteologin'. In B. Olsson (ed.) *Hela jorden är Herrens. Olika tro sida vid sida* (Lund: Teologiska institutionen). 71–78.

Angell, O.H. (2004). 'Welfare, church and gender in Norway'. In N. Edgardh Beckman (ed.) *Welfare, Church and Gender in Eight European Countries* (Uppsala: Uppsala Institute for Diaconal and Social Studies). 63–102.

—— (2010). 'Sacred welfare agents in secular welfare space: The Church of Norway in Drammen'. In A. Bäckström and G. Davie with N. Edgardh and P. Pettersson (eds) *Welfare and Religion in 21st Century Europe: Volume 1. Configuring the Connections* (Farnham: Ashgate). 57–76.

Angell, O.H. and T. Wyller (2006). 'The Church of Norway as an agent of welfare: The case of Drammen'. In A.B. Yeung, N. Edgardh Beckman and P. Pettersson (eds) *Churches in Europe as Agents of Welfare – Sweden, Norway and Finland* (Uppsala: Uppsala Institute for Diaconal and Social Studies). 86–141.

Archbishop of Canterbury's Commission on Urban Priority Areas (1985). *Faith in the City: A Call for Action by Church and Nation* (London: Church House Publishing).

Archbishops' Council, Commission on Urban Life and Faith (2006). *Faithful Cities: A Call for Celebration, Vision and Justice* (London: Church House Publishing and Methodist Publishing House).

Atherton, J. (2003). *Marginalization* (London: SCM).

Bäckström, A. (ed.) (1999). *From State Church to Free Folk Church: A Sociological, Service Theoretical and Theological Analysis in the Face of Disestablishment between the Church of Sweden and the State in 2000. Project Desciption* (Stockholm: Verbum).

—— (2001). *Svenska kyrkan som välfärdsaktör i en global kultur: En studie av religion och omsorg* (Stockholm: Verbum).

—— (2004). 'The church in a new century'. In O.G. Winsnes (ed.) *Contemporary Religion and Church: A Nordic Perspective* (Trondheim: Tapir). 81–99.

—— (2008). 'Religionens återkomst?' In L. Kanckos and R. Kauranen (eds) *Social samhörighet och religion. Festskrift till Susan Sundback* (Åbo: Åbo Akademi University Press). 19–30.

—— (2010). 'Religionens nya synlighet'. Unpublished lecture given at a Research Conference for the Swedish Police Force, Uppsala, 1 May.

Bäckström, A. and J. Bromander (1995). *Kyrkobyggnaden och det offentliga rummet: En undersökning av kyrkobyggnadens roll i det svenska samhället* (Uppsala: Svenska kyrkans centralstyrelse).

Bäckström, A. and G. Davie, with N. Edgardh and P. Pettersson (2010). *Welfare and Religion in 21st Century Europe: Volume 1. Configuring the Connections* (Farnham: Ashgate).

Bäckström, A., N. Edgardh Beckman and P. Pettersson (2004). *Religious Change in Northern Europe: The Case of Sweden* (Stockholm: Verbum).

Baines, C.T., P.M. Evans and S.M. Neysmith (eds) (1998). *Women's Caring: Feminist Perspectives on Social Welfare* (Toronto: Oxford University Press).

Bauman, Z. (2002). *Society under Siege (*Cambridge: Polity Press).

Beckford, J. (1989). *Religion and Advanced Industrial Society* (London: Unwin Hyman).

—— (2003). *Social Theory and Religion* (Cambridge: Cambridge University Press).

—— (2009). 'Post-secularity: Fashion and foible'. Unpublished paper presented at the 2009 annual meeting of the SSSR, Denver, CO.

Beckford, J. and S. Gilliat (1998). *Religion in Prison: Equal Rites in a Multi-Faith Society* (Cambridge: Cambridge University Press).

Bell, D. (1973). *The Coming of Post-Industrial Society: A Venture in Social Forecasting* (New York: Basic Books).

Belopopsky, A. (2004). 'Orthodox Diakonia'. Unpublished paper presented at a conference on the Social Witness and Service of Orthodox Churches, New Valamo Monastery, Finland. For more information, see http://www.rondtb.msk.ru.

Benedict XVI, Pope (2006). 'Deus caritas est'. Available at http://www.vatican.va.

—— (2009). 'Caritas in veritate'. Available at http://www.vatican.va.

Benne, R. (1998). 'Lutheran ethics: Perennial themes and contemporary challenges'. In K.L. Bloomquist and J.R. Stumme (eds) *The Promise of Lutheran Ethics* (Minneapolis, MN: Fortress Press). 11–30.

Berger, P.L. (1969). *The Sacred Canopy: Elements of a Sociological Theory of Religion* (New York: Doubleday).

—— (ed.) (1999). *The Desecularization of the World: Resurgent Religion and World Politics* (Grand Rapids, MI: Eerdmans).

—— (2001). 'Postscript'. In L. Woodhead, P. Heelas and D. Martin (eds) *Peter Berger and the Study of Religion* (London: Routledge). 189–198.

Berger, P.L., G. Davie and E. Fokas (2008). *Religious America, Secular Europe? A Theme and Variations (*Farnham: Ashgate).

Berger, P.L. and T. Luckmann (1979). *The Social Construction of Reality: A Treatise in the Sociology of Knowledge* (Harmondsworth: Penguin).

Beyer, P. (1994). *Religion and Globalization (*London: Sage).

Blennberger, E. (2004). 'Genusfrågor och civilt samhälle'. In E. Blennberger, U. Habermann and E. Jeppsson Grassman (eds) *Genus och civilt samhälle* (Stockholm: Sköndalsinstitutet). 48–65.

Borchorst, A. (1994). 'Welfare state regimes, women's interests and the EC'. In D. Sainsbury (ed.) *Gendering Welfare States* (London: Sage). 26–44.

Borchorst, A. and B. Siim (2002). 'The women-friendly welfare states revisited'. *Nordic Journal of Women's Studies* 10 (2): 90–98.

Bracke, S. (2008). 'Conjugating the modern/religious, conceptualizing female religious agency: Contours of a "post-secular" conjuncture'. *Theory, Culture and Society* 25 (6): 51–67.

Braidotti, R. (2008). 'In spite of the times: The postsecular turn in feminism'. *Theory, Culture and Society* 25 (6): 1–24.

Brodd, S.-E. (2006a). 'Guest editorial: Themes in operative ecclesiology'. *International Journal for the Study of the Christian Church* 6 (2): 124–125.

—— (2006b). 'Ecclesiology and church music: Towards a possible relationship'. *International Journal for the Study of the Christian Church* 6 (2): 126–143.

Bruce, S. (1996). *Religion in the Modern World: From Cathedrals to Cults* (Oxford: Oxford University Press).

—— (2002). *God is Dead: Secularization in the West* (Oxford: Blackwell).

Bruce, S. and D. Voas (2010). 'Vicarious religion: An examination and critique'. *Journal of Contemporary Religion* 25 (2): 243–259.

Buckser, A. (1996). 'Religion, science and secularization theory on a Danish island'. *Journal for the Scientific Study of Religion* 35 (4): 432–441.

Carroll, J.W. (1991). *As One with Authority: Reflective Leadership in Ministry* (Louisville, KY: Westminster John Knox Press).

Casanova, J. (1994). *Public Religions in the Modern World* (Chicago, IL: University of Chicago Press).

—— (2006). 'Rethinking secularization: A global comparative perspective'. *The Hedgehog Review: Critical Reflections on Contemporary Culture* 80(1–2): 7–22.

Castells, M. (1996). *The Information Age: Economy, Society and Culture. Vol. I, The Rise of the Network Society* (Oxford: Blackwell).

—— (1998). *The Information Age: Economy, Society and Culture. Vol. III, End of Millennium* (Oxford: Blackwell).

Catholic Church (1997). *Catechism of the Catholic Church*. Available at http://www.vatican.va.

Chapman, M.D. (2004). 'Ronald Preston, William Temple, and the future of Christian politics'. *Studies in Christian Ethics* 17 (2): 162–172.

Chopp, R.S. (1989). *The Power to Speak: Feminism, Language, God* (New York: Crossroad Publishing).

Christodoulos, Archbishop (1999a). '"The first of May" (Labour Day)'.

—— (1999b). 'Message to the Hellenic Gerontological and Geriatric Association'.

—— (1999c). 'The word and role of Orthodoxy in the European Union'.

—— (2003). 'The presence of the Church on the horizon of Europe'.

—— (2005). 'Letter to the President of the European Commission on social cohesion'.

Church of Norway (2005). *Når så vi deg fremmed og tok imot deg? Kirkelig ressursdokument om asyl- og flyktningpolitikk* (Oslo: Church of Norway). Available at http://www.kirken.no.

—— (2009). *Statistikk for Den norske kirke.* Available at http://www.kirken.no.

Church of Sweden (1993). *Rich and Poor: A Letter from the Bishops of the Church of Sweden about Justice and Morality in the Global Economy.* Published by the Bishops' Conference of the Church of Sweden. Available at http://www. svenskakyrkan.se/svk/englang.htm.

—— (2009). *Svenska kyrkans statistik.* Available at http://www.svenskakyrkan. se.

Clogg, R. (2002). *A Concise History of Greece* (Cambridge: Cambridge University Press).

Congregation for the Doctrine of the Faith (2004). *Letter to the Bishops of the Catholic Church on the Collaboration of Men and Women in the Church and in the World.* Available at http://www.vatican.va.

Constantelos, D.J. (2003). 'Some aspects of stewardship of the Church of Constantinople under Ottoman Turkish rule (1453–1800)'. In A. Scott (ed.) *Good and Faithful Servant: Stewardship in the Orthodox Church* (Crestwood, NY: St Vladimir's Seminary Press). 105–118.

—— (2004). 'Origins of Christian Orthodox Diakonia: Christian Orthodox philanthropy in Church history'. Unpublished paper presented at a conference on the Social Witness and Service of Orthodox Churches, New Valamo Monastery, Finland. For more information, see http://www.rondtb.msk.ru.

Croft, S. (ed.) (2006). *The Future of the Parish System* (London: Church House Publishing).

Curran, C.E. (2002). *Catholic Social Teaching 1891-Present: A Historical, Theological and Ethical Analysis* (Washington, DC: Georgetown University Press).

Dackson, W. (2006). 'Archbishop William Temple and public theology in a post-Christian context'. *Journal of Anglican Studies* 4 (2): 239–251.

Daly, M. (2000). *The Gender Division of Welfare: The Impact of the British and the German Welfare State* (Cambridge: Cambridge University Press).

Daly, M. and J. Lewis (1998). 'Introduction: Conceptualising social care in the context of welfare state restructuring'. In J. Lewis (ed.) *Gender, Social Care and Welfare State Restructuring in Europe* (Farnham: Ashgate). 1–24.

—— (2000). 'The concept of social care and the analysis of contemporary welfare states'. *British Journal of Sociology* 51 (2): 281–298.

Daly, M. and K. Rake (2003). *Gender and the Welfare State: Care, Work and Welfare in Europe and the USA* (Cambridge: Polity Press).

Davie, G. (1994). *Religion in Britain since 1945: Believing without Belonging* (Oxford, Blackwell).

—— (2000). *Religion in Modern Europe: A Memory Mutates* (Oxford: Oxford University Press).

—— (2002). *Europe: The Exceptional Case: Parameters of Faith in the Modern World* (London: Darton, Longman and Todd).

—— (2006). 'Religion in Europe in the 21st century: The factors to take into account'. *European Journal of Sociology* 47 (2): 271–296.

—— (2007a). *The Sociology of Religion* (London: Sage).

—— (2007b). 'Vicarious religion: A methodological challenge'. In N. Ammerman (ed.) *Everyday Religion: Observing Modern Religious Lives* (New York: Oxford University Press). 21–37.

—— (2010). 'Vicarious religion: A response'. *Journal of Contemporary Religion* 25 (2): 261–266.

Davies, D. (1994). 'Quality places for quality time'. Unpublished paper presented at the Department of Theology, University of Nottingham.

De Moor, R. (ed.) (1995). *Values in Western Societies* (Tilburg: Tilburg University Press).

Dinham, A., R. Furbey and V. Lowndes (eds) (2009). *Faith in the Public Realm: Controversies, Policies and Practices* (Bristol: Policy Press).

Diotallevi, L. (2002). 'Internal competition in a national religious monopoly: The Catholic effect and the Italian Case'. *Sociology of Religion* 63 (2): 137–155.

Dobbelaere, K. (1981). 'Secularization: A multi-dimensional concept'. *Current Sociology* 29 (2): 3–153.

Dulles, A. (2002). *Models of the Church* (New York: Doubleday).

Durkheim, E. (1897/1987). *Suicide: A Study in Sociology* (London: Routledge).

—— (1912/1995). *The Elementary Forms of Religious Life* (New York: The Free Press).

Edgardh, N. (2009). 'Social agent: A queer role for the church'. In J. Ideström (ed.) *For the Sake of the World: Swedish Ecclesiology in Dialogue with William T. Cavanaugh* (Eugene, OR: Pickwick Publications). 65–85.

Edgardh, N. and P. Pettersson (2010). 'The Church of Sweden: A church for all, especially the most vulnerable'. In A. Bäckström and G. Davie with N. Edgardh and P. Pettersson (eds) *Welfare and Religion in 21st Century Europe: Volume 1. Configuring the Connections* (Farnham: Ashgate). 39–56.

Edgardh Beckman, N. (ed.) (2004). *Welfare, Church and Gender in Eight European Countries: Working Paper 1 from the Project Welfare and Religion in a European Perspective* (Uppsala: Institute for Diaconal and Social Studies).

—— (2006). 'The theology of gathering and sending: A challenge from feminist liturgy'. *International Journal for the Study of the Christian Church* 6 (2): 144–165.

Edgardh Beckman, N., T. Ekstrand and P. Pettersson (2006). 'The Church of Sweden as an agent of welfare: The case of Gävle'. In A.B. Yeung, N. Edgardh Beckman and P. Pettersson (eds) *Churches in Europe as Agents of Welfare – Sweden, Norway and Finland* (Uppsala: Uppsala Institute for Diaconal and Social Studies). 20–85.

Edvardsson, B., A. Gustafsson, M.D. Johnson and B. Sandén (2000). *New Service Development and Innovation in the New Economy* (Lund: Studentlitteratur).

Egnell, H. (2006). *Other Voices: A Study of Christian Feminist Approaches to Religious Plurality* (Uppsala: Swedish Institute of Mission Research).

Ehrenreich, B. and A. Hochschild (2003). *Global Woman: Nannies, Maids and Sex Workers in the New Economy* (New York: Metropolitan Books; London: Granta Books).

Eisenstadt, S.N. (2003). *Comparative Civilizations and Multiple Modernities* (Leiden: Brill).

EKD (2002a). *Solidarität und Wettbewerb. Für mehr Verantwortung, Selbstbestimmung und Wirtschaftlichkeit im Gesundheitswesen. Eine Stellungnahme des Rates der EKD* (Hannover: EKD-Texte 74).

—— (2002b). *Zusammenleben gestalten. Ein Beitrag des Rates der EKD zu Fragen der Integration und des Zusammenlebens mit Menschen anderer Herkunft, Sprache oder Religion* (Hannover: EKD-Texte 76).

Ekstrand, T. (2000). *Max Weber in a Theological Perspective* (Leuven: Peeters).

—— (2002). *Folkkyrkans gränser. En teologisk analys av övergången från statskyrka till fri folkkyrka* (Stockholm: Verbum).

Esmer, Y. and T. Pettersson (eds) (2007). *Measuring and Mapping Cultures: 25 Years of Comparative Value Surveys* (Leiden: Brill).

Esping-Andersen, G. (1990). *The Three Worlds of Welfare Capitalism* (Cambridge: Polity Press).

—— (1999). *Social Foundations of Postindustrial Economies* (Oxford: Oxford University Press).

—— (2002). *Why We Need a New Welfare State* (Oxford: Oxford University Press).

EUMC (2006). *Muslims in the European Union: Discrimination and Islamophobia.* Report from the European Monitoring Centre on Racism and Xenophobia (Vienna: Manz Crossmedia). Available at http://fra.europa.eu/fraWebsite/attachments/Manifestations_EN.pdf.

European Union Constitution (2004). *Official Journal of the European Union,* C310, 47. Available at http://www.unizar.es/euroconstitucion/Treaties/Treaty_Const.htm.

Eurostat (2007). *Europe in Figures: Eurostat Yearbook 2006–07* (Luxembourg: European Commission).

Evangelical Lutheran Church of Finland (1999). *Towards the Common Good: Statement on the Future of the Welfare Society by the Bishops of the Evangelical Lutheran Church of Finland.* Published by the Bishops of the Church of Finland. Available at www.evl.fi/english.

—— (2009). *Kyrkan i siffror.* Available at http://evl.fi.

Fahlgren, S (2006). 'Preaching and preachership as fundamental expressions of being church'. *International Journal for the Study of the Christian Church* 6 (2): 180–199.

Fiorenza, E.S. (1993). *Discipleship of Equals: A Critical Feminist Ecclesia-logy of Liberation*. (New York: Crossroad Publishing).

—— (1994). *Jesus – Miriam's Child, Sophia's Prophet: Critical Issues in Feminist Christology* (New York: Continuum Press).

Fix, B. and E. Fix (2002). 'From charity to client-oriented social service production: A social profile of religious welfare associations in Western European comparison.' *European Journal of Social Work* 5 (1): 55–62.

—— (2005). *Kirche und Wohlfahrtsstaat* (Freiburg: Lambertus-Verlag).

Fokas, E. (2006). 'The Greek Orthodox Church as an agent of welfare: The case of Thiva and Livadeia'. In A.B. Yeung, N. Edgardh Beckman and P. Pettersson (eds) *Churches in Europe as Agents of Welfare – England, Germany, France, Italy and Greece*. (Uppsala: Uppsala Institute for Diaconal and Social Studies). 218–264.

—— (2007). 'Religion and politics: Examining the case of Greece through the prism of Europe'. In K. Zorbas (ed.) *Politics and Religions*. (Athens: Papazizis). 271–307 (original in Greek).

—— (2009). 'Welfare at the intersection between theology and politics: A global perspective'. *Journal of Theology for Southern Africa* 133 (a special issue on Churches, Welfare and Gender in Context: A South African-European Exchange of Perspectives): 126–144.

Fokas, E. and L. Molokotos-Liederman (2010). 'The disgraceful and the divine in Greek welfare: The cases of Thiva and Livadeia'. In A. Bäckström and G. Davie with N. Edgardh and P. Pettersson (eds) *Welfare and Religion in 21st Century Europe: Volume 1. Configuring the Connections* (Farnham: Ashgate). 167–182.

Forell, U. (1989). *Kärlekens motivstrukturer. En etisk och begreppsanalytisk studie* (Lund: Lund University Press).

Forrester, D. (1997). *Christian Justice and Public Policy* (Cambridge: Cambridge University Press).

Fraser, N. (1997). 'After the family wage: A postindustrial thought experiment'. In N. Fraser (ed.) *Justice Interruptus: Critical Reflections on the 'Postsocialist' Condition* (New York: Routledge). 41–66.

Frisina, A. (2004). 'Welfare, church and gender in Italy'. In N. Edgardh Beckman (ed.) *Welfare, Church and Gender in Eight European Countries* (Uppsala: Uppsala Institute for Diaconal and Social Studies). 269–287.

—— (2006). 'The Catholic Church in Italy as an agent of welfare: The case of Vicenza'. In A.B. Yeung, N. Edgardh Beckman and P. Pettersson (eds) *Churches in Europe as Agents of Welfare – England, Germany, France, Italy and Greece* (Uppsala: Uppsala Institute for Diaconal and Social Studies). 182–215.

—— (2010). What kind of church? What kind of welfare? Conflicting views in the Italian case'. In A. Bäckström and G. Davie with N. Edgardh and P. Pettersson (eds) *Welfare and Religion in 21st Century Europe: Volume 1. Configuring the Connections* (Farnham: Ashgate). 147–166.

General Synod Board for Social Responsibility, Social Policy Committee (1986). *Not Just for the Poor: Christian Perspectives on the Welfare State* (London: Church House Publishing).

Giddens, A. (1991). *Modernity and Self-identity: Self and Society in the Late Modern Age* (Palo Alto, CA: Stanford University Press).

Grenholm, C. (1990). *Romans Interpreted: A Comparative Analysis of the Commentaries of Barth, Nygren, Cranfield and Wilckens on Paul's Epistle to the Romans* (Uppsala: Uppsala University).

Grenholm, C.-H. (1994). 'Biskoparna, bibeln och rättvisan'. *Svensk kyrkotidning* 89 (39): 395–396.

Gustafsson, G. (1995). 'Svenska folket, Estonia och religionen'. In L. Ahlin and G. Gustafsson (eds) *Två undersökningar om Estonia och religionen* (Lund: Lunds universitet). 7–46.

Habermas, J. (2005). 'Religion in the public sphere'. Public lecture presented at the Holberg Prize Seminar, 28 November.

—— (2006) 'Religion in the public sphere'. *European Journal of Philosophy* 14 (1): 1–25.

Halman, L. (2001). *The European Values Survey: A Third Wave* (Tilburg: European Values Study).

Harris, M. (1998). *Organizing God's Work: Challenges for Churches and Synagogues* (London: Macmillan).

Hearn, J. and K. Pringle (2006). *European Perspectives on Men and Masculinities: National and Transnational Approaches* (Basingstoke: Palgrave Macmillan).

Heelas, P. and L. Woodhead (2005). *The Spiritual Revolution: Why Religion is Giving Way to Spirituality* (Oxford: Blackwell).

Heino, H., K. Salonen and J. Rusama (1997). *Response to Recession: The Evangelical Lutheran Church of Finland in the Years 1992–1996* (Tampere: Kirkon Tutkimuskeskus).

Held, V. (2006). *The Ethics of Care: Personal, Political, Global* (New York: Oxford University Press).

Henery, M. (2006). 'The selfish sex?' *Times 2*, 29 March.

Herbert, D. (2003). *Religion and Civil Society: Rethinking Public Religion in the Contemporary World* (Farnham: Ashgate).

Hernes, H. (1987). *Welfare State and Women Power: Essays in State Feminism* (Oslo: Norwegian University Press).

Hervieu-Léger, D. (1986). *Vers un nouveau christianisme* (Paris: Le Cerf).

—— (2000). *Religion as a Chain of Memory* (Cambridge: Polity Press).

Hobson, B., J. Lewis and B. Siim (2002). *Contested Concepts in Gender and Social Politics* (Cheltenham: Edward Elgar).

Hochschild, A.R. (1995). 'The culture of politics: Traditional, postmodern, cold-modern, and warm-modern ideals of care'. *Social Politics* 2 (3): 331–346.

Hopko, T. (2003). 'On stewardship and philanthropy: Forty sentences'. In A. Scott (ed.) *Good and Faithful Servant: Stewardship in the Orthodox Church* (Crestwood, NY: St Vladimir's Seminary Press). 133–151.

Hornsby-Smith, M. (2006). *An Introduction to Catholic Social Thought* (Cambridge: Cambridge University Press).

Ideström, J. (2009). *Lokal kyrklig identitet – en studie av implicit ecklesiologi med exemplet Svenska kyrkan i Flemingsberg* (Skellefteå: Artos).

Ingelstam, L. (1995). *Ekonomi för en ny tid* (Stockholm: Carlsson).

Inglehart, R. (1977). *The Silent Revolution: Changing Values and Political Styles among Western Publics* (Princeton, NJ: Princeton University Press).

—— (1990). *Culture Shift in Advanced Industrial Society* (Princeton, NJ: Princeton University Press).

Inglehart, R. and P. Norris (2003). *Rising Tide: Gender Equality and Cultural Change around the World* (Cambridge: Cambridge University Press).

ISSP (2007). *International Social Survey Programme*. Available at http://www.issp.org.

Jeanrond, W. (2001). *Gudstro. Teologiska reflexioner II* (Lund: Arcus).

Jeppsson Grassman, E. (2004). 'Welfare in Europe: New trends and old regimes'. In N. Edgardh Beckman (ed.) *Welfare, Church and Gender in Eight European Countries* (Uppsala: Uppsala Institute for Diaconal and Social Studies). 11–25.

—— (2010). 'Welfare in Western Europe: Existing regimes and patterns of change'. In A. Bäckström and G. Davie, with N. Edgardh and P. Pettersson (eds) *Welfare and Religion in 21st Century Europe: Volume 1. Configuring the Connections* (Farnham: Ashgate). 25–38.

Joas, H. (2002). *Do We Need Religion? On the Experience of Self-Transcendence* (Boulder, CO: Paradigm Publishers).

Joas, H. and K.W Wiegandt (eds) (2009). *Secularization and the World Religions* (Liverpool: Liverpool University Press).

John XXIII, Pope (1961/1992). 'Mater et magistra'. In D.J. O'Brien and T.A. Shannon (eds) *Catholic Social Thought: The Documentary Heritage* (Maryknoll, NY: Orbis). 82–128.

—— (1963/1992). 'Pacem in terris'. In D.J. O'Brien and T.A. Shannon (eds) *Catholic Social Thought: The Documentary Heritage* (Maryknoll, NY: Orbis). 129–162.

John Paul II, Pope (1981). 'Familiares consortio'. Available at http://www.vatican.va.

—— (1987/1992). 'Sollicitudo rei socialis'. In D.J. O'Brien and T.A. Shannon (eds) *Catholic Social Thought: The Documentary Heritage* (Maryknoll, NY: Orbis). 393–436.

—— (1988). 'Christifideles laici'. Available at http://www.vatican.va.

—— (1991/1992). 'Centesimus annus'. In D.J. O'Brien and T.A. Shannon (eds) *Catholic Social Thought: The Documentary Heritage* (Maryknoll, NY: Orbis). 437–488.

—— (2001). 'Novo millennio ineunte'. Available at http://www.vatican.va.

Jubilee Bishops' Council of the Russian Orthodox Church (2000). *Bases of the Social Concepts of the Russian Orthodox Church.* Available at http://www. orthodoxeurope.org.

July, F.O. (2005). *Diakonie und Kirche. Vortrag beim Sommerprogramm der Kirchen am 7. September 2005 in Freudenstadt.* Available at http://www.elk-wue.de/landeskirche/landesbischof.

Kärkkäinen, V.-M. (2002). *An Introduction to Ecclesiology: Ecumenical, Historical and Global Perspectives* (Downers Grove, IL: Inter Varsity Press).

Kahl, S. (2005). 'The religious roots of modern poverty policy: Catholic, Lutheran, and Reformed Protestant traditions compared.' *European Journal of Sociology* 46 (1): 91–126.

Kamergrauzis, N. (2001). *The Persistence of Christian Realism: A Study of the Social Ethics of Ronald H. Preston* (Uppsala: Uppsala University).

Kramer, R.M. (1981). *Voluntary Agencies in the Welfare State* (Berkeley, CA: University of California Press).

Lambeth Commission on Communion (2004). *The Windsor Report.* Available at www.anglicancommunion.org.

Lazareth, W.H. (2001). *Christians in Society: Luther, the Bible, and Social Ethics* (Minneapolis, MN: Fortress Press).

Leis, A. (2004). 'Welfare, church and gender in Germany'. In N. Edgardh Beckman (ed.) *Welfare, Church and Gender in Eight European Countries* (Uppsala: Uppsala Institute for Diaconal and Social Studies). 203–236.

Leis-Peters, A. (2006). 'Protestant agents of welfare in Germany: The case of Reutlingen'. In A.B. Yeung, N. Edgardh Beckman and P. Pettersson (eds) *Churches in Europe as Agents of Welfare – England, Germany, France, Italy and Greece* (Uppsala: Uppsala Institute for Diaconal and Social Studies). 56–122.

—— (2010). 'The German dilemma: Protestant agents of welfare in Reutlingen'. In A. Bäckström and G. Davie with N. Edgardh and P. Pettersson (eds) *Welfare and Religion in 21st Century Europe: Volume 1. Configuring the Connections* (Farnham: Ashgate). 95–112.

Leo XIII, Pope (1891/1992). 'Rerum novarum: The condition of labour'. In D.J. O'Brien and T.A. Shannon (eds) *Catholic Social Thought: The Documentary Heritage* (Maryknoll, NY: Orbis). 12–39.

Lewis, J. (1992). 'Gender and the development of welfare regimes'. *Journal of European Social Policy* 3 (2): 159–173.

—— (1997). 'Gender and welfare regimes: further thoughts.' *Social Politics* 4 (2): 160–177.

Lipset, S.M. and S. Rokkan (eds) (1964). *Party Systems and Voter Alignments* (New York: The Free Press).

Liveris, L.B. (2005). *Ancient Taboos and Gender Prejudice: Challenges for Orthodox Women and the Church* (Farnham: Ashgate).

Lohse, B. (1999). *Martin Luther's Theology: Its Historical and Systematic Development* (Minneapolis, MN: Fortress Press).

Lossky, V. (1978). *Orthodox Theology: An Introduction* (Crestwood, NY: St Vladimir's Seminary Press).

Luckmann, T. (1967). *The Invisible Religion: The Problem of Religion in Modern Society* (New York: Macmillan).

Luhmann, N. (1982). *The Differentiation of Society* (New York: Columbia University Press).

Lundström, T. and F. Wijkström (1997). *The Nonprofit Sector in Sweden* (Manchester: Manchester University Press).

Lusch, R.F. and S.L. Vargo (2006). *The Service-dominant Logic of Marketing: Dialog, Debate, and Directions* (Armonk, NY: M.E. Sharpe).

Luther, M. (1523/1900). 'Von weltlicher Obrigkeit, wie weit man ihr Gehorsam schuldig sei'. In P. Pietsch (ed.) *D. Martin Luthers Werke. Kritische Gesamtausgabe*. 11 Band (Weimar: Herman Böhlaus Nachfolger). 245–281.

Lutheran World Federation (LWF) (2004). *Reclaiming the Vocation of Government*. Statement from a Lutheran World Federation Consultation.

Lyon, D. and M. Glucksmann (2008). 'Comparative configurations of care work across Europe'. *Sociology* 42 (1): 101–118.

Mabille, F. and C. Valasik (2004). 'Welfare, church and gender in France'. In N. Edgardh Beckman (ed.) *Welfare, Church and Gender in Eight European Countries* (Uppsala: Uppsala Institute for Diaconal and Social Studies). 237–269.

McCann, D.P. (1981). *Christian Realism and Liberation Theology: Practical Theologies in Creative Conflict* (Maryknoll, NY: Orbis Books).

McFague, S. (1987). *Models of God: Theology for an Ecological, Nuclear Age* (Philadelphia, PA: Fortress Press).

McLennan, G. (2007). 'Towards postsecular sociology?' *Sociology* 41 (5): 857–870.

Manow, P. (2004). 'The "Good, the Bad and the Ugly". Esping-Andersen's welfare state typology and the religious roots of the Western welfare state'. Working paper 04/03, Max-Planck-Institut für Gesellschaftsforschung, Cologne.

Martin, D. (1978). *A General Theory of Secularization* (Oxford: Blackwell).

—— (2005). *On Secularization: Towards a Revised General Theory* (Farnham: Ashgate).

—— (2011). *The Future of Christianity: Reflections on Violence and Democracy, Secularization and Religion* (Farnham: Ashgate).

Marx, K. (1970). *Människans frigörelse. Ett urval ur Karl Marx skrifter av Sven-Eric Liedman* (Stockholm: Aldus/Bonniers).

Meyendorff, J. (1983). *Byzantine Theology: Historical Trends and Doctrinal Themes* (New York: Fordham University Press).

Micklethwait, J. and A. Wooldridge (2009). *God is Back: How the Global Rise of Faith is Changing the World* (London: Allen Lane).

Middlemiss, M. (2002). 'Anglican Christian social theory: An assessment of social welfare and the Church of England in the twentieth century'. Unpublished Master's thesis, Durham University.

—— (2004). 'Welfare, church and gender in England'. In N. Edgardh Beckman (ed.) *Welfare, Church and Gender in Eight European Countries* (Uppsala: Uppsala Institute for Diaconal and Social Studies). 152–202.

—— (2006). 'The Anglican Church as an agent of welfare: The case of Darlington'. In A.B. Yeung, N. Edgardh Beckman and P. Pettersson (eds) *Churches in Europe as Agents of Welfare – England, Germany, France, Italy and Greece* (Uppsala: Uppsala Institute for Diaconal and Social Studies). 1–55.

Middlemiss Lé Mon, M. (2009). *The In-between Church: A Study of the Church of England's Role in Society through the Prism of Welfare* (Uppsala: Uppsala University).

—— (2010). 'The "in-between" church: Church and welfare in Darlington'. In A. Bäckström and G. Davie with N. Edgardh and P. Pettersson (eds) *Welfare and Religion in 21st Century Europe: Volume 1. Configuring the Connections* (Farnham: Ashgate). 113–128.

Miller Kent, D. (2002). 'Competitive strategies of religious organizations'. *Strategic Management Journal* 23 (5): 435–456.

Molokotos-Liederman, L. and E. Fokas (2004). 'Welfare, church and gender in Greece'. In N. Edgardh Beckman (ed.) *Welfare, Church and Gender in Eight European Countries* (Uppsala: Uppsala Institute for Diaconal and Social Studies). 269–287.

Morgan, K.J. (2002). 'Forging the frontiers between state, church, and family: Religious cleavages and the origins of early childhood education and care policies in France, Sweden, and Germany'. *Politics and Society* 30 (1): 113–148.

—— (2006). *Working Mothers and the Welfare State: Religion and Politics of Work-Family Policies in Western Europe and the United States* (Palo Alto, CA: Stanford University Press).

—— (2009) 'The religious foundations of work-family policies in Western Europe.' In K. van Kersbergen and P. Manow (eds) *Religion, Class Coalitions, and Welfare States* (Cambridge: Cambridge University Press). 56–90.

Morrison, K. (1995). *Marx, Durkheim, Weber: Formations of Modern Social Thought* (London: Sage).

Namli, E. (2000). *Etikens ontologiska grund. En analys av Lev Karsavins personalism* (Skellefteå: Norma).

—— (2003). *Och på en enda kyrka: Ortodox etik i ekumenisk dialog* (Skellefteå: Artos).

Nielsen, J.S. (ed.) (2009). *Yearbook of Muslims in Europe, Volume 1* (Leiden: Brill).

Normann, R. (1998). *Quislingkyrkan: Nasjonal samlings kyrkopolitik 1940–1945* (Skellefteå: Norma).

Normann, R. and R. Ramírez (1994). *Designing Interactive Strategy: From Value Chain to Value Constellation* (Chichester: Wiley).

Norway, Department of Culture and Church (2008). *Staten og Den norske kirke*. Tilråding fra Kultur- og kirkedepartementet av 11. april 2008, St.meld. nr.

17 (2007–2008) (Oslo: Department of Culture and Church, Government of Norway).

O'Brien, D.J and T.A. Shannon (eds) (1992). *Catholic Social Thought: The Documentary Heritage* (Maryknoll, NY: Orbis).

OECD (2001). *Employment Outlook* (Paris: OECD).

Olk, T. (2001). 'Träger der Sozialen Arbeit'. In H.-U. Otto and H. Thiersch (eds) *Handbuch Sozialarbeit/Sozialpädagogik* (Neuwied/Kriftel: Luchterhand). 1910–1926.

ORB (2007). The Opinion Research Business, Church of England Omnibus Survey, CATI Fieldwork: 26–27 September 2007. Available at http://www.cofe.anglican.org/info/statistics/orb2007churchpowattendance.pdf.

Pace, E. (1998). *La nation italienne en crise. Perspectives européennes* (Paris: Bayard).

Papadakis, A. (1988). 'The historical tradition of church-state relations under Orthodoxy'. In P. Ramet (ed.) *Eastern Christianity and Politics in the Twentieth Century* (Durham, NC, and London: Duke University Press). 37–58.

Paul VI, Pope (1975/1992). 'Evangelii nuntiandi'. In D.J. O'Brien and T.A. Shannon (eds) *Catholic Social Thought: The Documentary Heritage* (Maryknoll, NY: Orbis). 301–346.

Persenius, R. (1987). *Kyrkans identitet: En studie i kyrkotänkandets profilering inom Svenska kyrkan i ekumeniskt perspektiv, 1937–1952* (Stockholm: Verbum).

Pessi, A.B. (2010). 'The church as a place of encounter: Communality and the good life in Finland'. In A. Bäckström and G. Davie with N. Edgardh and P. Pettersson (eds) *Welfare and Religion in 21st Century Europe: Volume 1. Configuring the Connections* (Farnham: Ashgate). 77–94.

Pettersson, P. (2000). *Kvalitet i livslånga tjänsterelationer: Svenska kyrkan ur tjänsteteoretiskt och religionssociologiskt perspektiv* (Stockholm: Verbum).

Pettersson, T. (2006). 'Religion in contemporary society: Eroded by human well-being, supported by cultural diversity'. *Comparative Sociology* 5 (2–3): 231–257.

Pfau-Effinger, B. and B. Geissler (2005). *Care and Social Integration in European Societies* (Bristol: Policy Press).

Phoenix, A. and P. Pattynama (2006). 'Intersectionality.' *European Journal of Women's Studies* 13 (3): 187–192.

Pius XI, Pope (1931/1992). 'Quadragesimo anno'. In D.J. O'Brien and T.A. Shannon (eds) *Catholic Social Thought: The Documentary Heritage* (Maryknoll, NY: Orbis). 40–80.

Plekon, M. (2007). 'Eastern Orthodox thought'. In P. Scott and W.T. Cavanaugh, *The Blackwell Companion to Political Theology* (Oxford: Blackwell). 93–106.

Pontifical Council for Justice and Peace (2004). *Compendium of the Social Doctrine of the Church* (London: Burns & Oates).

Post, P., R.L. Grimes, A. Nugteren, P. Pettersson and H. Zondag (2004). *Disaster Ritual: Explorations of an Emerging Ritual Repertoire*, Liturgia condenda 15 (Leuven: Peeters).

Preston, R. (1983). *Church and Society in the Late Twentieth Century: The Economic and Political Task* (London: SCM Press).

Putnam, R. (2000). *Bowling Alone: The Collapse and Revival of American Community*. (New York: Simon & Schuster).

Putnam, R., R. Leonardi and R.Y. Nanetti (1992). *Making Democracy Work: Civic Traditions in Modern Italy* (Princeton, NJ: Princeton University Press).

Radford Ruether, R. (1983). *Sexism and God-talk: Toward a Feminist Theology* (Boston, MA: Beacon Press).

—— (1992). 'Spirituality and justice: Popular church movements in the United States'. In E.C. Bianchi and R.R. Ruether (eds) *A Democratic Catholic Church: The Reconstruction of Roman Catholicism* (New York: Crossroad Publishing). 189–206.

Rapporto Eurispes (2006). *L'Italia non cresce più* (Roma: Eurispes-Link). Available at http://archivio.rassegna.it/2006/attualita/articoli/eurispes.htm.

Reimers, E. (1995). *Dopet som kult och kultur: Bilder av dopet i dopsamtal och föräldraintervjuer* (Stockholm: Verbum).

Repstad, P. (1996). 'A paradigm shift in the sociology of religion? In P. Repstad (ed.) *Religion and Modernity: Modes of Co-existence* (Oslo: Scandinavian University Press). 1–10.

Reuter, S. and A.G. Mazur (2003). 'The dynamics of French equality discourse'. In U. Liebert (ed.) *Gendering Europeanisation* (Brussels: Peter Lang). 47–83.

Riis, O. and L. Woodhead (2010). *A Sociology of Religion Emotion* (Oxford: Oxford University Press).

Runciman, S. (1968). *The Great Church in Captivity: A Study of the Patriarchate of Constantinople from the Eve of the Turkish Conquest to the Greek War of Independence* (Cambridge: Cambridge University Press).

Russell, L.M. (1993). *Church in the Round: Feminist Interpretation of the Church* (Louisville, KY: Westminster John Knox Press).

Sainsbury, D. (1994). *Gendering Welfare States* (London: Sage).

—— (ed.) (1999a). *Gender and Welfare State Regimes* (Oxford: Oxford University Press).

—— (1999b). Introduction. In D. Sainsbury (ed.) *Gender and Welfare State Regimes* (Oxford: Oxford University Press). 1–11.

Salamon, L.M. (1987). 'Market failure, government failure, and third-party government: Toward a theory of government – non-profit relations in the modern welfare state'. *Journal of Voluntary Action Research* 16 (1–2): 29–49.

Sayed, M. (2010). *Islam och arvsrätt i det mångkulturella Sverige: En internationellt privaträttslig och jämförande studie* (Uppsala: Uppsala University).

Schmidt, U. (2006). *Endring og tilhørighet. Statskirkespørsmålet i perspektiv* (Trondheim: Tapir Akademisk Forlag).

Schulz, A.D., A. Klein, R. Kleinfeld and F. Nullmeier (eds) (2007). *Organisationen zwischen Markt, Staat und Zivilgesellschaft. Arbeitsmarktförderung von Langzeitarbeitslosen im Deutschen Caritasverband* (Wiesbaden: VS-Verlag).

Second Vatican Council (1964). 'Lumen gentium: Dogmatic constitution on the church'. Available at http://www.vatican.va.

—— (1965/1992). 'Gaudium et spes: Pastoral constitution on the church in the modern world'. In D.J. O'Brien and T.A. Shannon (eds) *Catholic Social Thought: The Documentary Heritage* (Maryknoll, NY: Orbis). 164–237.

SFS (1998). *Lag om Svenska kyrkan* (Svensk författningssamling 1998:1591). Available at http://62.95.69.3/SFSdoc/98/981591.PDF

Sigurdson, O. (2009). *Det postsekulära tillståndet: Religion, modernitet, politik* (Göteborg: Glänta).

—— (2010). 'Beyond secularism? Towards a post-secular political theology'. *Modern Theology* 26 (2): 177–196.

Slater, D. (1997). *Consumer Culture and Modernity* (Cambridge: Polity Press).

Sörensdotter, R. (2004). 'Idealiserad omsorg och hindrande strukturer'. In R. Sörensdotter and I. Michaeli (eds) *Att vara i omsorgens mitt* (Hedemora: Gidlunds). 48–65.

Sörensdotter, R. and I. Michaeli (eds) (2004). *Att vara i omsorgens mitt* (Hedemora: Gidlunds).

Stadt Reutlingen (2005). *Reutlingen im Spiegel der Statistik* (Reutlingen: Stadtverwaltung).

Stark, A. and Å. Regnér (2002). *In Whose Hands? Work, Gender, Aging and Care in Three EU-countries* (Linköping: Linköpings Universitet).

Stark, R. and L.R. Iannaccone (1994). 'A supply-side reinterpretation of the "secularization" of Europe'. *Journal for the Scientific Study of Religion* 33 (3): 230–252.

Stathopoulou, T. (2007). 'Religiosity and trust in institutions: Emerging trends in Greece and Europe'. In K. Zorbas (ed.) *Politics and Religions* (Athens: Papazisis). 161–187 (original in Greek).

Statistisches Bundesamt Deutschland (2010). *Bevölkerung nach Altersgruppen, Familienstand und Religionszugehörigkeit*. Available at http://kuerzer.org/27d.

Storrar, W.F. (2004). 'Scottish civil society and devolution: The new case for Ronald Preston's defense of middle axioms'. *Studies in Christian Ethics* 17 (2): 37–46.

Suggate, A. (1987). *William Temple and Christian Social Ethics* (Edinburgh: T. and T. Clark).

Swatos, W.H. and K.J. Christiano (1999). 'Secularization theory: The course of a concept'. *Sociology of Religion* 60 (3): 209–228.

Szebehely, M. (2005). 'Care as employment and welfare provision: Child care and elder care in Sweden at the dawn of the 21st century'. In H.M. Dahl and T.R. Eriksen (eds) *Dilemmas of Care in the Nordic Welfare State* (Farnham: Ashgate). 88–97.

Temple, W. (1942). *Christianity and Social Order* (Harmondsworth: Penguin).

Toffler, A. (1980). *The Third Wave* (London: Collins).

Torry, M. (2005). *Managing God's Business* (Farnham: Ashgate).

Trifiletti, R. (1999). 'Southern European welfare regimes and the worsening position of women'. *Journal of European Social Policy* 9 (1): 49–64.

Troeltsch, E. (1931/1992). *The Social Teaching of the Christian Churches* (Louisville, KY: Westminster John Knox Press).

Valasik, C. (2006). 'The Catholic Church in France as an agent of welfare: The case of Evreux'. In A.B. Yeung, N. Edgardh Beckman and P. Pettersson (eds) *Churches in Europe as Agents of Welfare – England, Germany, France, Italy and Greece* (Uppsala: Uppsala Institute for Diaconal and Social Studies). 123–181.

—— (2010). 'Church-state relations in France in the field of welfare: A hidden complementarity'. In A. Bäckström and G. Davie with N. Edgardh and P. Pettersson (eds) *Welfare and Religion in 21st Century Europe: Volume 1. Configuring the Connections* (Farnham: Ashgate). 129–146.

van der Ven, J. (1996). *Ecclesiology in Context* (Grand Rapids, MI: Eerdmans).

van Kersbergen, K. and P. Manow (eds) (2009a). *Religion, Class Coalitions and Welfare State Regimes*. (Cambridge: Cambridge University Press).

—— (2009b). 'Religion and the Western welfare state: The theoretical context'. In K. van Kersbergen and P. Manow (eds) *Religion, Class Coalitions and Welfare State Regimes* (Cambridge: Cambridge University Press). 1–38.

Visser't Hooft, W.A. and J.H. Oldham (1937). *The Church and its Function in Society* (London: Allen and Unwin).

Voas, D. and A. Crockett (2005). 'Religion in Britain: Neither believing nor belonging'. *Sociology* 39 (1): 11–28.

Warner, S. (2008). 'Parameters of paradigms'. Unpublished paper presented at the Nordic Conference in Sociology of Religion, Turku, Finland.

Watson, N.K. (2002). *Introducing Feminist Ecclesiology* (London: Sheffield Academic Press).

'We are Church'. Available at http://www.we-are-church.org.

Weber, M. (1906/1990). *Letter to Adolf von Harnack*. In *Max Weber Gesamtausgabe II/5* (Tübingen: Mohr/Siebeck).

—— (1920/1996). *Gesammelte Aufsätze Zur Religionssoziologie I*. Selected Swedish translation (Lund: Argos).

—— (1922). *Die protestantische Ethik und der Geist des Kapitalismus*. In *Gesammelte Aufsätze Zur Religionssoziologie I* (Tübingen: Mohr/Siebeck).

Wedberg, A. (1968). *Filosofins historia: Antiken och medeltiden* (Stockholm: Thales).

Weisbrod, B.A. (1988). *The Nonprofit Economy* (Cambridge, MA: Harvard University Press).

Wharton, A.S. (2005). *The Sociology of Gender: An Introduction to Theory and Research* (Oxford: Blackwell).

Wijkström, F., S. Einarsson and O. Larsson (2004). *Staten och det civila samhället. Idétraditioner och tankemodeller i den statliga bidragsgivningen till ideella organisationer* (Stockholm: Socialstyrelsen).

Wijkström, F. and T. Lundström (2002). *Den ideella sektorn: organisationerna i det civila samhället* (Stockholm: Sober).

Williams, R. (2006). Contribution to the House of Lords debate on 'The Churches' Role in the Civic Life of the Nation'. *House of Lords Hansard*, 19 May 2006: 501–506. Also available at http://www.archbishopofcanterbury.org.

—— (2007). 'Christianity: Public religion and the common good'. Lecture given in St. Andrew's Cathedral, Singapore. Available at http://www. archbishopofcanterbury.org.

Wolf, A. (2006). 'Working girls'. *Prospect Magazine* 121. 23 April. Available at http://www.prospectmagazine.co.uk/2006/04/workinggirls.

Woodhead, L. (2005). 'Gendering secularisation theory'. *Kvinder, køn og forskning* 14 (1/2): 20–33.

—— (2007). 'Gender differences in religious practice and significance'. In J.A. Beckford and N.J. Demerath III (eds) *The Sage Handbook of the Sociology of Religion* (London: Sage). 566–586.

—— (2008a). 'Gendering secularization theory'. *Social Compass* 55 (2): 187–193.

—— (2008b). 'Locality studies of religion: Methods and approaches'. Unpublished paper presented at the Nordic Conference in Sociology of Religion, Turku, Finland.

Woodhead, L. with R. Catto (2009). *'Religion or Belief': Identifying Issues and Priorities*. Equality and Human Rights Commission. Research report 48 (Manchester: Equality and Human Right Commission). Available at http://www.equalityhumanrights.com/uploaded_files/research/research_report_48_ _religion_or_belief.pdf.

Woodhead, L. and P. Heelas (eds) (2000). *Religion in Modern Times: An Interpretive Anthology* (Oxford: Blackwell).

World Council of Churches (1997). *Living Letters: A Report of Visits to the Churches during the Ecumenical Decade – Churches in Solidarity with Women* (Geneva: World Council of Churches).

Yanagawa, K. (1987). 'Introductory thesis: Beyond the secularization thesis'. *The Journal of Oriental Studies* 26 (1): 1–4.

Yannoulatos, A. (2003). *Facing the World: Orthodox Christian Essays on Global Concerns*. Crestwood, NY: St Vladimir's Seminary Press.

Yeung, A.B. (2003). 'The re-emergence of the church in the Finnish public life? Christian social work as an indicator of the public status of the church'. *Journal of Contemporary Religion* 18 (2): 197–211.

—— (2004). 'Welfare, church and gender in Finland'. In N. Edgardh Beckman (ed.) *Welfare, Church and Gender in Eight European Countries* (Uppsala: Uppsala Institute for Diaconal and Social Studies). 103–151.

—— (2006). 'The Finnish Lutheran Church as an agent of welfare: The case of Lahti'. In A.B. Yeung, N. Edgardh Beckman and P. Pettersson (eds) *Churches in Europe as Agents of Welfare – Sweden, Norway and Finland* (Uppsala: Uppsala Institute for Diaconal and Social Studies). 142–203.

—— (2008). 'Servant of solidarity, institution of authenticity: The dilemma of welfare in the Church of Finland'. *Nordic Journal of Religion and Society* 21 (1): 1–21.

Yeung, A.B., N.E. Beckman and P. Pettersson (eds) (2006a). *Churches in Europe as Agents of Welfare – Sweden, Norway and Finland. Working Paper 2.1 from the project Welfare and Religion in a European Perspective* (Uppsala: Uppsala Institute for Diaconal and Social Studies).

—— (eds) (2006b). *Churches in Europe as Agents of Welfare – England, Germany, France, Italy and Greece. Working Paper 2:2 from the project Welfare and Religion in a European Perspective* (Uppsala: Uppsala Institute for Diaconal and Social Studies).

Index

abortion 92, 94–5
ageing of populations 5, 16
agricultural economies 6, 28, 56
Ahlstrand, Kajsa 99–100
Alleanza Nazionale (Italy) 6
Angell, Olav Helge 134
Anglican Communion 126–31; *see also*
    Church of England
Archbishops of Canterbury 126–8

baptism 158
Baptist church 37, 38
Bases of the Social Concepts of the Russian
    Orthodox Church 118–19
Beckford, Jim 170
Benedict XVI 115
Benne, Robert 123–4, 125, 126
Berger, Peter 105
Blue Cross 134
Brodd, Sven-Erik 109
Bruce, Steve 166
Bruderhaus Diakonie 34, 76, 134
Buddhism 4
Byzantine Empire 116–17

Calvinist Church 7, 8
care deficit 65–7, 95–7, 153
care homes 34–5, 73, 82
Caritas-Diakonia 6, 35, 40–41, 51, 75
Caritas in Veritate 115
Caritas Internationalis 134
Caritas Italiana 134
Caritasverband 29
Carrefour Rural 91–2
Casanova, José 159
Catechism of the Catholic Church 113
Catholic Church 4, 5–6, 7, 18, 22, 24,
    25–6, 27, 29, 30, 32–3, 35–6,
    40–41, 47–8, 68, 69, 75, 76–7,
    80–81, 89–93, 111–15, 132, 134–6,

140–41, 142, 144–5, 146, 148–9,
    152, 158
Centesimus Annus 112, 114
chaplaincy services 31, 36
children 34, 36, 74, 75–6, 78, 93
Christian Democratic Party (Italy) 6
Christianity 18–19, 99–100; *see also*
    churches
Christifideles Laici 134
Christodoulos, Archbishop 41–2, 116, 118,
    120, 121, 136, 145
church buildings 20, 23, 32
Church City Mission (Drammen) 50–51,
    80, 133–4, 140, 147, 154
Church of England 5, 22, 23, 25, 36–7, 38,
    77–8, 93–4, 126–31, 135, 143, 146,
    148, 152, 158
Church of Finland *see* Evangelical
    Lutheran Church of Finland
Church of Norway 3–4, 22, 25, 38, 80,
    122, 134; *see also* Lutheran Church
Church of Sweden 2, 14, 18, 22, 24–5, 26,
    38, 78–9, 80–81, 94, 107, 122, 132,
    142, 147; *see also* Lutheran Church
churches
    as communion 142, 145
    conservatism of 90, 93, 97
    contexts 132, 133–7
    as contracted agents 17, 43–6, 154
    defining 107, 141–2
    as direct service providers 38–41,
        50–51, 146–9, 154
    and education 69, 75
    financial resources 38, 59, 96, 97
    and gender 67, 68–9, 70–71, 73–95,
        96–106
    human resources 15, 38, 59, 96, 97
    identity of 17, 46–7, 58, 123–4,
        131–49, 153–4
    importance of individuals 47–52

increasing role of 15, 52, 96–7, 154–7
as institution 142, 145
as linking individuals to society 23, 52
as major institutions 22–4
membership numbers 15, 21–2, 38,
    59, 97, 154–6
missions 132, 141–2, 146–9
opinions on role of 38–46
ordained ministers of 80–82
perceived neutrality of 23, 31–2
as professional organizations 46–7, 152
as providers of social activities 20,
    35–6, 37
and public debate 16–17, 38–9, 41–3,
    50–51, 146–9, 154, 156–7
public expectations of 30, 31–2,
    38–43, 50, 59
quality of services 47–9
related organizations *see* church-related
    organizations
relationships with states 24–6, 43–6,
    58, 117–19, 125–6, 127–8
as semi-public organizations 31–2
separation from state 19
social doctrines 111–31
and the social economy 20–22
symbolic functions of 37, 48–9, 57
as transmitting cultural values 19
unique nature of 18–20
visions 132, 141–6
as voluntary organizations 21, 31–2,
    46–7
volunteer workers 38, 46–7, 49–50,
    67, 74, 75, 76, 77–9, 81–3, 152–3
as welfare providers 16–17, 29–30,
    33–43, 47–52, 96–7, 141–2, 146–9
see also individual churches/countries
church-related organizations 32–3, 36,
    45, 77, 82, 83, 133–7; *see also*
    voluntary organizations
common good 112–13, 130–31
communion 136–7, 142, 145
*Compendium of the Social Doctrine of the
    Church* 111–15
competition 44, 56, 95, 154
complementary services 33, 36, 37
Congar, Yves 109
Conservative Party (England) 5

conservative welfare model 7
contraception 5, 91, 92
contracting 17, 43–6, 154
convictions 132, 137–41
counselling services 34, 35, 36
cultural values 19

Daly, Mary 63–4, 65, 66, 68
Darlington 5, 36–7, 38, 93–4, 135, 143,
    148; *see also* England
Davie, Grace 57, 165–6
deacons 80–81
Debré, Jean-Louis 5
Deus Caritas Est 115
diakonia 119
Diakonisches Werk 29, 34
disabled people 34, 36
divorce 91
Drammen 3–4, 36, 38, 50–51, 79–80,
    133–4, 147, 154; *see also* Norway
Durkheim, Emile 54

ecclesiology 101–2, 109, 131–3, 141–2
Edgardh, Ninna 145, 151, 154
education 35, 69, 75, 78
Egnell, Helene 100
Ekstrand, Thomas 151–2, 153–4
EKD; *see* Evangelical Churches in
    Germany
elderly people 34, 35, 36, 73, 75–6, 82
employment 62–3, 75–6
England
    baptisms 158
    case study summary 5
    church involvement in debate 50, 148
    church membership 22
    church-related organizations 135
    church–state relationship 25, 127–8
    church visions 143
    church welfare activities 36–7, 38
    controversial gender issues 93–4
    female employment levels 62, 77
    legitimization of inequality 84–5, 87
    Muslim population 19
    perceptions of the state 27, 41
    public expectations of the church
        31–2, 41, 50
    responses to pluralism 164

role of individuals 50
unequal gender influence 81
uneven gender representation 77–8
welfare mix 30
welfare system 30, 77
eschatology 116–19
Esping-Andersen, Gøsta 7, 8, 63, 65, 67, 160, 161
ethnic minorities 2, 4, 6, 66
European Economic and Monetary Union (EMU) 16, 53
European Union (EU) 17–18, 53, 118
European Values Survey 52
Evangelical Churches in Germany (EKD) 4–5, 22, 25–6, 34, 42–4, 58, 69, 122, 134, 143–4, 158; *see also* Lutheran Church; Protestant Church
Evangelical Lutheran Church of Finland 4, 22, 26, 36, 41, 79, 80, 122; *see also* Lutheran Church
Evreux 4–5, 76–7, 83, 91–2, 115, 135–6, 144–5; *see also* France

Faith in the City report 127, 131
Faithful Cities report 128, 130, 131
Familiaris Consortio 114
families
    need for care provision 62, 64, 65
    as providers of welfare 18, 27, 28, 30, 34–5, 62, 64, 65, 68, 73, 74–6
    traditional model of 68–9, 74–6, 90, 93, 120
feminism 83, 88–9, 90, 103
feminist ecclesiology 101–2
feminist theology 71, 72, 98, 101–3
Femmes et Hommes en Eglise 91
financial support services 35, 36
Finland
    baptisms 158
    case study summary 4
    church involvement in debate 43, 147
    church membership 22
    church resources 38
    church–state relationship 26, 69
    church welfare activities 36
    controversial gender issues 94–5
    convictions 140

education 69
female employment levels 62, 78
gender equality 69, 78, 87–8, 94
Muslim population 19
perceptions of the state 27
public expectations of the church 41, 43
unequal gender influence 80
uneven gender representation 78–80
welfare system 18, 78
Fiorenza, Elisabeth Schüssler 101
Fix, Birgit 7–8
Fix, Elizabeth 7–8
Forward in Faith movement 93–4
Forza Italia 6
France
    case study summary 5–6
    church involvement in debate 42, 148
    church membership 22
    church-related organizations 32–3, 45, 77, 134
    church–state relationship 26, 45–6, 58, 69, 77; *see also laïcité*
    church visions 144–5
    church welfare activities 35–6
    contracting of welfare provision 45
    controversial gender issues 91–2
    education 69
    female employment levels 62, 76
    legitimization of inequality 84–5, 87
    Muslim population 19
    perceptions of the state 27, 41
    public expectations of the church 41, 42
    quality of services 48
    responses to pluralism 163–4
    unequal gender influence 81, 82–3
    uneven gender representation 76–7
    welfare mix 30
    welfare system 30, 45, 76
Fraser, Nancy 83, 87, 103

Gaillot, Monsignor 5, 92, 115, 135, 144
Gaudium et Spes 112–13
Gävle 2–3, 36, 78–9, 94, 133, 143, 147; *see also* Sweden
Gävle Diaconal Council 36
gender
    and care deficit 65–7, 95–7

and the church 67, 68–9, 70–71,
73–95, 96–106
defining 70–72
equality of 69, 78, 85, 87–8, 94, 97,
103
legitimization of inequality 83–8
points of conflict concerning 88–95
religious influence on roles 68–9,
70–71
as social construction 71
and unequal influence 80–83, 99–100
and uneven representation 73–80
and welfare 62–9, 73–95
see also men; women
gender roles 54, 62–9, 70–71, 73–4, 77,
95, 96–103
General Synod Board for Social
Responsibility 129
Germany
baptisms 158
case study summary 4–5
church involvement in debate 42–3, 148
church membership 22
church-related organizations 32, 134
church–state relationship 25, 44, 58, 69
church visions 143–4
church welfare activities 34
contracting of welfare provision 44
controversial gender issues 93
education 69
female employment levels 62, 75–6
legitimization of inequality 87
Muslim population 19
perceptions of the state 27
professionalism 46
public expectations of the church 30,
40, 42–3, 59
unequal gender influence 81, 82
uneven gender representation 75–6
welfare mix 29–30
welfare system 17, 18, 29–30, 44, 46
globalization 20, 167–8
Greece
case study summary 6
church involvement in debate 42, 148
church membership 22
church-related organizations 32, 135
church resources 38

church–state relationship 25, 117–19
church visions 145
church welfare activities 34–5, 38
controversial gender issues 89
convictions 139
female employment levels 62, 74
legitimization of inequality 84–5
Muslim population 19
perceptions of the state 27, 40, 48, 49
public expectations of the church 30,
39, 40, 41–2
quality of services 48, 49
role of individuals 50
unequal gender influence 82
uneven gender representation 73–4
welfare mix 30
welfare system 18, 30
Greek Orthodox Church *see* Orthodox
Church
Grenholm, Cristina 109, 122

Habermas, Jürgen 168–9
health care provision 18
Hearn, Jeff 64
Held, Virginia 103
Hernes, Helga 68
Hinduism 4
Hochschild, Arlie Russell 65
holism 47, 56–7
Holy Trinity Association for Diaconal
Work 133
homeless people, services for 35, 82
homosexuality 91, 93, 94, 95
Hopko, Thomas 120
House of Lords 25, 127–8, 148
human dignity 111–12, 117–18
human nature 126
human rights 112, 117–18
Humanae Vitae 91
humanism 164–5

identity 17, 22, 46–7, 58, 123–4, 131–49,
153–4
immigrant communities 2, 4, 6, 19, 36, 66,
74, 75, 90–91
individuals
as adding quality 49–50
importance of 50–51

linking to wider society 23, 52
provision of services to 47–9
as recipients of welfare 64
and spirituality 20, 52, 157–61
industrial economies 3, 5, 6, 56
industrialization 8, 28
inequality, legitimising of 70–71, 74, 83–8
institutional separation 8–9, 55
*International Journal for the Study of the
Christian Church* 109
invisibility 10, 12, 61, 153
Islam 4, 6, 19, 163, 164, 166, 167
Italian Council of Bishops 90
Italy
    case study summary 6
    church involvement in debate 148–9
    church membership 22
    church-related organizations 32, 134
    church–state relationship 25, 69
    church visions 144–5
    church welfare activities 35
    controversial gender issues 89–91
    convictions 139–40
    education 69
    female employment levels 62, 75
    legitimization of inequality 84–5
    Muslim population 19
    perceptions of the state 27, 40
    public expectations of the church
        40–41
    quality of services 47
    role of individuals 51
    unequal gender influence 82
    uneven gender representation 74–5
    welfare mix 30
    welfare system 18, 30

Jeanrond, Werner 136
Jehovah's Witnesses 4
Jenkins, David 127
Joas, Hans 169
John Chrysostom, Saint 116
John Paul II 112, 113, 114, 115, 134, 135
Judaism 4
justice 138–41

Kahl, Sigrun 7
Kamergrauzis, Normunds 138–9

kingdom of God 116–19, 139

Labour Party (England) 5
Lahti 4, 36, 79, 95, 140; *see also* Finland
laïcité 26, 30, 32, 42, 132, 148, 163–4
Lega Nord (Italy) 6
legitimation 70–71, 74, 83–8
Leis-Peters, Annette 134, 143
Leo XIII 113, 115
Lewis, Jane 63, 66, 78
Liberal Democrat Party (England) 5
liberal welfare model 7
Lipset, Seymour Martin 8
Livadeia *see* Thiva and Livadeia
love 86, 107, 109, 118–20, 125, 136,
    138–41
Luckmann, Thomas 54
Lumen Gentium 145
Lutheran Church 4, 7, 78, 122–6, 134,
    136, 143, 147–8, 152, 158; *see
    also* Church of Norway; Church
    of Sweden; Evangelical Lutheran
    Church of Finland; EKD
Lutheran World Federation 126

McLennan, Gregor 168
Manow, Philip 7, 108–9
market economy *see* competition
marriage 74, 91–2
Martin, David 8, 159, 160, 169–70
Martino, Cardinal 111
Marx, Karl 54, 105
men
    as bread-winners 62, 63–4, 69, 75, 77,
        78, 103
    as care-givers 61, 67, 103–4
    as decision-makers 80–82, 95, 99
    need for change in social roles 103–4
    see also gender
mental health 34, 36
Meyendorff, John 117
middle axioms 128–9
Middlemiss, Martha 127, 129, 131, 143
migration 16, 19; *see also* immigrant
    communities
Mikaeli, Inga 67
minority religions 4, 6, 7, 19, 157, 162–5
missions 132, 141–2, 146–9

Morgan, Kimberly J. 68–9
Mother of God image 74
motherhood 74; *see also* families
multiculturalism 18

Namli, Elena 119
National Coalition Party (Finland) 4
national identity 22, 158
neutrality, perceptions of 23, 31–2
Norway
    case study summary 3–4
    church involvement in debate 50–51,
        147
    church membership 22
    church-related organizations 133–4
    church–state relationship 25, 69
    church welfare activities 36, 38
    convictions 140
    education 69
    female employment levels 62, 78
    gender equality 69, 78, 87, 94
    legitimization of inequality 84–5
    Muslim population 19
    perceptions of the state 27, 40
    public expectations of the church 30,
        41
    responses to pluralism 164–5
    role of individuals 50–51
    unequal gender influence 80, 83
    uneven gender representation 78–80
    welfare system 18, 78
Norwegian Humanist Association 165
Not Just for the Poor (General Synod
        Board for Social Responsibility)
        129, 131
Novo Millennio Ineunte 115
nursing homes *see* care homes
nursing services 34

Obama, Barack 18
Oldham, Joseph H. 128
operative ecclesiology 109, 141–2
ordination
    of married men 91
    of women 5, 72, 80, 89, 93–4, 95, 97,
        98
organizational management 46–7

Orthodox Church 6, 7, 18, 22, 25, 30,
        32, 34–5, 41–2, 74, 80–82, 88–9,
        115–21, 135, 137, 139, 140–41,
        145, 146, 158

parishes 32–3, 135
part-time working 62, 76
party politics 41, 53
Pentecostal Church 4
personalism 119–20, 139
Pessi, Anne Birgitta 49
Petterson, Per 136, 147, 151–2, 153–4,
        156, 166
philanthropia 119–20
Pius XI 113–14
Plein Jour 91
Plekon, Michael 115–16
pluralism 19–20, 52, 54, 161–5
post-secularism 166–9, 170
primary services 33, 34, 35
Pringle, Keith 64
private sector welfare provision 28–9
privatization 165–6, 169–70
professionalism 46–7, 49, 66–7, 152
Protestant Church 4, 7, 18, 24, 26, 29,
        34, 40, 69, 76, 80–81, 89, 93–4,
        158; *see also* Church of England;
        Church of Norway; Church of
        Sweden; Evangelical Lutheran
        Church of Finland; EKD; Lutheran
        Church
psychotherapy 34, 35, 50
public debate 16–17, 38–9, 41–3, 50–51,
        146–9, 154, 156–7
Putnam, Robert 22

Quadragesimo Anno 113–14
Quakers 5
quality 47–50

Radford Ruether, Rosemary 101
Rake, Katherine 63–4, 65, 66, 68
Rawls, John 168
Reclaiming the Vocation of Government
        (Lutheran World Federation) 126
reconstructive interpretation 109–10
Redfield, Robert 99
Reformed Church 7

religious change 15, 53, 55, 169–70
religious orders 81–3, 90, 140
Rerum Novarum 113, 115
Reutlingen 4–5, 34, 75–6, 93, 134, 143–4;
    see also Germany
Rich and Poor (Church of Sweden) 122
rites of passage 20, 22, 23, 158
Rokkan, Stein 8
Rubin, Edgar 99
Rubin's vase 99, 100
rural issues 91–2
Russell, Letty 101

Sainsbury, Diane 63
salvation 107, 116, 120–21, 123, 137
Secours Catholique France 134
secular elites 161–5
secularization 8, 15, 55–6, 68, 69, 105,
    155–7, 158, 159–60, 166, 169–70
service economies 3, 4, 5, 56–7
service-provider activities 33
sexuality 71, 91, 92, 94
Sigurdson, Ola 169
Sikhism 4
sin 112, 123, 124, 126
social activities 20, 35–6, 37
social capital 22, 24
social care 66–7, 95
social democratic welfare model 7, 29
Social Democrats (Finland) 4
Social Democrats (Norway) 3
Social Democrats (Sweden) 2
social doctines
    Anglican 126–31
    Catholic 111–15
    Lutheran 122–6
    Orthodox 115–21
social economy 20–22, 24
Socialist Party (Greece) 6
solidarity 17–18, 44, 95, 114–15
Sollicitudo Rei Socialis 113
Sörensdotter, Renita 67
specialization 54–5, 57
spirituality 20, 49, 52
standardization 16, 18, 43–4, 45–6
Stark, Agneta 65
'The State and the Individual' (Swedish
    Research Council) 14

states
    contracting of welfare provision 17,
        43–6, 154
    cutbacks in welfare provision 16–17,
        39–40
    perceptions of 26–7, 39–41, 48
    relationships with churches 24–6,
        43–6, 58, 117–19, 125–6, 127–8
    role in welfare provision 28–30,
        39–41, 48
subsidiarity 27, 68, 69, 113–14
Suggate, Alan M. 131
supplementary services 33
Sweden
    case study summary 2–3
    church involvement in debate 43, 147
    church membership 22
    church-related organizations 133
    church resources 38
    church–state relationship 24–5, 26,
        58, 69
    church visions 143
    church welfare activities 36
    controversial gender issues 94–5
    education 69
    female employment levels 62, 78
    gender equality 69, 78, 85, 94
    Muslim population 19
    perceptions of the state 27, 48
    public expectations of the church 41,
        43
    quality of services 48
    unequal gender influence 80–81
    uneven gender representation 78–80,
        83
    welfare system 18, 78
Swedish Research Council 14
symbolic values 37, 48–9, 57

Temple, William 127, 128–9
theological reflection 128–30
theology, defining 107–8
theory extension 109
Thiva and Livadeia 6, 34–5, 50, 73–4, 82,
    89, 135, 139, 145; *see also* Greece
Towards the Common Good (Evangelical
    Lutheran Church of Finland) 122,
    124, 125, 148

Town Centre Churches' Group
(Darlington) 135
Town City Mission (Darlington) 135
transcendence 37, 48–9
transformation 120–21
transnational financial structures 16, 18, 53
transnational political structures 16, 18
Troeltsch, Ernst 124
two kingdoms doctrine 124–6, 147–8

unemployment 5, 6
United Kingdom *see* England
Uppsala Religion and Society Research
Centre 14
urbanization 8, 28

Valasik, Corinne 148
value-guardianship activities 33, 37
van der Ven, Johannes A. 131–2, 136
vanguard activities 33, 35, 36, 37
Vicenza 6, 35, 74–5, 89–91, 135, 139–40,
144–5, 148–9; *see also* Italy
La Vie 91
visions, churches 132, 141–6
Voas, David 166
voluntary organizations
churches as 21, 31–2, 46–7
role in welfare provision 28–30, 37,
41, 43–6
role of women in 67
see also church-related organizations
volunteer workers 38, 46–7, 49–50, 67,
74, 75, 76, 77–9, 81–3, 152–3

Watson, Natalie 102
We Are Church movement 90, 100
Weber, Max 55, 105, 107, 124
Wedberg, Anders 109
Welfare and Religion in a European
Perspective (WREP) 1, 2, 14, 151,
153, 155, 156, 161, 162
Welfare and Values in Europe (WaVE) 7,
14, 71, 157, 160
welfare mix 27–30
welfare provision
by churches 16–17, 29–30, 33–43,
47–52, 96–7, 141–2, 146–9

competition in 44, 95, 154
contracting of 17, 43–6, 154
cutbacks in 16–17, 39–40
deficit of care 65–7, 95–7, 153
division of roles in 27–30
by families 18, 27, 28, 30, 34–5, 62,
64, 68, 73, 74–6
and gender 62–9, 73–95
individualization of 64
influence of religion upon 68–9
by the private sector 28–9
public opinion on provision 38–43
quality of 47–9
standardization of 16, 18, 43–4, 45–6
by the state 28–30, 39–41, 48
unequal gender influence 80–83
uneven gender representation 73–80
by voluntary organizations 28–30, 37,
41, 43–6
welfare systems
changes in 159–60
characteristics of 17–18
comparative measures 68
models of 7–9, 63, 83
Wharton, Amy S. 70
Williams, Rowan 127–8, 130
Wolf, Alison 67
women
as care-givers 62, 63, 64, 65–7, 73–4,
77, 95, 97, 98, 103
devaluation of 96, 97
labour market participation 62–3, 64,
65, 67, 74, 75–6, 77, 78
ordination of 5, 72, 80, 89, 93–4, 95,
97, 98
women's organizations 82
see also feminism; gender
Women-Church movement 101
Woodhead, Linda 105–6
World Values Survey 52
Wyller, Trygve 134

Yannoulatos, Archbishop Anastasios 118,
119, 121, 145

Zentrum Party (Germany) 76